EMORY UNIVERSITY STUDIES IN LAW AND RELIGION

John Witte Jr., General Editor

BOOKS IN THE SERIES

Religious Liberty in Western Thought
Noel B. Reynolds and W. Cole Durham Jr., eds.

Political Order and the Plural Structure of Society
James W. Skillen and Rockne M. McCarthy

The Idea of Natural Rights:
Studies on Natural Rights, Natural Law, and Church Law, 1150-1625
Brian Tierney

The Fabric of Hope: An Essay
Glenn Tinder

Liberty: Rethinking an Imperiled Ideal
Glenn Tinder

Religious Human Rights in Global Perspective: Legal Perspectives
Johan D. van der Vyver and John Witte Jr., eds.

Natural Law and the Two Kingdoms:
A Study in the Development of Reformed Social Thought
David VanDrunen

Early New England: A Covenanted Society
David A. Weir

God's Joust, God's Justice: Law and Religion in the Western Tradition
John Witte Jr.

Religious Human Rights in Global Perspective: Religious Perspectives
John Witte Jr. and Johan D. van der Vyver, eds.

Justice in Love
Nicholas Wolterstorff

Justice in Love

Nicholas Wolterstorff

WILLIAM B. EERDMANS PUBLISHING COMPANY
GRAND RAPIDS, MICHIGAN / CAMBRIDGE, U.K.

Published 2011 by
Wm. B. Eerdmans Publishing Co.
2140 Oak Industrial Drive N.E., Grand Rapids, Michigan 49505 /
P.O. Box 163, Cambridge CB3 9PU U.K.

Printed in the United States of America

17 16 15 14 13 12 11   7 6 5 4 3 2 1

Library of Congress Cataloging-in-Publication Data

Wolterstorff, Nicholas.
Justice in love / Nicholas Wolterstorff.
p.   cm.   — (Emory University studies in law and religion)
ISBN 978-0-8028-6615-8 (cloth: alk. paper)
1. Agape.   2. Love — Religious aspects.   3. Love — Philosophy.
4. Christianity and justice.   5. Justice (Philosophy)   I. Title.

BV4639.W63   2011
241′.677 — dc22

2010046704

www.eerdmans.com

Contents

Part Three   *Just and Unjust Love*

Part Four   *The Justice of God's Love*

Two concepts long prominent in the moral culture of the West are those of *love* and *justice*. One can imagine a society in which either or both of these was absent; in such a society, nobody would think in terms of love or nobody would think in terms of justice. In our society, most of us think in terms of both.

We are the present day recipients of two comprehensive imperatives issued by the writers of antiquity that employ these concepts. One is the imperative to do justice, coming to us from both the Athens-Rome strand of our heritage and the Jerusalem strand. "Do justice," said the prophet Micah in a well-known passage. The ancient Roman jurist Ulpian said that we are to render to each person his or her *right* or *due* *(ius)*. The other imperative comes to us only from the Jerusalem strand: love your neighbor as yourself, even if that neighbor is an enemy. Do not return evil for evil, said Jesus. The ancient Greek writers praised *eros*-love and *philia*-love. Jesus, quoting the Torah, enjoined *agape*-love.

These two imperatives, do justice and love your neighbor as yourself, do not reveal on their face how they are related to each other. It is this, plus their persistence and prominence in our inheritance, that accounts for the fact that over and over the question has been raised, what do justice and love have to do with each other? And it was the persistence and prominence of the question that made it natural for me to project a chapter on the relation between justice and love when planning my book *Justice: Rights and Wrongs*.[1] But *Justice* became too long for any additional chapters. And in any case it became clear to me, after no more than preliminary reflection, that a serious treatment of the topic would require not a chapter but a book.

Prominent in the literature on justice and love is the theme of tension or conflict. Sometimes this theme takes the form of writers arguing that one cannot follow the two imperatives simultaneously; they are inherently conflictual. To act out of love is perforce not to treat the recipient as one does because justice requires it; to treat someone as one does because justice requires it is perforce not to be acting out of love. At other times the theme takes the form of writers arguing that following

---

1. (Princeton: Princeton University Press, 2008).

the love-imperative will sometimes wreak injustice, or arguing that following the justice-imperative will sometimes be unloving.

The examples offered of unjust love fall, for the most part, into three categories. The way generosity is sometimes dispensed is unjust. The way in which benevolent paternalism is sometimes exercised is unjust. And a persistent charge against forgiveness, mercy, pardon, amnesty, commutation of sentence, and the like is that, in mercifully foregoing or diminishing punishment of the wrongdoer, justice is violated. This charge is at the center of the controversies swirling around truth and reconciliation commissions of the past thirty years or so.

There are different kinds of justice, as there are different kinds of love. So a question that naturally comes to mind, once one has noted the prominence of the agonistic theme in the literature, is what kind of justice and what kind of love do writers see as coming into conflict with each other?

With respect to justice, all kinds: commutative, distributive, corrective; they all turn up in discussions about justice and love. Not so for love. Among the various phenomena that we use the English word "love" to refer to is that of being drawn or attracted to something on account of its worth or excellence — as when one says, "I love the late Beethoven string quartets." That's not the kind of love that those who write about love and justice have in mind. Invariably they are thinking of love as benevolence, generosity, charity. Admittedly most writers don't say this; they don't clearly differentiate love as benevolence from other kinds of love and declare that it is love as benevolence that they have in mind. But close attention to what they say reveals that it is in fact always benevolence that they are talking about.

The response of some writers to the perceived tension between the justice-imperative and the love-imperative is to prefer love to justice. They propose eliminating the concept of justice from our moral culture, or giving priority to love over justice whenever there is conflict, or confining the use of the category of justice to a few, carefully delimited, situations. The response of others is the opposite, to prefer justice to love.

Rather than accepting tension between these two imperatives as an unalterable fact of life, I argue in the following pages that our perception of tension between them is the sign of something having gone wrong in our understanding of them. I propose and argue for a way of understanding love and a way of understanding justice such that the two imperatives are fully in harmony with each other.

In Part One I argue for the desirability of a compatibilist way of understanding the relation between the two imperatives; in Part Two I work out such an understanding. Then in Part Three and Part Four I

analyze cases of perceived conflict between love and justice. Is it true
that forgiveness is inherently unjust, as many have charged? What
makes generosity sometimes unjust? What makes benevolent paternalism sometimes unjust? What accounts for the malformations of love represented by unjust generosity and unjust paternalism? For that, so I argue, is what they are, malformations of love. Love that perpetrates
injustice is malformed love.

Let me emphasize that this is neither a discourse on justice with some
ancillary reflections on love, nor is it a discourse on love with some ancillary reflections on justice. My *Justice: Rights and Wrongs,* is an expansive discussion of justice; those who expect a similarly expansive discussion of love in this companion volume will be disappointed. My focus is
on the relation between justice and love; there is much about love that
falls outside that focus.

Parts of this volume were delivered as lectures at Azusa Pacific University, Columbia Theological Seminary, Geneva College, Oxford University, Regent College, Tyndale College, the University of Oklahoma,
the University of Tennessee, the University of Virginia, and Western
Theological Seminary. I thank these institutions for the honor of being
invited to give the lectures and for the vigorous and helpful discussions
that they provoked. And I thank the Institute for Advanced Studies in
Culture (University of Virginia), of which I am a senior fellow, for financial support and for the extraordinarily pleasant atmosphere it provides
for thinking, reading, and writing.

Chapter One

INTRODUCTION

IT WAS ALMOST INEVITABLE that we in the West would return over and over to the topic of love and justice in our literature, our philosophy, our theology. As I observed in the Preface, the topic was placed on our agenda by two comprehensive imperatives handed down to us from antiquity: the imperative to do justice and the imperative to love one's neighbor as oneself.

It was by no means inevitable, however, that justice in the former imperative and love in the latter would be understood in such a way that the most pervasive theme in discussions about love and justice would be the theme of conflict. But so it is. The perceived conflict includes, but goes deeper than, incidents of unjust love and incidents of unloving justice. It is said or assumed that to act out of love is not to act as one does because justice requires it, and that to act as one does because justice requires it is not to act out of love. Some then choose love, whether or not they perpetrate injustice in so doing; some choose justice, whether or not they are unloving.

My argument in this volume is that when these two imperatives are rightly understood, they are not in conflict. To suppose that they are is to misunderstand either justice in the justice-imperative or love in the love-imperative — or both. Where so many for so long have thought they saw conflict, I aim to show harmony.

Comprehensive though the justice-imperative may be, nobody has ever proposed that seeking justice should constitute the whole of one's ethical orientation. Not so for love. Many have held that love should be the totality of one's orientation toward one's fellow human beings. The Greek word most commonly used in the Septuagint and New Testament for love is *agapē*. For that reason, this ethical orientation has come to be called *agapism*. My goal in this first chapter is to introduce, in preliminary fashion, that ethical orientation which is agapism.

I think the best way to get a sense both of the structure and the significance of agapism is to contrast it with the three alternative ethical orientations most commonly discussed by philosophers: namely, egoism, eudaimonism, and utilitarianism. In order to do this, we must first identify and distinguish certain types of goods. It would not be a mistake to think of our entire subsequent discussion as all about different

1

kinds of goods and different ways of being related to those different kinds of goods.

WELLBEING, AND WHAT IS GOOD FOR SOMEONE

Every ethical system, whether embedded in the practices of a society or articulated by some theorist, employs the idea of certain states and events in a person's life as good *for* that person.[1] Likewise every ethical system employs the idea of certain actions and activities on the part of a person as good *for* that person. My being of good health is one of the states in my life that is good for me; my listening to a good performance of a Beethoven string quartet is one of the activities that is good for me. The states and events in a person's life that are good for the person, combined with the actions and activities of that person that are good for him or her, together make up the whole of what is good for that person.

Let us agree that if some state or event in a person's life is good *for* that person, then it is a good *in* that person's life, a life-good. So too for the actions and activities a person performs that are good *for* her: those are goods *in* her life, life-goods.

Some of the states and events in a person's life that are good for him or her are intrinsically good; some are instrumentally good. So too for the actions and activities that he or she performs. Something is an *instrumental* good for someone just in case it makes a causal contribution to something else that is a good for him or her; something is an *intrinsic* good for someone just in case its being good for her does not consist at all, or not only, in its being an instrumental good for her. If getting bifocal eye glasses would be good for me, it would obviously not be an intrinsic but an instrumental good for me; its worth for me lies entirely in the fact that bifocals will bring about the good for me of my being able to see better.

The distinction between instrumental and intrinsic goods makes reference to causation. A parallel distinction can be made concerning the relation among intended actions within the action-plans of persons. A person may intend to do something because he judges that performing that action will be a means to something else that he wants to bring about. Alternatively, he may do it not at all, or not only, as a means to something else but for its own sake; in the latter case, it is an end in itself for him.

---

1. Throughout this and subsequent chapters I will usually speak of persons rather than human beings, even though what I say applies, and is meant to apply, both to persons and to those human beings who are not capable of functioning as persons.

It is commonly assumed nowadays that something is good *for* someone just in case it contributes positively to his or her wellbeing or welfare.[2] This seems to me correct. When we say such things as "Exercising
regularly would be good for you" and "It would be good for me to get bifocals," we mean that exercising regularly would contribute to your
wellbeing, as would getting bifocal glasses to mine. So let me use the
term "wellbeing-goods" for both the states and events in a person's life
that are good for the person and the actions and activities of a person
that are good for him or her.

We can make sound judgments about whether or not something is
good for someone without being able to explain what it is for something
to be good for someone. One of the challenges facing the theorist, however, is to explain this idea; and that has proved difficult. Robert Adams
observes that explaining "what human well-being consists in — what it is
for something to be good for a person" is in fact "one of the most difficult tasks of ethical theory."[3] In this book I will not attempt that task.

A negative point is worth making, however. A position widely shared
nowadays, in the debates concerning the nature of wellbeing, is that
what makes something intrinsically good for a person is that it bears
some connection to the satisfaction of that person's desires or preferences. Those attracted to this position have found it difficult to specify
exactly what that connection is. In *What Is Good and Why: The Ethics of
Well-Being,* Richard Kraut offers what seems to me a decisive objection to
the position — an objection that saves us the labor of scrutinizing all the
different accounts that have been proposed, concerning the supposedly
essential connection between wellbeing and desire-satisfaction, to see
whether any of them work. He observes that we speak of something as
good for a plant and that, in doing so, we use the term "good for" in the
same sense that we do when we apply it to human beings. But plants
don't have desires.[4] In my discussion, I will assume that Kraut is right
about this; something's being good for someone has no essential connection to desire-satisfaction.

All ethical systems, in addition to employing the idea of states and
events, actions and activities, in a person's life that are good *for* him or
her, also employ the idea of *acting so as to bring about* some wellbeing-

2. A recent example of someone who defends this identification is Richard Kraut, in
What Is Good and Why: The Ethics of Well-Being (Cambridge, MA: Harvard University Press,
2007).

3. *Finite and Infinite Goods: A Framework for Ethics* (Oxford: Oxford University Press,
1999), 84.

4. An objection to Kraut's own account of something's being good for something,
which is of the same sort as his objection to the desire-satisfaction account, is that we
speak of things as *good for* an institution.

good in the life of someone or other. Bringing about some wellbeing-good in someone's life may either be an end in itself in the structure of one's action or activity, or a mere means to something else.

Among the diverse phenomena that we use the English word "love" to refer to, prominent is that of seeking to promote some wellbeing-good of someone or other as an end in itself. Every ethical system operates with the idea of love so understood. Most systems do not call it love; but whether or not they call it love, every ethical system operates with the idea.

RULES FOR THE PROMOTION OF WELLBEING: EGOISM, EUDAIMONISM, AND UTILITARIANISM

Ethical systems do not just *have* the ideas mentioned; they *apply* them. In particular, they apply them in formulating rules as to which wellbeing-goods of which persons one may or should seek to bring about, and under what conditions and in what manner. One of the most fundamental points of difference among such systems concerns which rules of application are correct.

I must explain how I will be using the terms "should" and "may" in my discussion. In ordinary English, "should" and "ought" often function as synonyms, as do "may" and "permitted." I will not be using them as synonyms. When I say that S *may* do X, or that it is *acceptable* for S to do X, I will mean that it would be a good thing for S to do X; and when I say that S *should* do X, I will mean that, of the alternatives on offer, doing X is the best thing for S to do. By contrast, when I say that S *ought to* do X, I will mean that it is *morally obligatory* for S to do X; and when I say that it is *permissible* for S to do X, I will mean that it is not morally obligatory for S to refrain from doing X.

The assumption underlying this regimentation of language is that not everything one should do is something that one is morally obligated to do. When a friend asks me for advice on whether he should apply for some position advertised in the newspaper, I may say that I think he should apply. Usually I will not mean that he is obligated to apply; I mean that applying for the position is the best thing for him to do in his circumstance. On the other hand, if one is morally obligated to do something, then one should do it; moral obligation trumps other considerations.

The rule of application easiest to explain and grasp is that of ethical *egoism*. The egoist holds that the only wellbeing-goods one should seek as ends in themselves to bring about are one's own; only as a means to the enhancement of one's own overall wellbeing should one seek to bring about some wellbeing-good of another. The well-lived life is the life animated entirely by self-love.

Eudaimonism, the position of almost all the ancient Greek and Roman ethical theorists, is considerably more complex than egoism.[5] It's similar to egoism in that it too is agent-oriented. The eudaimonists observed, however, that not only do we promote the wellbeing of another as a *means* to enhancing our own wellbeing; sometimes promoting another person's wellbeing *as an end* in itself enhances one's own wellbeing. Promoting her wellbeing is not a *means* to enhancement of one's own wellbeing but a *component* therein, a *constituent.* The ancients often cited friendship as an example. Overall wellbeing requires friends. Friends do sometimes promote the wellbeing of the friend as a means to enhancing their own overall wellbeing. In true friendship, however, one goes beyond this; one promotes the wellbeing of one's friend as an end in itself. Promoting her wellbeing is a *component* within one's own wellbeing, not just a means to enhancing it.

These observations led the ancient eudaimonists to the position that one may seek to promote the wellbeing of anyone whatsoever as an end in itself provided that doing so promises to enhance one's own overall wellbeing. It makes no sense, they said, to promote the wellbeing of another, whether as a means or as an end in itself, if doing so does not promise to enhance one's own overall wellbeing. No wise person would do such a thing. The fact that such-and-such would be good for another person is never complete as a reason for its being a good thing for one to try to bring about.

Interpreting the ancient eudaimonists as affirming this *agent-wellbeing proviso* is not uncontested. In discussions of the matter one hears it said that though this interpretation may hold for the Stoics, it does not hold for Aristotle. But I know of no passage in Aristotle that contradicts this interpretation. Nor I do know of any plausible alternative interpretation. And it seems to me the plain sense of the passage in the *Nicomachean Ethics* where Aristotle says that "It is thought to be a mark of a man of practical wisdom to be able to deliberate well about what is good and expedient for himself, not in some particular respect, e.g., about what sorts of things conduce to health or to strength, but about what sorts of things conduce to the good life in general" (6.5; 1140a 25-28).[6]

---

5. I discuss eudaimonism more fully in the seventh chapter of my *Justice: Rights and Wrongs* than I will here.

6. The translation I am using is that by W. D. Ross (revised by J. O. Urmson) in Jonathan Barnes, ed., *The Complete Works of Aristotle,* vol. 2 (Princeton: Princeton University Press, 1984). Exactly the same point that Aristotle makes is somewhat more fully stated in the following passage from one of the most notable of our contemporary eudaimonists, Alasdair MacIntyre: "What constitutes a good reason for my doing this rather than that,

Let it be noted that eudaimonism is not a thesis about motivation. It was not the position of the eudaimonists that one should seek to promote the wellbeing of another only if one does so *for the reason that* one judges that doing so will enhance one's own wellbeing; far better to have a virtuous character that leads one to act thus in appropriate circumstances without deliberation. Eudaimonism affirms a thesis concerning the conditions under which it is acceptable to seek to promote the wellbeing of someone as an end in itself; that thesis concerning conditions is not a thesis concerning acceptable motivations.

I opened this chapter by distinguishing, within the goods that constitute a person's wellbeing, between those that are states and events in the person's life and those that are actions or activities on the part of the person. Eudaimonism made more of this distinction than any other movement in the history of philosophy. They insisted that one's happiness, the estimability of one's life, is determined entirely by the actions and activities one performs, not by states and events in one's life. We may call this their *activity thesis* concerning the estimable life. Describing ancient eudaimonism in general, Julia Annas says that "Happiness is . . . thought of as active rather than passive, and as something that involves the agent's activity, and thus as being, commonsensically, up to the agent. This kind of consideration would rule out wealth, for example, right away. Happiness cannot just be a thing, however good, that someone might present you with. At the very least it involves what you *do* with wealth, the kind of *use* you put it to."[7] She quotes Arius's paraphrasing of Aristotle: "[Since the final good is not the fulfilment of bodily and external goods, but living according to virtue], therefore happiness is activity. . . . Happiness is life, and life is the fulfilment of action. No bodily or external good is in itself an action or in general an activity."[8]

activity.
thesis: is
Happiness is
determined by
action

Aristotle
- Happiness
is activity

---

for my acting from this particular desire rather than that, is that my doing this rather than that serves my good, will contribute to my flourishing qua human being." In *Dependent Rational Animals* (Chicago and LaSalle: Open Court, 1999), 86. What MacIntyre says here is of course compatible with holding that this is not the only sort of good reason for acting. Nowhere in his discussion does he even so much as suggest this.

7. *Platonic Ethics: Old and New* (Cornell: Cornell University Press, 1999), 45. Here is what John Cooper says on the same point: "According to Aristotle's account, [external goods] are needed as antecedently existing conditions that make possible the full exercise of the happy man's virtuous qualities of mind and character. In each case the value to the happy man consists in what the external goods make it possible for him, as a result of having them, to do. Any value goods other than virtuous action itself might have just for their own sakes is denied, or at least left out of account on this theory." "Aristotle on the Goods of Fortune," in *Aristotle's Ethics*, ed. Terence Irwin (New York and London: Garland, 1995), 189.

8. Annas, *Platonic Ethics*, 189. The passage from Aristotle that Arius was paraphrasing is to be found in *Nicomachean Ethics* 1.7; 1098a 16-19: "Human good turns out to be activity

Commentators, both ancient and modern, have found the sharp distinction within a person's life-goods that the eudaimonists drew, between actions and activities that the person performs and states and events that she undergoes, either baffling or purely verbal. The eudaimonists did not deny that states and events in a person's life have worth. The Stoics called them indifferents, but then added that some indifferents are *preferable* to others. They insisted on reserving the term "goods" for virtuous actions. Cicero and Augustine insisted that this distinction between goods and preferables was purely verbal. In *City of God* Augustine remarks that "when [the Stoics] say that these things are not to be called goods but advantages [*commoda*], we are to regard this as a dispute over words, not as a genuine distinction between things" (*City of God*, 9.5).[9]

But suppose we take seriously the eudaimonists' insistence that the estimability (happiness) of one's life is determined by what one does, not by what happens to one. This claim is fully compatible with holding that states and events in one's life have worth; the claim being made is that they lack the sort of worth that contributes to determining the estimability of a person's life. The Stoic distinction between goods and preferables is not purely verbal; nor, indeed, is it baffling. What's baffling is not the distinction but the thesis, that it is only what one does that counts toward the estimability of one's life.

I know of no passage in which any of the eudaimonists directly addresses this question in its full generality. To the best of my knowledge they all content themselves with arguing against specific versions of the alternative: being wealthy does not contribute to the estimability of a person's life, having honors bestowed on one does not contribute to its estimability, experiencing lots of pleasure does not, etc.

Though the ancient eudaimonist theorists may have found the activity thesis more or less obvious, what makes you and me ask for a defense is that, on this point, Judaism and Christianity differ sharply from ancient eudaimonism. What determines the estimability of one's life is not only what one does but how one fares. That's what lies behind the cry of the psalmist in the Hebrew Bible/Old Testament: "Why do the righteous suffer?" The biblical Job was a virtuous man who lamented the misery of his life. To the eudaimonist, Job was a crybaby.

I mentioned above that every ethical system proposes one or more

---

of soul in conformity with excellence, and if there are more than one excellence, in conformity with the best and most complete. But we must add, 'in a complete life.' For one swallow does not make a summer, nor does one day; and so too one day, or a short time, does not make a man blessed and happy."

9. I am using the translation by R. W. Dyson, *Augustine: The City of God against the Pagans* (Cambridge: Cambridge University Press, 1998), here 364.

rules as to which wellbeing-goods of which persons one may or should
seek to bring about as an end in itself, and under what circumstances
and in what manner. To my formulation of their agent-wellbeing proviso the ancient eudaimonists would all insist on adding a point about
the manner in which one should seek to enhance one's own wellbeing
and that of others, insofar as theirs is intertwined with one's own: one
should always do so in accord with virtue. Thus it is that we get Arius's
apothegmatic paraphrase of Aristotle, quoted earlier: happiness "is living in accord with virtue." The virtues are habituated skills in assessing
priorities among the actual and potential preferables in one's life and
acting accordingly.

When we put together the activity principle for the estimability of a
person's life with the principle that the estimable life is the life lived in
accord with virtue, what we then get is this: "The indifferents — conventional goods and evils — have value for happiness only in being the ma-
terials for and context within which the virtuous life is lived. On their
own they neither add to the happiness of a life nor subtract from it."[10]

The third major ethical position commonly articulated and discussed
by philosophical theorists, far less complex than eudaimonism, is *utilitarianism.* The utilitarian agrees with the eudaimonist that, in principle,
one may seek to promote the wellbeing of anyone whatsoever as an end
in itself. He attaches a different condition, however. One should always
do what promises to maximize the total amount of wellbeing in people's
lives, taking due account, in this way, of everyone whose wellbeing
would be affected by the alternative courses of action open to one. If
maximizing wellbeing requires, in a given case, that one promote the
wellbeing of some particular person, be that person oneself or another,
then that is what one should do. If it does not require that one should
not promote the wellbeing of that person, be the person oneself or another, then one *may* do so. Essential to utilitarianism is the maximizing
principle.

Defending Our Description of Eudaimonism

It is often said to be definitive and distinctive of eudaimonism that it
takes, as the fundamental question to be addressed by each of us, how
can I live my life well, whereas other systems of ethics take, as their fundamental question, which action should I perform of those available to
me? This claim seems to me not correct. It's true that the ancient
eudaimonists did take as fundamental that question about one's life as a

10. Annas, *Platonic Ethics*, 43.

whole whereas modern ethicists typically focus on individual actions. But the connection is purely contingent. Egoists and utilitarians could also take, as their fundamental question, how to live one's life well; I think they should. But doing so would not turn them into eudaimonists. The answer they give to that fundamental question would be an egoist or utilitarian answer, not a eudaimonist answer.

Another thing often said to be definitive and distinctive of eudaimonism is its emphasis on the virtues. And it is certainly true that a striking difference between ancient eudaimonism and modern utilitarianism is the prominence of virtues in the former and their near-absence in the latter. The recent resurgence of interest in virtue ethics has in good measure been spurred by a resurgence of interest in ancient eudaimonism. But the fact that modern utilitarians have not talked about virtue is purely contingent; they can and should. The virtues would be different, however. The virtues necessary and appropriate for living as a modern utilitarian are not those praised and cultivated by the ancient eudaimonists.

WHY THESE POSITIONS FAIL

Let us now reflect, all too briefly, on the acceptability of these three positions, taking them in the order of mention. The egoist is not making the claim that we human beings are so constituted psychologically that it is impossible for us to seek to promote the wellbeing of someone other than oneself as an end in itself. That is the position that the eighteenth-century writer, Francis Hutcheson, argued against in his *Inquiry concerning Moral Good and Evil;* but it is not the position of the egoist. Nor is it the position of the egoist that though it is psychologically possible to seek to promote the wellbeing of someone other than oneself as an end in itself, there is something in our circumstances that renders futile all or most attempts to do so — lack of sufficient knowledge about other persons, perhaps. The egoist concedes, implicitly if not explicitly, that some of us do successfully aim at promoting the wellbeing of someone else as an end in itself; his position is that we should not do this. It makes no sense.

The love of parents for their children is like the love of persons for their friends in that, though it typically contains an element of self-love, rarely if ever will that constitute the totality of a parent's love. Parents seek to advance the wellbeing of their children as an end in itself; they do so for the sake of the child. The egoist tells us that such love makes no sense; we should work to eliminate all such love. Such a radical re-orientation of ourselves would make sense only if we were given a powerful reason for undertaking it. The egoist offers no such reason.[11]

What then about the eudaimonist's principle, that one should seek to promote the wellbeing of another as an end in itself only if doing so promises to enhance one's own wellbeing? It's easy to think of situations in which someone seeks to promote the wellbeing of another as an end in itself even though doing so neither promises nor proves to be a component in his own wellbeing; sometimes it promises to diminish, and does in fact diminish, one's own wellbeing. In Jesus' parable of the good Samaritan, the Samaritan's going to the aid of the wounded man alongside the road did not enhance, nor did it promise to enhance, his own wellbeing. Jesus said that the Samaritan was moved by compassion. It is true of human beings in general that compassion often moves us to come to the aid of those who are neither friends nor family members, people to whom we have no prior attachment and with whom we are unlikely to have any significant relationship in the future, sometimes doing so at considerable cost to ourselves, even the cost of death.

The position of the eudaimonist is that the good Samaritan was misguided. Rather than holding him up for praise, we should declare that acting as he did makes no sense; such indiscriminate bleeding-heart behavior is not to be admired. Going to the aid of friends, that makes sense. Going to the aid of family members, that makes sense. Going to the aid of fellow members of one's nation or people, sometimes that makes sense. But going to the aid of a stranger who is a member of an alien and hostile people — an "enemy" — makes no sense whatsoever. No wise person would do that.

As for myself, I hold that the good Samaritan did a fine and noble thing even if it did diminish his wellbeing. I would need a powerful argument against this position before I set about trying to extirpate my admiration for the good Samaritans of the world. The eudaimonist offers no such argument.

That leaves us with utilitarianism. As will become clear in Part Two of our discussion, I hold that the utilitarian is correct in his insistence that, in deciding what to do, one should take into account all those who will be affected by one's action. But in my judgment the utilitarian has not succeeded in identifying the right way of taking their wellbeing into account. His position is that we should take their wellbeing into account by seeking to maximize net utility, that is, the overall amount of wellbeing-goods in people's lives.

An old objection to this position is that it permits unacceptable trade-offs. If I find myself in a situation where maximizing overall

11. Richard Kraut makes this point in *What Is Good, and Why*.

wellbeing requires that I drastically diminish the wellbeing of someone who has done no wrong, I may do so; indeed, I *should* do so. The objection seems to me on target; it's a *reductio ad absurdum* of the position. It would be unacceptable for a judge to impose a prison sentence on someone widely thought to be guilty of some crime, but whom he knows to be innocent, for the sake of the social good of deterrence.

Richard Kraut offers a different objection, one that focuses on the universalism of the utilitarian principle. The principle tells us that, when deciding what form our love for children and spouse should take, we are to take into account everybody whose wellbeing would be affected by the alternative courses of action open to us; we are to think in universal terms. I endorse what Kraut says about this in the following passage:

> Just as the promise-maker should give heightened attention to one small part of the world and should provide the good he said he would provide, so a parent who has a responsibility to care for his child should also give heightened attention to one small part of the world. If parents adopted the principle that they should produce the greatest amount of good for the universe, giving their children only as much attention as will contribute to this final sum and treating the needs of their children as having no more importance than anyone else's, then not only would the children of the world suffer greatly, but their parents would themselves lose the good that consists in having a special relationship with their children. (44)

Utilitarians have resorted to various strategies for blocking such objections as the two mentioned, prominent among them that of replacing so-called act-utilitarianism with so-called rule-utilitarianism. It's not the net utility of individual actions that is to be considered but the net utility of following general rules for action. I fail to see that this recourse saves utilitarianism.

Consider a rule such that the following of the rule by the members of society does yield greater overall wellbeing than their not following it would yield. But now suppose that, in a given case, I see that I can violate the rule in such a way that I can bring about a greater net utility while in no way impairing general adherence to the rule. I violate the rule in secret; nobody ever discovers the violation. Rule-utilitarianism says that only the utility of following rules is to be taken into account, not the utility of individual actions. But what could be the rationale for not also taking into account, in the sort of case described, the utility of the individual action? It seems thoroughly ad hoc. The core "intuition" of the utilitarian is that maximizing net utility is the great desideratum in action; in this case, the greatest net utility is achieved by violating the rule while making sure that this violation has no negative impact on the social practice of following the rule.

But suppose the rule-utilitarian has a rationale for his contention that the utility of individual actions is never to be taken into account. Then consider the following two rules for action. Rule One: prurient spying on someone is never to be done. Rule Two: prurient spying on someone is only to be done in such a way that it has no effect on anyone's wellbeing other than that of the spy, whose wellbeing it enhances. General adherence to Rule Two has somewhat greater net utility than adherence to Rule One. But surely prurient spying on someone ought not to be done, period; persons have a right not to be pruriently spied upon.

INTRODUCING AGAPISM

Egoism, eudaimonism, utilitarianism — none of them offers an acceptable rule as to whose wellbeing one may or should promote as an end in itself, and under what conditions. To be acceptable, a rule would have to resemble the rules offered by eudaimonism and utilitarianism in affirming or implying that we may and should sometimes seek to promote the wellbeing of another as an end in itself; it will have to differ from them in rejecting the agent-wellbeing proviso of the eudaimonist and the maximizing proviso of the utilitarian.

Kraut, whom I just quoted and whose discussion of these issues is excellent, sees no such rule on the horizon. The failure of all the main philosophical systems of ethics suggests, he says, "that the question to which they are responses is too broad, too general, too abstract. Philosophy is in the business of posing broad, general, abstract questions; but when all the answers prove defective, it is time to ask whether we really need to work at so high a level of generality. And in fact, we do not need a formula that tells all people whatsoever, regardless of their circumstances, whose good they should promote. We can instead rely on common sense and recognize that the world as it is already offers countless opportunities for doing what is good" (56).

Kraut is right, of course, in saying that we can recognize that something is a good for someone, and can decide whether or not to promote that good, without having in hand explanations and general rules of the sort that philosophers seek. Indeed, if we were not able to recognize pre-theoretically what is the case in such matters, we would be unable to employ one of the most important strategies for appraising the explanations and rules offered by philosophers, that of appealing to examples and counter-examples.

But I think Kraut misdescribes the "failure," as he calls it, of "all the main philosophical systems of ethics." He understands those systems as aiming at finding "a formula that tells all people whatsoever, regardless of their circumstances, whose good they should promote." This fits egoism and utilitarianism, those being the two systems that Kraut discusses. And I agree that it is impossible to find such a formula, for reasons that I will explain in Chapter Eleven. But a rule of application need not take that form; the eudaimonist rule does not. I described the eudaimonists as holding that one may seek to promote the wellbeing of anyone whatsoever as an end in itself provided that doing so promises to enhance one's own overall wellbeing. This does not even purport to tell us, for everybody whatsoever, whose good they should promote in every circumstance in which they may find themselves. It is not on that account pointless, however; it offers definite guidance. And so too for the system of ethics that I will be developing in what follows, namely, agapism.

Agapism is a way of thinking about the issues at hand that Kraut, along with most other philosophers, takes no note of, mainly, I think, because its foundational sources are religious texts rather than philosophical texts. William Frankena is an exception to the generalization. In his well-known book *Ethics*, Frankena remarks that "there is an ethical theory that has been and still is widely accepted, especially in Judeo-Christian circles, the ethics of love. This holds that there is only one basic ethical imperative — to love — and that the others are to be derived from it. . . . We may call this view *agapism*. In spite of its prevalence, it is generally neglected in philosophical introductions to ethics like this, yet just because of its prevalence, it is desirable to . . . say something about it" (56). Frankena then proceeds to devote a chapter to a discussion of agapism.

It will be evident from the foregoing that I do not think we can identify the sort of theory Frankena has in mind by saying that it is an ethic of love. If by "love" one means seeking to promote the wellbeing of someone as an end in itself — and Frankena's subsequent discussion shows that that is what he means — then every ethical system is an ethic of love, whether or not it uses the term "love."[12] And though it is open to egoists, eudaimonists, and utilitarians to hold that the concept of *seeking to promote the wellbeing of someone as an end in itself* is not the only concept to be employed in deciding what one should do and how one

Agapism

---

12. Though egoists, eudaimonists, and utilitarians do not usually employ the term "love," it is interesting that in his exposition of egoism and utilitarianism, Richard Kraut often does employ it, along with other terms that he uses as synonyms of "love," namely, "care for," "care about," and "concern for." I count fifteen occurrences of these terms on just two pages, 53-54.

should live, it is also open to them to insist that it is the only relevant concept. It is open to them to insist "that there is only one basic ethical imperative — to love," that "the others are to be derived from it."

If agapism is not to be identified as the ethic of love, how then is it to be identified? There are different versions of agapism, just as there are different versions of egoism, eudaimonism, and utilitarianism. How can we identify the type? Given that agapism is distinct from all three of the ethical systems thus far considered, we can infer that the agapist holds that we should sometimes seek to promote the wellbeing of another as an end in itself even though neither the eudaimonist nor the utilitarian proviso is satisfied. But that only describes the general region within which agapism is located; it does not pick it out.

Agapism is a way of thinking about ethics that has its origin in the injunction in the Pentateuch to love one's neighbor as oneself and in the declaration by Jesus and other rabbis that that commandment is the heart of the Jewish Torah. The identity of agapism is not first of all a systematic identity but the identity of an intellectual tradition, viz., the tradition of reflecting on the implications of what I called, in the Preface, the *love-imperative.*

Of course eudaimonism and utilitarianism are also intellectual traditions. Eudaimonists and utilitarians see themselves as thinking within an intellectual tradition handed down to them, a tradition full of internal controversies and novel developments. It is typical of present day eudaimonists to spend considerable time engaging the founding documents of the tradition, the writings of the ancient Peripatetics and Stoics. Because the founding documents of eudaimonism and utilitarianism were philosophical, however, there is a tighter systematic unity to those traditions than there is to the agapist tradition.

That said, let me be so bold as to identify some points of systematic unity in the agapist tradition. In order to do so, we need a more expansive idea of someone's good than we have thus far been working with.

FLOURISHING, AND GOODS OF SOMEONE

The utilitarian rule of application introduced an innovation into our understanding of a person's good that is easy to miss but fraught with import. On the utilitarian principle, the good thing to do in a given case, the thing one should do, may well be something that is not good for one; maximizing overall wellbeing may diminish one's own wellbeing. To accommodate the utilitarian principle, we must introduce the idea of a good in a person's life that is not a good *for* the person but is nonetheless a good *of* the person. Those actions and activities that are goods of the person will include those that are goods for the person but will include other life-goods as well.

We not only need this more expansive concept of life-goods to accommodate those actions and activities that are goods of the person but not goods for the person; we also need it to accommodate states and events in a person's life that are goods of, but not for, the person — states and events that contribute nothing to the person's wellbeing even though they are goods in that person's life. Let me explain why.

It was possible to formulate the egoist, eudaimonist, and utilitarian rules of application without employing the concept of a right. What I will be arguing in Part Two of our discussion is that it is impossible to formulate the agapist rule of application without employing the concept of a right. Let us, for the time being, set off to the side corrective rights — the rights we acquire by being wronged — and focus on primary rights. With minor exceptions, if I have a right to being treated a certain way, then being treated that way would be a good in my life. So suppose that my email correspondence has been read by a hacker who does nothing with the information gleaned other than enjoy it. I would say that he has deprived me of a life-good to which I have a right, the good of not having my privacy violated for prurient reasons. But he has in no way diminished my wellbeing; he has not deprived me of anything that is a good for me.

Rights

In short, acknowledging the full range of rights requires acknowledging that some state or event in a person's life, some action or activity, may be a good of the person without being a good for the person. Let me call such goods, life-goods.[13] What I have been calling "wellbeing-goods" are a species of life-goods. And as a parallel to saying that something is a good for a person in case it contributes positively to her wellbeing, let me say that something is a good of a person in case it contributes positively to her flourishing. Wellbeing is a component of flourishing.

life goods

Near the beginning of this chapter I remarked that one of the phenomena that we use the English word "love" to refer to is that of seeking to promote some wellbeing-good of someone or other as an end in itself; and I added that every ethical system operates with the idea of love so understood. This remark requires an amplification that is now obvious. We use the English word "love" to refer to seeking to promote not just wellbeing-goods but life-goods in general; some ethical systems, utilitarianism and agapism in particular, operate with this broader idea of love.

13. Bringing about a diminution in someone's wellbeing is often called *harming* them, and the diminution itself, *a harm*. Using this terminology, what the above argument shows is that one may be wronged without being harmed.

THE AGAPIST TRADITION

Back to agapism. The agapist tradition, like the eudaimonist and utilitarian traditions, has texts that those in the tradition regard as classical,
along with texts that they regard as belonging to the tradition but that
they would not hold up as classical expressions of the tradition. So let's
distinguish between a *classical* agapist and a *non-classical* agapist. A classical agapist is a thinker who locates himself in the agapist tradition and
agrees with the classical texts on fundamental points; a non-classical
agapist is a thinker who locates himself in the agapist tradition but
whose thought differs on fundamental points from that found in the
classics of the tradition. The two great classical texts in the modern day
agapist tradition are Søren Kierkegaard's *Works of Love* and Anders
Nygren's *Agape and Eros*. Various texts of Reinhold Niebuhr represent a
non-classical version of modern day agapism.

All agapists, classical and non-classical alike, hold that one should
seek to promote life-goods of everyone who is one's neighbor as ends in
themselves, in the sense of "neighbor" that Jesus gave to the term; and
all of them reject both the agent-wellbeing proviso of the eudaimonist
and the maximizing proviso of the utilitarian. Contrary to the utilitarian, who holds that if maximizing the overall amount of wellbeing requires that one impair the wellbeing of someone, then that's what one
should do, the classical agapist holds that one may impair someone's
flourishing (i.e., their life-goods) only if doing so is necessary to promoting *that* person's greater flourishing. In seeking to promote some
life-good of someone who is one's neighbor as an end in itself, one is
never to diminish the life-goods of anyone else; no such trade-offs. All
classical agapists likewise hold the thesis Frankena mentions, that love is
the only basic ethical imperative; all other imperatives are to be derived
from this one.

In Part Two of our discussion I will expand on these points as I articulate and defend a non-classical version of agapism, paying special attention to how the justice-imperative is related to the love-imperative. As
preparation for that, I propose engaging modern day agapism, both
classical and non-classical forms thereof. Not only will such engagement
prove interesting in its own right. Uncovering the points at which modern day agapism proves inadequate, particularly the points at which its
understanding of the relation between love and justice proves inadequate, will also be instructive for working out our own version.

As Frankena observed, and as I mentioned earlier, philosophers for
the most part have ignored agapism. The most articulate agapists have
been theologians rather than philosophers — Søren Kierkegaard being
the great exception. And all of them have worked out their systematic

views in dialogue with the founding texts of the agapist tradition, viz.,
the Hebrew and Christian scriptures. Accordingly, to fully explore modern day agapism we will have to look at both theologians and philosophers; and to appraise it, we will have to engage both in systematic reflection and interpretation of the founding texts of the tradition. When
I develop my own version of agapism in Part Two, I too will combine systematic reflection with interpretation of the founding texts.

PART ONE

Benevolence-Agapism

Chapter Two

MODERN DAY AGAPISM

IN THE TWENTIETH CENTURY there emerged, among Christian (especially Protestant) ethicists and theologians, a highly articulate and provocative version of agapism, with Søren Kierkegaard as its great nineteenth-century forebear. Prominent members of the movement were Anders Nygren, Karl Barth, Reinhold Niebuhr, and Paul Ramsey. The classic texts of the movement are Kierkegaard's *Works of Love* and Nygren's *Agape and Eros*.[2] At the core of the movement was a distinctive and sharply delineated interpretation of what Jesus meant by "love" (Gk. *agapē*) when he said, "You shall love your neighbor as yourself" and "God so loved the world that he gave his only Son." It became common to call such love *agape, agapic love,* and *neighbor-love.* Kierkegaard often called it *Christian love.* We are to love our neighbors with that distinctive form of love that is agape.[3]

Nobody questions the profundity of Kierkegaard's *Works of Love.* Not so for *Agape and Eros,* published in the early 1930s by the Swedish Lutheran bishop, Anders Nygren. *Agape and Eros* has come in for an enormous amount of criticism. Mention Nygren's name in circles where his work is known and one almost always gets a dismissive comment: Nygren had no doctrine of creation, Nygren misinterpreted Plato and Augustine, Nygren misinterpreted the New Testament, Nygren was hostile to Judaism, Nygren thought of divine love as deterministically causing human love, and so forth, on and on. All true. There is indeed defective theology in *Agape and Eros,* defective intellectual history, defective biblical interpretation, defective philosophy, overtones of anti-Semitism. Nonetheless, Nygren deserves to be defended against his cultured despisers on two important points.

First, on the matter of influence. Nygren's interpretation of what Jesus meant with the Aramaic term that the writers of the New Testament translated with the Greek *agapē,* and his insistence that obedience to Jesus requires that one love every one who is one's neighbor with that form of

---

1. *Works of Love,* ed. and trans. Howard V. Hong and Edna H. Hong (Princeton: Princeton University Press, 1995), 55.

2. Anders Nygren, *Agape and Eros,* trans. Philip S. Watson (London: SPCK, 1953), 78.

3. For a history of the movement see Gene Outka, *Agape* (New Haven: Yale University Press, 1972).

love, proved to be compelling for many. The framework of Old Testament interpretation, intellectual history, and so forth, within which he set his interpretation of Jesus' love command has caught the fire of unrelenting criticism; his agapism itself gained wide acceptance as an interpretation of the New Testament texts. My attention will be focused on Nygren's version of agapism; I will attend to the framework only as necessary.

Second, Nygren deserves praise for his systematic rigor. With a determination wonderful to behold he pursued the implications of his way of understanding Jesus' love command. Arguments in Nygren that I regard as *reductio ad absurdum* arguments were viewed by him as simply unfolding the radical and surprising implications of New Testament thought. After Nygren, the implications of his line of interpretation are much clearer than they were before.

An Initial Characterization of Modern Day Agapism

Before we look at what the modern day agapists had to say, let me make a few comments about the overall character of their discussion. First, articulation of their systematic position is intimately interwoven with interpretation of the relevant biblical texts, and those texts are treated as authoritative. What this means, in practice, is that the modern day agapists present their position as a plausible interpretation of, and extrapolation from, the texts, and defensible as a systematic position; for the most part, they do not take the next step of assembling arguments in favor of the position which do not assume the authority of the text. That's what a philosopher would typically do. The contrast should not be overdrawn, however. Though a philosopher will seldom if ever say that he accepts some thesis because it was propounded by a certain philosopher, those familiar with the work of historians of philosophy will have noticed that it is the habit of scholars of Aristotle, Aquinas, Kant, and Heidegger, to struggle hard to avoid interpreting their philosopher as having said something false or in some other way indefensible; they implicitly treat the texts they are interpreting as authoritative.

Second, though agapic love for someone is a form of love that seeks to promote the good of that person as an end in itself, the modern day agapists made no attempt to explain the nature either of flourishing in general or of wellbeing in particular. They did, of course, have views concerning the good of human beings and concerning what's good for them; but they did not try to explain the nature of these two kinds of good. They took for granted that we all understand well enough what is a person's good, and concentrated on explaining the nature of agapic love and how that form of love differs from other forms. Kierkegaard interwove his articulation of the nature and distinctiveness of agapic love with substantial comments on how such love fits into a person's life along with other forms of love; Nygren interwove his discussion with substantial comments on how such love is related to justice.

I will not follow the modern day agapists in calling the form of love they had in mind, *neighbor-love.* I have three reasons for not doing so. First, using the term "neighbor-love" for that form of love makes it all-too-easy to forget that what the agapists had in mind was not love of whatever sort whose object is the neighbor but a special kind of love. Second, it was Kierkegaard's view that one should include oneself among the recipients of one's agapic love; it would be overly paradoxical to express this view by saying that we should have neighbor-love for ourselves. Third, the modern day agapists all held that God loves us with love of the same sort that we should have for our neighbors. It would be odd to say that we are one and all recipients of God's neighbor-love.

The term I will use is "agapic love." When I want to refer to the kind of love that Jesus *actually* had in mind when he enjoined us to love our neighbors and when he attributed love for us to God, rather than the kind of love that the modern day agapists *thought* he had in mind, I will call it *New Testament agape,* or, when there is no danger of confusion, simply *agape.*

The Nature of Agapic Love and the Rule for Application

Our main project in this chapter is, first, to identify the sort of love that the modern day agapists typically called neighbor-love; second, to take note of the rule of application that they propounded for this sort of love; and third, to see what they had to say about the relation, both conceptual and existential, between that form of love and other forms of love. For the most part, I will refrain from critique. Critique will come in later chapters.

All modern day agapists held that agapic love is a species of that sort of love which consists of seeking to promote the good of someone as an end in itself, provided one does not do so because justice requires it. Such love, when the recipient is someone other than oneself, is *benevolence,* or *generosity;* agapic love for the other is a species of benevolence. Those who held that one should not include oneself among the recipients of one's agapic love often described it as *self-sacrificial* love. As Barth was fond of saying, agape is *being for* the other.

Let me offer a few supporting quotations for this interpretation. In agapic love, says Barth, a person "gives himself to another with no expectation of a return, in a pure venture." He identifies "with [the other's] interests in utter independence of the question of [the other's] attractiveness, of what [the other] has to offer."[4] In his book on Niebuhr, Robin Lovin declares that love "is the disposition to seek the well-being of persons generally that theologians and moral philosophers have called 'benevolence'."[5] "To love another is to wish that person's good" (200). And speaking of the movement as a whole, Outka says that "agape is, in both its genesis and continuation, an active concern for the neighbor's well-being which is somehow independent of particular actions of the other" (260). The person who treats others with agape considers "the interests of others and not simply his own. Others are to be regarded for their own sakes, for what *they* may want or need, and not finally because they bring benefits to the agent" (8).

In the course of presenting his version of agapism, Paul Ramsey mentions what he says is the other main interpretation "of the meaning of Christian love contending for acceptance in present-day theological discussion."[6] The main alternative, he says, is *mutual love* — that is, love that both loves and seeks to be loved. In mutual love, "self-referential motives . . . are co-present with other-regarding motives" (106).

Ramsey brusquely rejects this alternative. "Surely," he says, the benevolence interpretation "is the more correct reading of Biblical and New Testament texts. While the national life of the people of the Old Testament was based on covenant, this covenant among men was in turn measured by the standard of the extraordinary righteousness of God. God's *hesed*, or his steadfast faithfulness to men even when there was on their part no returning love, gave the standard for the covenant. . . . When the scripture enjoins: 'Let love be among you,' it does not mean, 'Let "among-you-ness" be among you.' It is one thing to say, 'Let mutual love be mutual,' and quite another to say in the New Testament meaning of the word, 'Let *love* be mutual.' For the love in question takes its measure from Christ's love for the church when he 'gave himself up for her'" (106).

Agapic love, I said, was understood by the modern day agapists as a species of seeking to promote the good of someone as an end in itself, provided one does not do so because justice requires it. Our question now is, what species?

The term "neighbor-love" suggests the answer. The modern day agapists all held that agapic love is that species of benevolence in which

4. Karl Barth, *Church Dogmatics*, Vol. 4, Part 2: *The Doctrine of Reconciliation*, ed. T. F. Torrance, trans. G. W. Bromiley (Edinburgh: T & T Clark, 1958), 745.

5. Robin W. Lovin, *Reinhold Niebuhr and Christian Realism* (Cambridge: Cambridge University Press, 1995), 199.

6. Paul Ramsey, "Love and Law," in Charles W. Kegley and Robert W. Bretall, eds., *Reinhold Niebuhr: His Religious, Social, and Political Thought* (New York: Macmillan, 1961), 104.

one loves someone *because* she is one's neighbor, as Jesus understood "neighbor" — not because she is one's spouse, not because he is one's friend, not because she is someone whom one admires, not because he is someone to whom one is attached, but because he or she is one's neighbor.

The agapists disagreed among themselves as to who is one's neighbor. The neighbor is anyone affected by one's actions, says Outka (13). "The neighbor is all people," says Kierkegaard (55), every human being. And since the lover is himself a human being, each of us is neighbor to himself.[7] On that last point, Nygren vigorously disagreed. Agape, he says, "excludes all self-love. Christianity does not recognize self-love as a legitimate form of love. Christian love moves in two directions, towards God and toward its neighbor; and in self-love it finds its chief adversary, which must be fought and conquered. . . . Agape recognizes no kind of self-love as legitimate" (217).

That explains the nature of agapic love. What is the rule for its application? Who should be the recipient of one's agapic love? Quite obviously, anyone who is one's neighbor. The Christian doctrine, says Kierkegaard, "is to love the neighbor, to love the whole human race, all people, even the enemy, and not to make exceptions, neither of preference nor of aversion" (19). Under what conditions is one to love agapically everyone who is one's neighbor? Under all conditions, said the classical modern day agapists. Reinhold Niebuhr, a prominent non-classical member of the modern day agapist movement, disagreed; there are conditions under which one should treat one's neighbor as justice requires rather than loving him agapically. We will look at Niebuhr's view in Chapter Five.

What Accounts for Agapic Love?

Running throughout Kierkegaard's discussion is the contrast between agapic love and natural love; all forms of love other than agapic love are natural. Ordinary self-love, romantic love, familial love, love of country, love of friends for each other: all are manifestation of dynamics belonging to human nature.[8] Not so for agapic love. But if this is so, what ac-

---

7. In *Works of Love*, Kierkegaard observes that whereas the second love command says "You shall love your neighbor as yourself," if "properly understood it also says the opposite, *You shall love yourself in the right way*" (22). What then follows is an extended passage on right and wrong ways of loving oneself.

8. In *Works of Love*, 154-55, Kierkegaard sounds the corresponding theme, that the "need of love" and the "need of companionship" are innate in human beings. For that reason, Christ also had these needs. To be the recipient of love is a "blessing" (157).

counts for the existence of agapic love among us? What accounts for this unnatural form of love?

Over and over Kierkegaard emphasizes the partiality of all natural forms of love; they all have certain human beings as their recipients and not others. His examples of such love were almost always examples of loving someone on account of being attached to him or her. About love grounded in attachment, there is no mystery; it's as natural as anything could be. But what would move one to seek to promote the good of someone other than oneself as an end in itself even though one has no attachment to that person — indeed, even though one feels no empathy for him or her (for empathy is also natural)? What would evoke in one a form of benevolence that is impartial as among all those who count as one's neighbor? Or to rephrase the question so as to take account of Kierkegaard's view that one is neighbor to oneself: what would evoke in one a form of seeking the good of someone as an end in itself that is impartial as among all human beings? What would account for so unnatural a form of love as agapic love?

Running throughout Nygren's discussion was the contrast between agape and eros. All forms of love other than agapic love are manifestations of love as eros; Nygren thought that eros always has within it a tinge of neediness, thus of self-love. About self-love, there is no mystery; it's as natural as anything could be. But, to quote Nygren, "What can induce a man to love just simply his neighbour, with no further object in view? What, above all, can induce him to love an enemy?" (215).

Nygren prefaced his answer to this question with an insistence that agape "has nothing to do with the kind of love that depends on the recognition of a valuable quality in its object" (78). His argument for this position was that, if this were not so, "God's love would not in the last resort be spontaneous and unmotivated but would have an adequate motive in the infinite value inherent in human nature. The forgiveness of sins would then imply merely the recognition of an already existing value. But it is evident enough that this is not the forgiveness of sins as Jesus understands it. When He says 'Thy sins are forgiven thee', this is no merely formal attestation of the presence of a value which justifies the overlooking of faults; it is the bestowal of a gift" (79-80). Coming to the surface in this passage is Nygren's conviction that God's forgiveness of the sinner is the paradigmatic example of agapic love. When one is reading Nygren and puzzled as to why he says what he does say about love, it often helps to recall that he viewed agape through the lens of God's gratuitous forgiveness of the sinner. The same is true for most of his twentieth-century successors.

But if recognition of worth in the recipient is dismissed as motivating agapic love, what's left? As we have just seen, "there is no motive for the love in the loved object itself"; but neither is there any motive "outside the object, in some ulterior purpose, or else the love will not be true and unfeigned, will not be Agape. For unless love for one's neighbour is directed to the neighbour alone, unless it is concerned exclusively with him and has literally no other end in view — not even that of gaining God's love — then it has no right to the name of neighbourly love" (Nygren, 216).

Since nothing outside the lover can account for agapic love, it has to be something within the lover; what other option is there? What might that be? Begin with God. God's love of human beings is agapic. Hence "we look in vain for an explanation of God's love in the character of the man who is the object of His love. . . . The only ground for [God's love] is to be found in God Himself. God's love is altogether *spontaneous*" (75). God loves "quite simply because it is His nature to love" (201).

Our love, if it is likewise to be agapic, will have to be like God's love in that its explanation also lies in the one loving. We must step carefully here, however. The explanation, in our case, is not that it belongs to our nature or essence as human beings to love the other with agapic love, for it does not. The explanation is rather that God's love has been infused into us. "God is the starting point and permanent basis of neighbourly love. He is not its *causa finalis*, but its *causa efficiens*. . . . Being Himself Agape, He brings forth Agape. . . . Everyone who is loved by Him and has been gripped and mastered by His love cannot but pass on this love to his neighbour. In this way God's love passes over directly into the Christian's love for his neighbour" (216).[9]

Kierkegaard's answer was different. Insofar as agapic love is present among us, it is present because we have acknowledged such love to be our duty. Only this can account for why one would do something so unnatural as to love agapically everyone who is one's neighbor, even one's enemies. It is "the very mark of Christian love and . . . its distinctive characteristic — that it contains this apparent contradiction: to love is a duty" (24). Christian love "is a matter of conscience and thus is not a matter of drives and inclination, or a matter of feeling, or a matter of intellectual calculation" (143). Kierkegaard calls erotic love and friendship "spontaneous love" (*passim*, 29-43). Their works are done out of passion; that's what accounts for their selective and preferential character. The works of agapic love are done out of duty.[10]

The duty is laid on us by Christ's command. Christ's command gener-

Yes. That's how it feels.

---

9. Barth objected strenuously to the deterministic character of Nygren's account.

10. There are unmistakable echoes of Kant in Kierkegaard's discussion of this point. "Erotic love and friendship, as the poet understands them, contain no moral task. . . . On the other hand, when one *shall* love the neighbor, then the task is the moral task, which in turn is the origin of all tasks. . . . Christianity is the true morality" (51).

or, the over-flowing nature of God's love in us.

ates in us the duty to love each and every neighbor with agapic love. We acknowledge the duty because we love the one who issues the command. In that way, it is our love for God that accounts for the presence of agapic love among us. From "love for God . . . originates love for the neighbor" (57). "Love God above all else; then you also love the neighbor, and in the neighbor every human being. Only by loving God above all else can one love the neighbor in the other human being" (58).

Though obedience to Christ's command out of love for the one who commands is what Kierkegaard emphasizes, it is not the whole of his thought on these matters. In the Conclusion of *Works of Love*, Kierkegaard observes that in the New Testament book of First John we find, instead of the command to love, the more gentle optative, "Beloved, let us love one another." This difference leads Kierkegaard to remark that "the commandment is not changed in the slightest way, least of all by an apostle. The change then can be only that the person who loves becomes more and more intimate with the commandment, becomes at one with the commandment, which he loves. This is why he can speak so gently. . . . If, however, you forget that it is the apostle of love who is speaking, you misunderstand him, because such words are not the beginning of the discourse about love but are the completion. Therefore we do not dare to speak this way" (375-76).

The "apostle of love" has come to love the command so much that he acts in accord with it out of love for it rather than out of duty. In addition, the apostle has discerned, says Kierkegaard, that "to love people is the only thing worth living for, and without this love you are not really living" (375). What does Kierkegaard mean? How is he thinking?

He doesn't say. But what I assume to be the answer is to be found in a rhetorically remarkable passage that occurs much earlier in *Works of Love* (86-89), where Kierkegaard makes metaphorical use of the contrast between an actor in costume and out of costume. Most of us deal with each other most of the time as costumed; some of us never allow ourselves to be seen in any other way. But beneath our costumes there is, in all of us, "the inner glory of equality" (87) — or to change the metaphor, "a common watermark" (89). "The Christian doctrine addresses itself equally to each individual, teaches him that God has created him and Christ has redeemed him" (69). If we could consistently manage to see past all our costumes and their dissimilarities, agapic love for each human being could be evoked in us by our perception of the equal inner glory in each. In this life, however, only such sanctified individuals as St. John consistently discern the inner glory present equally in all human beings. The rest of us must wait until "at death the curtain falls on the stage of actuality" to discern that "all of [us] are what [we] essentially were, what [we had not seen] because of the dissimilarity [of the costumes, namely, that we] are human beings" (87). In the meanwhile, "if someone is truly to love his neighbor, it must be kept in mind at all times that his dissimilarity is a disguise. . . . In each individual there continually glimmers that essential other, which is common to all, the eternal resemblance, the likeness" (88).[11]

I assume Kierkegaard's thought to be that agapic love for a human being *befits* the inner glory that is to be found in that human being. St. John arrived at the point of sanctification where he was able to look through or past our costumes in all their dissimilarities to the equal inner glory present in each; he was moved to act as befits that inner glory rather than out of dutiful obedience to Christ. "Love for the neighbor makes a person blind" to the dissimilarities, "so that he blindly loves every human being" (69). Or to change the metaphor, agapic love "sees the neighbor only with closed eyes, or by looking *away from* all dissimilarities" (68).

Kierkegaard takes note of the egalitarianism implicit in this picture of human beings. "None of us is pure humanity" (70). We are dissimilar in all sorts of ways; and Christianity neither pretends that that's not so nor does it try to get rid of all dissimilarities — if that were even possible. It does not "storm forth to abolish dissimilarity, neither the dissimilarity of distinction nor of lowliness." Instead, "it wants the dissimilarity to hang loosely on the individual" (88). If "you should see the ruler, cheerfully and respectfully bring him your homage, but you would still see in the ruler the inner glory, the equality of the glory that his magnificence conceals. If . . . you should see the beggar, . . . you would still see in him the inner glory, the equality of the glory, that his wretched outer garment conceals" (88).

Kierkegaard never spells out what he sees as the connection between, on the one hand, the inner glory that is equally present in all human beings and, on the other hand, agapic love for a human being. When formulating his view above, I said that agapic love for someone *befits* his inner glory; I let it go at that. But someone who holds, as I do, that justice is what due respect for the worth of someone requires, will naturally wonder whether we would be faithful to Kierkegaard's thought if we went beyond what he says to hold that, in at least some cases, loving someone because she is a neighbor is doing what justice requires and that, in those cases, one's love is required not only by obedience to the command of Christ but also by due respect for the worth of the neighbor.

We have to distinguish between acting *in accord with* what justice requires and acting as one does *because* justice requires it. I see nothing in
Kierkegaard's thought that would lead him to resist saying that love for
the other, concern for her good, is sometimes *required by* her worth. But
he makes it unmistakably clear that, in his view, treating someone as one
does *because* justice requires it is not an instance of the sort of love that
Jesus requires of us. Justice, he says, "is identified by its giving each his
own, just as it also in turn claims its own. . . . As soon as someone is de-
frauded of his own, or as soon as someone defrauds another of his own,
justice intervenes, because it safeguards the common security in which
everyone has his own, what he rightfully has" (265). But in Christian
love, the distinction between *mine* and *yours* disappears. The more it disappears, "the more justice shudders" and "the more perfect is the love"
(266). Agapic love is blind and deaf to what justice requires.

CAN AGAPIC LOVE CO-EXIST WITH OTHER FORMS OF LOVE?

In considering what could evoke agapic love in someone, we have already moved beyond discussing the modern day agapists' account of the
nature of agapic love to discussing what they had to say about its place
in human life. Another question concerning its place in life, equally important, is this: can agapic love co-exist with at least some natural forms
of love? Or does its presence drive out all natural forms of love?

Though I know of no passage in which Nygren is fully explicit on the
matter, I think it almost certain that it was his view that agapic love cannot co-exist with any other form of love. Agapic love is jealous; it toler-
ates no other forms. To make room for agapic love, one has to root out
all other forms of love.

Why exactly Nygren held this view, assuming that he did, is not entirely clear, however. Nygren regards every form of love other than
agapic love as a species of eros; and between agape and eros he sees a
fundamental difference. Eros always seeks the satisfaction of some need
of the lover; in eros there is always a tinge of self-love. Agape, by contrast, gives itself completely to and for the flourishing of the other with
no consideration of how this affects one's own flourishing. But from the
fact that any instance of eros is perforce not an instance of agape, and
vice versa, it does not follow that agape cannot *co-exist* with eros. Why
can it not be the case sometimes that one seeks to promote the good of
the other as an end in itself because she is one's neighbor and also seeks
to promote her good because doing so promises to enhance one's own
flourishing? To the best of my knowledge, Nygren never addressed this
question.

Deep and intense conflicts of interpretation surround Kierkegaard's views on the matter; to say that he could have been more clear is an understatement. He says that agapic love "drives out all preferential love, just as it drives out all self-love" (55). Yet he also says that "Christianity presupposes that a person loves himself," and then adds to this only the phrase about "the neighbor *as yourself*" (18). He says, "Take away the distinction of preferential love so that you can love the neighbor" (61). Yet he also says that "It was always a mistake to think that Christianity had something against erotic love because it was based upon a drive. . . . Christianity is very far from unreasonably wanting to incite the sensuous against a person himself" (52). After all, human beings have "not given to themselves" the drives that produce such loves (52). He says that "Insofar as you love the beloved, you are not like God, because for God there is no preference. . . . Therefore, go and do likewise. Forsake the dissimilarities so that you can love the neighbor" (63). Yet he also says that "Christianity has nothing against the husband loving his wife in particular" (141).

One way of dealing with such pairs of texts — and there are more that I could cite — is to conclude that Kierkegaard was contradicting himself. That seems to me implausible. Genuine contradictions in the writings of a serious thinker are either inadvertent or the result of the writer having changed his mind over time. The apparent contradictions that I just now cited are not inadvertent; they are "in your face," far from subtle. And they are not spread out over time but occur within a single book. Kierkegaard was in full possession of his powers when he wrote *Works of Love*.

Another way of handling the problem is to concede the apparent contradictions but give one member of each pair interpretive priority over the other member, doing whatever is necessary, in one's interpretation of the latter, to make it consistent with the former. Two fine recent commentaries on *Works of Love* are those by C. Stephen Evans[12] and M. Jamie Ferreira.[13] Both adopt this prioritizing strategy, and both make the same decision concerning priority. They interpret Kierkegaard as speaking literally and strictly in those passages in which he appears to affirm the legitimacy of our natural preferential forms of love; they interpret the contrasting passages so as to make them consistent with the prioritized passages: he's speaking loosely in these passages, speaking hyperbolically, speaking ironically, or whatever.[14] Their reason

12. *Kierkegaard's Ethic of Love: Divine Commands and Moral Obligations* (Oxford: Oxford University Press, 2004).

13. *Love's Grateful Striving* (Oxford: Oxford University Press, 2001).

14. In an earlier draft of this chapter I adopted the same strategy of prioritizing, but made the opposite decision as to which texts should be given interpretive priority. In as-

for prioritizing as they do is, to quote Evans, that "understanding neighbour-love in such a way that it precludes all special relations would be altogether too offensive" (206).[15]

On this strategy of interpretation, what should we make of Kierkegaard's statement that agapic love "drives out all preferential love, just as it drives out all self-love"? Evans suggests that we should interpret Kierkegaard, in this passage and others like it, as saying no more than that we should root out all forms of love that lead us into not loving some people at all. "It becomes clear," he says, "that Kierkegaard is not making the absurd claim that a wife must treat her husband exactly as she would any other man, or that a husband should treat his wife exactly as he would treat any other woman. Rather, he means that we must not 'make distinctions' in the sense that we exclude some people from the scope of our moral concern" (205-6). Ferreira's interpretation is similar: "We must remove the restrictions of preference when we face someone in need. . . . The point is that our responsibility is not limited to those we incline to or prefer" (46).[16]

These seem to me strained interpretations. What Kierkegaard means, says Evans, when he says that agapic love drives out all preferential love and all self-love is that preferential love and self-love should not lead us to exclude some people from the scope of our love. If this is the best we can do by way of interpretation, then so be it. But I think it is not the best we can do. Let me propose a way of interpreting Kierkegaard such that he is saying exactly what his words mean in both members of the contrasting pairs of clauses and sentences.

Recall that the modern day agapists all share the view that when Jesus enunciates the second love command, he is not merely enjoining us to love everyone who is our neighbor but enjoining us to do so with that special kind of love that I have been calling *agapic love* — what Kierkegaard often calls *Christian love,* and what others generally called *neighbor-love.* I suggest that when Kierkegaard says that agapic love drives

---

signing priority as I did, I was following many, if not most, of the commentators. Forceful objections by Evans led me to see that there are too many passages in which Kierkegaard cannot plausibly be interpreted as doing anything other than affirming the legitimacy of preferential love. I thank Evans for thus forcing me to acknowledge the error of my ways.

15. Cf. Ferreira, *Love's Grateful Striving,* 44-47.

16. Ferreira (47) quotes the following clause in support of her interpretation: "self-denial's boundlessness in giving itself means not to exclude a single one." But when one reads the clause in connection with the clause that precedes it, this interpretation loses its plausibility: "But preferential love's most passionate boundlessness in excluding means to love only one single person" (52). Kierkegaard's thought, surely, is that the most extreme example of preferential love is when one loves only one person. In that case, the contrast between preferential and agapic love is that whereas the former includes just one person, the latter excludes no person.

out all preferential love and other things of the same sort, he is talking about the *nature* of agapic love; he is making a conceptual point.[17] It is the nature of agapic love to be devoid of preference as among those who are one's neighbors; agapic love is that form of benevolent love which is bestowed on someone just because she is a neighbor. Any form of love that is preferential as among one's neighbors is perforce not an instance of agapic love. By contrast, when Kierkegaard affirms the legitimacy of natural preferential loves, he is talking concretely about the place of various forms of love in our lives. Agapic love can and should co-exist in a person with natural preferential forms of love.

On this way of reading Kierkegaard, we do not have to give interpretive priority to one set of passages over another; we can give all of them equal status. And we can interpret Kierkegaard as saying in each of them what his words mean. The things he says all fit together.

As such this proposal is, of course, purely schematic; it's only a strategy for interpreting, not an actual interpretation. But in my discussion of Kierkegaard's analysis of the nature of agapic love I was already implementing the conceptual aspect of the strategy. We must now implement the concrete aspect by filling in some of the details of how Kierkegaard thinks agapic love does relate and should be related in a person's life to natural preferential forms of love.

Kierkegaard is resolutely opposed to regarding Christianity's contribution to discussions about love as consisting of proposals for revisions in, and additions to, our preferential loves — as consisting of proposing "this or that change in how you are to love your wife and your friend" (143), "adding a little or subtracting something" (147).[18] Christianity "has changed everything, has changed love as a whole" (147).

In what way has it done this? First, it has done this by declaring that it is one's duty to love everyone who is one's neighbor *because* she is one's neighbor, *for the reason that* she is one's neighbor. Christianity does not tell us that we are to supplement our natural loves by dutifully loving those neighbors whom we do not love naturally. We have a duty to love *everyone* who is a neighbor *because* she is a neighbor. And as Kierkegaard sees it, every human being is one's neighbor. "The category 'neighbor' is like the category 'human being.' Each one of us is a human being and then in turn the distinctive individual that he is in particular, but to be a human being is the fundamental category. . . . No person is an exception to being a human being because of his particular dissimilarity but is

17. In a passing comment, Ferreira makes the same point: "In one sense there is a kind of either/or about preference — preferential love can be sharply contrasted *conceptually* with nonpreferential love" (45).

18. The text has "added" rather than "adding" and "subtracted" rather than "subtracting."

a human being and then what he is in particular" (141). Thus "your wife must first and foremost be to you the neighbor" (141). I love my wife out of affection for her. But that does not take away from the fact that I must also love her — and everyone else — because it is my duty to love every creature who is a human being, and she is a human being.

How do I know whether I love my wife out of my duty to love every human being and not just because I have affection for her? How do I know whether I love her agapically? Kierkegaard doesn't say. But presumably one asks oneself the counterfactual question: would I continue to love her even if my affection withered away, even if she became an enemy? If the answer to that question is "Yes," then I love her agapically. Do any of us know with certainty the answer to such a question? Perhaps not. Perhaps only God knows.

There is a second way in which Christianity "has changed everything." It declares that one's agapic love for someone must become *foundational* for whatever other forms of love one has for that person; it must "lie at the base of and be present in every other expression of love" (146). All natural preferential forms of love for someone are to be so formed and shaped that they become manifestations or specifications of one's agapic love for that person. The sentence from which a fragment was quoted above, "your wife must first and foremost be to you the neighbor," continues as follows: "that she is your wife is then a more precise specification of your particular relationship to each other. . . . The eternal foundation must also be the foundation of every expression of the particular" (141).

Kierkegaard's thought here is that loving everyone agapically does not imply loving everyone identically. My love for my spouse is to take a different form from my love for a colleague — because my spouse is different from my colleague and because my relation to her is different. "The wife and the friend are not loved in the same way, nor the friends and the neighbor, but this is not an essential dissimilarity, because the fundamental similarity is implicit in the category 'neighbor'" (141). "The truly loving one . . . loves every human being according to his distinctiveness. . . . Let us look for a moment at nature. With what infinite love nature, or God in nature, encompasses all the diverse things that have life and existence! Just recollect what you yourself have so often delighted in looking at, recollect the beauty of the meadows! There is no difference in the love, no, none — yet what a difference in the flowers! . . . So it is also in the relationships of love among human beings; only true love loves every human being according to the person's distinctiveness" (269-70).

In short, "Christianity has nothing against the husband's loving his wife in particular, but he must never love her in particular in such a way that she is an exception to being the neighbor that every human being is, because in that case he confuses what is essentially Christian — the wife does not become for him the neighbor, and thus all other people do not become for him the neighbor either. . . . Christianity . . . knows only one kind of love, the spirit's love, but this can lie at the base of and be present in every other expression of love" (141-42, 146). "Love the beloved faithfully and tenderly, but let love for the neighbor be the sanctifying element in your union's covenant with God. Love your friend honestly and devotedly; but let love for the neighbor be what you learn from each other in your friendship's confidential relationship with God" (62).

Kierkegaard begs off from explaining in any detail how agapic love "Christianly changes erotic love and friendship" (143), his reason for begging off being that Christianity "recognizes really only one kind of love, the spirit's love, and does not concern itself much with working out in detail the different ways in which this fundamental universal love can manifest itself. Christianly, the entire distinction between the different kinds of love is essentially abolished" (143).

CAN THE PERSON WHO LOVES AGAPICALLY LOVE SOME MORE THAN OTHERS?

My argument against the Evans-Ferreira line of interpretation was that it forces us to give a strained interpretation to such comments as agapic love "drives out all preferential love" when there is another line of interpretation available that requires no such strained interpretation of these or any other passages. In the course of applying this alternative strategy of interpretation we have seen that Kierkegaard holds that whatever form of natural preferential love one has for someone must be so formed and shaped that it becomes a specification and manifestation of one's agapic love for that person. That does not settle another issue of interpretation raised earlier, however.

Evans and Ferreira hold that one may be loving all one's neighbors agapically even when one's natural forms of love lead one to love some of them *more* than others (though not when they lead one to love some of them not at all). Having agapic love for all one's neighbors does not mean that one is overall just as committed to the flourishing of the neighbor who is an enemy as to the neighbor who is one's child. Are they right about that?

Let's divide the question. Are we talking about the *nature* of agapic love or are we talking about how agapic love fits concretely into a person's life? If the topic is the nature of agapic love, then I think it was

✓ clearly Kierkegaard's view that agapic love loves every neighbor equally.
Recall that agapic love is love that befits, in some way that Kierkegaard
does not explain, the "inner glory" that is equally present in every human being. The point of Christ's command, to love everyone who is
one's neighbor, is that one is to treat every neighbor as befits his or her
inner glory. But surely any love whose fundamental *ratio* is to treat everyone as befits the inner glory that we all possess equally has to be correspondingly equal. Agapic love, in its essence, is equal-regarding love.

From this it does not follow, however, that if overall one loves some
persons more than others — one's children more than one's enemies,
for example — then one does not fully possess agapic love. One's agapic
love might be equal-regarding even though one's natural loves are not.
How would one determine whether or not one does love everybody with
equal-regarding agapic love when overall one has more love for some
people than for others? Presumably, once again, by discerning the answer to some counterfactual question — though what that question
might be, I will not try to figure out.[19]

So what was Kierkegaard's view on this issue? Was it his view that our
natural loves are true specifications or manifestations of our agapic love
only if they do not lead us to love some people more than others? Or
was it his view that they may be true specifications or manifestations of
agapic love even if they differ not only in mode but also in intensity? I
know of no passage in which Kierkegaard addresses the issue, nor do I
know of any in which it is clear that he is implicitly taking a position one
way or the other.

Some readers might observe that there is something inhumane
about insisting that we must so reform our natural loves that our love
overall for any one person is equal to that for any other — less inhumane than insisting, with Nygren, that we must root out all natural
loves, but inhumane nonetheless. And they might then go on to argue
that the inhumanity of the position is a reason for not attributing it to
Kierkegaard.

I think that, in general, the supposed inhumanity of some position is
a very poor reason for concluding that Kierkegaard did not hold it.
Kierkegaard conceded that to make agapic love for the neighbor fundamental "is no doubt a strange, chilling inversion" (141). He realized
that some of his readers would probably be "shocked" by his insistence
that in erotic love and friendship, one is always to "preserve love for the

19. One's first thought is that that question is this: Would one love everybody equally if
one had no affections and aversions for anyone — and no empathy, no feelings of solidarity, and the like. But the answer to that question might be "Yes" even though, in actuality,
one's affections and aversions provoke such a pinched form of love for some people that
one has to conclude that agapic love for them is absent or seriously deformed.

neighbor." His response is that "the essentially Christian is always attended by signs of offense" (62).

What *should* Kierkegaard have said? So far as I can see, his line of thought implies neither of the two positions. He could have gone either way. However, it seems to me exceedingly implausible to suppose that we have it in our power to so govern our attachments and sympathies that our overall love for any one human being is equal to that for any other. So I think that Kierkegaard should have rejected the position for ✓ that reason.

DISTINGUISHING KINDS OF LOVE

As we have seen, the modern day agapists identified New Testament agape as a species of that form of love which consists of seeking to promote the good of someone as an end in itself, provided one does not do so because justice requires it. Such love, if its recipient is someone other than oneself, is *benevolence*. Kierkegaard held that agapic love includes oneself along with others in its scope; it was for that reason that I have refrained from saying, without qualification, that the modern day agapists identified agapic love as a species of benevolence. But if we keep Kierkegaard's view in mind, I think there will be no harm in henceforth following the practice of many, if not most, modern day agapists and say that agapic love is a species of benevolence.

In their attempt to articulate the nature of agapic love, the modern day agapists not only tried to pick out that particular species of benevolence which is agapic love; they also devoted time to distinguishing benevolence in all its species from other forms of love. It will aid our grasp of their position and be useful for subsequent purposes if we briefly follow them in this.

Nygren's overarching thesis in *Agape and Eros* was that there are three "fundamental motifs" locked in a struggle for the mind and heart of the West: the *eros*-motif, which received its best articulation in Plato and the Platonic tradition; the *nomos*-motif, which received its best articulation in the testimony of the Old Testament writers concerning law and justice; and the *agape*-motif, which received its best articulation in certain of Jesus' parables, in Paul's teaching about God's love, and, much later, in Luther's writings.

Eros is the love of attraction. Eros is being in the grip of something, drawn to it, attracted to it: persons, animals and plants, landscapes, institutions and groups, projects, ideals, God, whatever. We love persons and things for something about them that we find of worth. Sometimes it is difficult, even impossible, to put into words what that is. But whether describable or not, it is for some estimable features of mind, of character, of body, of commitment, of achievement, that we love the person. Something about her makes her love-worthy in our eyes, something about the tree makes it love-worthy, something about the institution. Love as attraction is the love of being drawn to something by its worth, its excellence. The love Plato had in mind in the *Symposium,* and the love Augustine had in mind when he spoke of our love of God, was attraction-love.

Kierkegaard contrasted agapic love not only with erotic love but with friendship. Though friendship usually if not always incorporates an element of love as attraction, it incorporates another form of love as well, namely, love as attachment. I find myself attached to this person who is my friend, as I do to my child, my house, my cat. If I can manage to view the situation objectively I may concede that, were I just going for excellence, I would not have fastened onto this child, this house, this cat. But it was not the recognized excellence of the thing that caused my attachment. In one way or another I became bonded; that's what accounts for it. I recognize that your cat is a finer cat than mine. No matter. Mine is the cat I am attached to; mine is the one that I found huddled on my doorstep one cold winter morning with a pleading look on its face; mine is the one I love.

If the thing to which one is attached is susceptible to variations in flourishing, attachment-love is invariably accompanied, so it seems to me, by love as benevolence. One seeks to preserve or enhance the flourishing of the child, the cat, as an end in itself. On the other hand, the modern day agapists rightly insisted that benevolence-love can occur in the absence of both attachment-love and attraction-love. I may seek to promote as an end in itself the flourishing of someone to whom I am neither attached nor attracted, someone whose company I don't like. I may do so out of duty.

Love of each of these three sorts — attraction-love, attachment-love, and benevolence-love — is manifested in desires with respect to the thing loved, the desire to be in the presence of the person to whom one is attracted, for example. But while it may be plausible to *identify* benevolence with desires of a certain sort, it would be implausible to identify attraction-love and attachment-love with desires. For one thing, love of these sorts is manifested not only in desires but also in admiration, praise, reveling in the presence of the person or thing loved, and so forth. Second, these loves give rise to desires that, in good measure, come and go while the love abides. The desires I now have with respect to my children, on account of my attachment to them, are considerably different from those I had when they were young.

Diminution in the worth of something to which one is attached need not weaken one's attachment; it may, in fact, intensify it. Typically it will, however, cause grief, as will death or destruction of that to which one is attached. Love as attraction is different. If the qualities that drew one to the object disappear, or are impaired and not replaced by other qualities that one finds equally attractive, one's attraction weakens to the point of disappearing. The emotion one then feels is not so much grief as disappointment and regret. So too one feels disappointment and regret when the object is destroyed or taken away.

Kierkegaard dwelt at length on the imperturbability of agapic love, contrasting it with the perturbability of erotic love and friendship. Whether he was right or wrong about that depends on the sort of commitment that we understand love as benevolence to be. Benevolence is commitment to enhancing the good of the other for its own sake. There are two forms that such commitment might take: one might be committed to *actually* enhancing her good, or one might be committed to *trying to* enhance her good. Commitment of the former sort is far from imperturbable; if I do not succeed in enhancing the good of the other, I am disappointed. But if my commitment is only to *trying* to enhance her good, then the fact that my endeavors bear no fruit will not disappoint me. I will be disappointed only if I prove irresolute in my commitment to try.

Kierkegaard was thinking about benevolence in the latter way; any disappointment connected with benevolence is disappointment with oneself. It's a Stoic way of thinking. I see no reason to align the modern day agapist movement in general with either of the two positions.

There is yet another kind of love. In addition to love as attraction, love as attachment, and love as benevolence, there is advantage-love, self-love. Advantage-love consists of desiring that something come about because, so one believes, it would be to one's own advantage, would enhance one's own good. The agapists talked often and at length about self-love, contrasting it with agapic love. It was advantage-love they had in mind. Rather often they claimed that every form of love other than agapic love amounts to self-love, advantage-love.[20] I think they were wrong about that. When I am gripped by a performance of one of Schubert's late sonatas, it's the sonata in this performance that I love, not myself.

I have presented this typology of forms of love in order to sharpen our perception of what the modern day agapists had in mind when they

20. Cf. Kierkegaard, *Works of Love,* 53: "Christianity has misgivings about erotic love and friendship simply because preferential love in passion or passionate preference is actually another form of self-love." Outka discusses Barth at some length on the issue of whether every form of love other than agape is self-love (the love of advantage), and concludes that Barth speaks inconsistently on the matter.

spoke of love. The typology also serves to highlight just how striking their position was. The love that Hebrew and Christian scripture predicates of God and enjoins on us, so they said, is not love as attraction, not love as attachment, not the love of advantage. It is pure benevolence.[21]

21. A question that some will ask is how my typology compares to that of C. S. Lewis in his *The Four Loves* (London: Geoffrey Bles, 1960). It's not entirely clear to me what Lewis took the four loves to be. He devotes separate chapters to affection, friendship, eros, and charity; perhaps those are his four loves. On the other hand, he identifies four other loves of which the first four are manifestations — with the exception of one point of identity. These other four are need-love, gift-love, appreciation, and affection. Lewis's need-love is the same as what I call love of advantage, his gift-love is the same as what I call benevolence, his appreciation is the same as what I call attraction, and his affection is the same as what I call attachment.

Chapter Three

CLASSICAL MODERN DAY AGAPISM
ON THE RELATION OF LOVE TO JUSTICE

OUR TOPIC IN THIS CHAPTER is the relation between agapic love and justice in the thought of the classical modern day agapists. First, though, I must qualify something I said in the preceding chapter. I said that the agapists presented their account of love as an interpretation of, and extrapolation from, what the term *agapē* was used to mean in the Greek New Testament. They did indeed offer it as an interpretation of what Jesus meant when he attributed love for us to God and enjoined love for the neighbor on us. But Jesus also enjoined love for God on us, using the same term, *agapē*. And none of the agapists thought that, in so doing, he was enjoining us to treat God with agapic love — or with any other sort of benevolence. ∨

On this point, as on most points, Nygren had the courage of his convictions. In reporting what Jesus said, the New Testament writers sometimes used the noun *agapē* and the verb *agapaō* loosely. They were speaking loosely when they reported Jesus as saying that we are to love God; what Jesus really meant, said Nygren, is that we are to have *faith* in God. Paul tended to speak with greater precision on this point than Jesus. Paul's preferred word for our proper stance toward God was *pistis* rather than *agapē* (*Agape and Eros*, 94ff., 124ff.).

This is a good example of what I had in mind when I remarked that many arguments in Nygren that he regards as unfolding the surprising implications of New Testament thought I regard as *reductio ad absurdum* arguments. If Jesus meant *faith* in God, why didn't the gospel writers report him as saying that? The Greek word *pistis* was, after all, available to them for translating and reporting what he said.

AGAPIC LOVE EXCLUDES ACTING AS ONE DOES
BECAUSE JUSTICE REQUIRES IT

We saw in the preceding chapter that the modern day agapists were all of the view that, when Jesus enjoined us to love our neighbors, he did not mean that we should love them with some form or other of love but

that we should love them with that special form of love that the agapists
typically called *neighbor-love,* that Kierkegaard called *Christian love,* and
that I have been calling *agapic love.* The modern day agapists disagreed
on whether agapic love could have oneself as recipient. But I suggested
that, if we keep this point of disagreement in mind, it will do no harm to
ignore the linguistic fact that we would not call love for oneself "benevolence" and say that the modern day agapists held that agapic love is a
species of benevolence, of generosity, of charity.

To say that someone acted benevolently toward someone is to imply
that he did not act as he did because justice required it. And all the
modern day agapists agreed that if one loves someone agapically, one
does not treat him as one does because justice requires it, and conversely, if one treats someone as one does because justice requires it,
one is not loving him agapically. Loving someone agapically and treating him as one does because justice requires it are conceptually incompatible. Agapic love casts out all thought of justice and injustice. Agapic
love is blind and deaf to justice and injustice. Justice and injustice do
not enter into its purview. Agapic love is *gratuitous* generosity.

The question before us now is why the modern day agapists held this
view. When I aim to treat you justly I do, after all, aim to promote some
aspect of your good; how else could I render you justice? So why did
they hold that the love Jesus requires of us is inherently indifferent to
justice and injustice?

Kierkegaard's reason, as we saw in the preceding chapter, was that
whereas justice "is identified by its giving each his own," in agapic love
the distinction between *mine* and *yours* disappears. Kierkegaard does not
develop this thought. Since Nygren was more forthcoming and articulate in his reasons for holding that agapic love pays no attention to what
justice requires, let's look at what he had to say on the matter.

It is distinctive of agapic love that it is *spontaneous,* says Nygren; it
spontaneously seeks to enhance the good of the neighbor.[1] To cite
again a passage quoted in the preceding chapter, "We look in vain for
an explanation of God's love in the character of the man who is the object of His love. . . . The only ground for [God's love] is to be found in
God Himself. God's love is altogether *spontaneous*" (75). The spontaneity of agapic love makes it inherently different from seeking justice.

I do not find Nygren ever completing the argument by explicitly
pointing out what it is about seeking to treat the neighbor justly that
makes such action non-spontaneous. But I think we can surmise how
he was thinking. When I seek to treat someone justly, I seek to enhance some aspect of her flourishing because my doing so is *due* her.

1. Kierkegaard sometimes describes *natural* loves as spontaneous.

The recognition of a certain kind of requiredness enters my intentions when I seek to treat someone justly. Given that this person crossed the finish line first, I am *required* to give her the prize for first place; if I do not, I do not render to her what is due her. I surmise that this is what led Nygren to hold that seeking to treat someone justly is not spontaneous.

Agapic love is blind to all requiredness coming from the side of the recipient. It is in that way spontaneous. But when I seek to treat you justly, I treat you as I do because your worth requires it.

Love is spontaneous
Justice is due.

WHY IS AGAPIC LOVE SPONTANEOUS?

Suppose all this is true. Agapic love, as the modern day agapists understand it, is spontaneous in a way that seeking to treat someone justly is not. Pointing this out does not answer our question, however; it only invites us to ask it in a different way. Why did the modern day agapists all hold that agapic love is spontaneous in this way? Why did they all hold that in enjoining us to love our neighbors, Jesus was enjoining us to treat our neighbors with that sort of love which takes no note of what justice to the neighbor requires of us? ✓

I observed in the preceding chapter that the modern day agapists presented their position as a plausible interpretation of, and extrapolation from, Christian scripture, especially the New Testament, and as defensible against systematic objections. Since they regarded the biblical text as authoritative, they viewed this line of argument as sufficient; they had no interest in developing a positive case in favor of their view that did not presuppose the authority of scripture. Up to this point in my exposition, however, I have given no indication of why they thought they were giving a plausible interpretation of Christian scripture; I have said nothing about their hermeneutical case. It is time to ask why they thought that New Testament agape takes no account of what justice requires.

To put the question more pointedly: why did Nygren regard his conclusion, that agapic love for someone is conceptually incompatible with seeking to treat that person justly, as an implication of New Testament agape rather than as *reductio ad absurdum* of his interpretation? When he and the other agapists reached this point in their thought, why did they not back up and conclude that they had misinterpreted the texts?

Nygren's hermeneutical case rested almost entirely on his conviction that scripture presents God's loving forgiveness of the sinner as the paradigmatic form of God's love for us and as the model for our love of the neighbor.[2] It is of the very nature of forgiveness, said Nygren, that the one forgiven does not have a right to be forgiven. The malefactor cannot claim, were he not forgiven, that he would be wronged, treated unjustly; he cannot claim, were he not forgiven, that he would be deprived of what is due him. Forgiveness, when granted, is gratuitous. God's love in its entirety is like that. God's love is pure grace, grace all the way down. God's love is pure spontaneity. Our love is to be like God's love.

Speaking of Jesus' teaching, Nygren says that "fellowship with God is not governed by law but by love. God's attitude to men is not character- ized by *justitia distributiva,* but by agape, not by retributive righteous- ness, but by freely giving and forgiving love" (70). If

> God, the Holy One, loves the sinner, it cannot be because of his sin, but in spite of his sin. . . . When God's love is shown to the righteous and godly, there is always the risk of our thinking that God loves the man on account of his righteousness and godliness. But this is a de- nial of Agape — as if God's love for the "righteous" were not just as unmotivated and spontaneous as His love for the sinner! . . . It is only when all thought of the worthiness of the object is abandoned that we can understand what Agape is. God's love allows no limits to be set for it by the character or conduct of man. The distinction be- tween the worthy and the unworthy, the righteous and the sinner, sets no bounds to His love. (77-78)

In short, forgiveness in particular and agape in general are "indiffer- ent to value" — that is, indifferent to whatever might be the worth or value of the person loved and to what recognition of that worth might require of us. Agape does not represent a "transvaluation" of ordinary values. Jesus does not reverse "the generally accepted standard of values and [hold] that the sinner is 'better' than the righteous" (77). Rather, when God's love is directed to the sinner, then . . . all thought of valua- tion is excluded in advance" (77).

One of the most striking and provocative aspects of Nygren's thought is his insistence that not only is God's love of human beings *not* moti- vated by recognition of their worth or conditioned thereon, but also that human beings simply have no worth except that which is created in them by God's agapic love for them. "God does not love that which is al- ready in itself worthy of love, but on the contrary, that which in itself has no worth acquires worth just by becoming the object of God's love.

---

2. From the passage quoted from Paul Ramsey in the preceding chapter (n. 6) it's clear that Ramsey shared this assumption about the role of God's forgiveness of the sinner in our thinking about love.

Agape has nothing to do with the kind of love that depends on the recognition of a valuable quality in the object; Agape does not recognize value but creates it. . . . The man who is loved by God has no value in himself; what gives him value is precisely the fact that God loves him. *Agape is a value-creating principle*" (78). Few of the other modern day agapists were willing to go this far.

Nygren is not forthcoming on why he denies all worth to human beings other than the worth created in them by God's agapic love for them. From the fact that God's agapic love for human beings is neither motivated by recognition of their worth nor conditioned thereon, it does not follow, nor does Nygren anywhere claim it follows, that they have no worth other than that created in them by God's love. But here, too, I think we can surmise how he was thinking.

He is assuming that, in general, if human beings have worth, then there are ways of treating them that respect for their worth requires. If God were confronted by human beings who had worth antecedent to God's love of them, God's treating them in certain ways would be required of God by due respect for their worth. Not to treat them thus would be to treat them unjustly. It does not follow that to do what justice requires, God would have to act *for the sake of* securing justice. In principle it might be the case that, acting out of gratuitous generosity, God always did what the antecedent worth of human beings required of God. Nonetheless, the serpent of requirement would have wriggled its way into the garden of pure agape. There would be ways of treating us that were in fact required of God. Even if God did not treat us as God does *because* it is required of God, nonetheless God's love would constitute doing what is required of God.

Agape cannot tolerate even that trace of requiredness. Not only does God always act toward us out of pure generosity and never out of requirement; there is nothing in God's treatment of us that is in fact required of God. None of love's works is required of God. Agape in general, like forgiveness in particular, is generosity all the way down. I surmise that that is how Nygren was thinking.

It's an interesting near-reversal of a traditional line of thought. Nygren's argument is that God's love is pure unalloyed generosity; hence there cannot be some way of treating us that is required of God by what is due us. Traditionally it was argued that God's aseity implies that there is no way of treating us that is required of God by what is due us; hence God's love of us has to be pure unalloyed generosity.

Can the Pursuit of Justice Co-Exist with Agapic Love?

We have been exploring Nygren's reason for holding the view he shared with all the modern day agapists, that agapic love, the sort of love they believed Jesus enjoined on us, is purely spontaneous and gratuitous, taking no note of what justice requires. But there remains the question of the *concrete* relation, as I called it in the preceding chapter, between agapic love and justice. Let us grant, for the sake of the argument, that if one acts out of agapic love, one is not acting as one does because justice requires it, and that if one acts as one does because justice requires it, one is not acting out of agapic love. May it nonetheless be the case that these two ways of acting can co-exist in a person? May it even be the case that they can co-exist in the strong sense that one may seek to promote some good of someone both out of agapic love for her and because justice requires it?

Nygren's position on the matter is clear. Extending agapic love to all one's neighbors requires rooting out of one's life all concern for doing justice. Jesus "enters into fellowship with those who are not worthy of it." His doing so is directed "against every attempt to regulate fellowship with God by the principle of justice" (86). Those whom Jesus opposed in word and deed were "the spokesmen for justice in the relation between God and man" (83). "That Jesus should take lost sinners to Himself was bound to appear, not only to the Pharisees, but to anyone brought up and rooted in Jewish legal righteousness, as a violation of the order established by God Himself and guaranteed by His justice" (83). For them it was "a violation, not merely of the human, but above all of the Divine, order of justice, and therefore of God's majesty" (70).

The point is unmistakable: the moral vision of the New Testament is opposed not only to Platonic *eros* but to Old Testament *nomos,* that is, law and justice. The New Testament is not a fulfillment of the Old but a repudiation thereof and the proclamation of an alternative. Agape "shatters completely the legal conception of the relationship between God and man. That is the reason for the conflict of Jesus with the Pharisees and Paul's campaign against 'the Law'. Agape is the opposite of 'Nomos', and therefore a denial of the foundation on which the entire Jewish scale of values rested" (200-201).

In the New Testament, agapic love does not supplement justice but supersedes it. The love of God for us, and our love for the neighbor that God's love evokes in us, are not only conceptually distinct from seeking justice but concretely incompatible therewith. "'Motivated' justice must give place . . . to 'unmotivated' love" (74). We are not to love the neighbor agapically *in addition to* seeking to treat her as justice requires; we are to love the neighbor agapically *instead of* seeking to treat her as justice requires.

WHAT LED NYGREN TO HIS STRONG POSITION?

Nygren was led to this strong position in part, so I suggest, by failing to keep clearly in mind the distinction between conceptual and concrete incompatibility between loving agapically and seeking justice; he slides from arguing that agapic love is a species of gratuitous benevolence to holding that one cannot seek to promote some good of someone both out of gratuitous benevolence and because justice requires it. But confusion on this point was not the only thing that led him to his position. From what he says, it's possible to construct an argument. He says in one place that "Where spontaneous love and generosity are found, the order of justice is obsolete and invalidated" (90). That's the clue. Agapic love renders the pursuit of justice obsolete and invalidated.

When agapic love does what justice requires, seeking justice is rendered otiose, or as Nygren puts it, "obsolete." When agapic love would do what justice forbids, we are to prefer love to justice; all the classical modern day agapists agreed that we are always to treat every neighbor with agapic love. Put the two together, and we have the conclusion: agapic love renders the pursuit of justice obsolete in some cases and invalid in the others.

On the second point, that agapic love sometimes does what justice forbids, Nygren might have cited examples from ordinary affairs in which agapic love perpetrates injustice; as we shall see in Chapter Five, that's what Niebuhr does. Nygren instead confines himself to citing two parables of Jesus, the parable of the laborers in the vineyard (Matthew 20:1-16) and the parable of the prodigal son (Luke 15:11-32). The advantage for Nygren of citing these parables is that, on his interpretation, they not only exemplify the conflict between love and justice but also present Jesus as telling us that we are to be like God in not allowing such injustice as agapic love may perpetrate to deter us from loving the neighbor agapically.

The kingdom of heaven, said Jesus, is like a landowner who went out early in the morning to hire day-laborers for his vineyard. After agreeing with the laborers to pay them the going daily wage, he sent them into the vineyard. Around nine o'clock he went out again and saw that there were some laborers standing idle in the marketplace. So he sent them to work in the vineyard as well, saying that he would pay them whatever was just.[3] The same sequence was repeated around noon, around three o'clock, and, for the final time, around five o'clock. Each

---

3. The NRSV, which is the translation I am using, has "whatever is right"; the Greek that the NRSV translates as "right" and which I translate as "just" is *dikaios*.

time the landowner found day-laborers standing around idle; each time
he told them, "You also go into the vineyard."

When the workday ended, the landowner instructed his manager to
give the workers their pay, beginning with those hired last and concluding with those hired first. Those hired last were given "the usual daily
wage" — to their surprise, no doubt. Those hired first took note and expected to receive considerably more than the latecomers. But they too
were given the usual daily wage. So they grumbled, complaining to the
landowner that the latecomers worked only one hour, yet you have
made them equal to us who worked all day and bore the burden of the
scorching heat. Equal pay for unequal work: it's not fair, it's not just.
The landowner rejected the complaint. Friend, he said to one of them,
"am I not allowed to do what I choose with what belongs to me? Or are
you envious because I am generous?"

Nygren's interpretation of the parable is that "if it were really a question of merit and worthiness, then the labourers who complained were
undoubtedly in the right. It is impossible to make a simple addition of
the exercise of kindness and the non-infringement of justice. If the
principle of merit and reward is laid down as finally decisive, then
there is an 'infringement of justice', not only when the good lose their
reward and the evil receive it, but also when the more deserving and
the less deserving are treated in the same way. The principle of justice
requires a due proportion between work and wages" (88). "It is futile,"
he adds, "to try to eliminate from the Parable that which is offensive in
it from a juridical point of view. The offence only ceases when the principle of justice is eliminated as inapplicable to the religious relationship" (87-89).[4]

Emil Brunner, in *Justice and the Social Order,* offers a similar interpretation: our "natural sense of justice is violated . . . by Christ's parable of
the labourers in the vineyard. . . . It is love, the incomprehensible gift,
bound to no law of retributive justice and standing in absolute contrast
to what we must call just in the things of this world, which is shown here
as God's manner of action. . . . The substance of the parable is not the
justitia civilis but the *justitia evangelica* which consists precisely in the ces-

---

4. Nygren also says, "The Householder replies: If you come with the demands of justice, let us stick to justice. 'Friend, I do thee no wrong; didst not thou agree with me for a
penny? Take that which is thine, and go thy way.' Where spontaneous love and generosity
are found, the order of justice is obsolete and invalidated" (90). This is baffling. But apparently what Nygren is saying is that had the landowner paid each worker what he had
earned, everybody, including the grumblers, would have been treated justly. The insertion of "spontaneous love and generosity" into the situation changes things, however.
The insertion of "spontaneous love and generosity" makes "the order of justice . . . obsolete and invalidated."

sation of all deserving, in the denial of all lawful claims, and is hence the antithesis of the law of worldly justice."[5]

Nygren's interpretation of the parable of the prodigal son is more cursory, but along the same lines. The elder brother "stands in the background representing the legal order. From his point of view, from the point of view of justice, [he] is entirely right; his younger brother's conduct has furnished no grounds whatever for such a love as his father has shown him" (90). It is he, the hard-working, responsible, elder brother who deserves a party, not this dissolute wastrel brother of his. But the father has never thrown a party for him and his friends. It's not fair, it's not just. Unjust love.

Where agapic love and justice conflict, God chooses love over justice; we are to do likewise. Where they do not conflict, love does what justice would do. Nygren's conclusion follows: where spontaneous love and generosity are found, the order of justice is rendered either invalid or obsolete. Agapic love supersedes the pursuit of justice.

does it have to, in human affairs?

5. (New York: Harper & Brothers, 1945), 111.

Chapter Four

IRONY AND IMPOSSIBILITY IN
CLASSICAL MODERN DAY AGAPISM

MODERN DAY AGAPISM, in its classical form, is neither plausible as an interpretation of the founding texts of agapism nor defensible as a systematic position. Something has to give; we have to think of love differently, find a different rule of application, or both. That's the thesis that I will defend in this chapter. In the fifth chapter of *Justice: Rights and Wrongs* I argued that rather than being superseded in the New Testament, justice lies at the heart of the New Testament gospels. That argument, which I will not repeat here, is an important component of the larger case for the implausibility of classical modern day agapism as an interpretation of the founding texts of agapism.

THE IMPOSSIBILITY OF FOLLOWING THE MODERN DAY
AGAPIST'S RULE OF APPLICATION

There are a number of points at which we could press the charge that modern day agapism in its classical form is systematically indefensible. Modern day agapism first explains what it calls, variously, neighbor-love, agapic love, and Christian love as that species of benevolence which consists of seeking to promote the good of someone as an end itself *because* he is one's neighbor. Classical modern day agapism then offers, as its rule of application, that one is *always* to treat *everyone* who is one's neighbor with equal-regarding agapic love. To this rule Nygren added the rule that one is not to treat one's neighbor in any other way than with agapic love. Kierkegaard held, to the contrary, that one can treat a neighbor with other forms of love as well, provided those other forms are so shaped and formed that they become specifications or manifestations of one's agapic love for the neighbor. Kierkegaard left open whether such forming and shaping must satisfy the principle that one's overall love for any one neighbor is to be equal to that for every other neighbor.

I submit that it is impossible to follow the classical modern day agapist's rule of application. It's clearly impossible if one follows

Kierkegaard in counting every human being presently existing as one's neighbor. How could one possibly promote the good of six billion human beings? But it's also impossible if one adopts a narrower understanding of *neighbor* — for example, if one counts as neighbor only someone whose flourishing would be affected by the actions one is considering performing.

Though the modern day agapists are seldom explicit on the point, we should no doubt interpret them as holding that it is permissible to impair someone's good if doing so is the best available means to that person's greater good; it is permissible to subject someone to the misery of cardiac bypass surgery if doing so is the best way to lift the imminent threat of a heart attack. What the application-rule of the classical modern day agapists forbids is impairing one person's good for the sake of enhancing another's. Yet in this world of ours we often find ourselves in the unhappy situation of being forced to do exactly that; we find that we can promote the good of one neighbor only by neglecting or even impairing the good of another. We cannot always treat all of them with agapic love, let alone treat all of them equally.

It is especially this fact about life in our world that leads the utilitarian to his maximizing principle: in such situations, choose the greater overall good. But if the agapist goes down that road, he is no longer an agapist; he changes stripes. At the very heart of the position of the classical modern day agapist is the rejection of utilitarian trade-offs. I am always to treat each neighbor with agapic love. I am to impair some aspect of a neighbor's flourishing only if doing so serves *that* neighbor's greater flourishing.

I will have more to say in subsequent chapters about this problem with the modern day agapist's rule of application. In the remainder of this chapter, let me focus on various points of irony and impossibility in what the classical form of modern day agapism says about the relation between agapic love and seeking justice.

THE IRONIC INTRUSION OF JUSTICE INTO CLASSICAL MODERN DAY AGAPISM

Since Nygren discussed the relation between love and justice in more detail than any other classical modern day agapist, we looked at what he had to say on the matter. Nygren took for granted, as did the modern day agapists in general, that when Jesus enjoined us to love our neighbors as ourselves, he was not instructing us to love our neighbors with one or another form of love but instructing us to love our neighbors with that special form of love which is agapic love. The reason he and the other modern day agapists gave for holding that treating one's neighbor as justice requires is not an instance of treating him with the sort of love that Jesus enjoins on us is that we are to take, as the paradigmatic form of such love, God's forgiveness of the sinner. It's true of forgiveness in general that a person who has wronged one cannot rightly claim that justice requires that he be forgiven.

That leaves open, as we saw, the existential question of whether it is acceptable to supplement agapic love with seeking justice. Why not love one's neighbor agapically and also treat him as justice requires? Nygren's argument on this point, as I reconstructed it, is that loving a person agapically will sometimes lead one to treat someone unjustly; when that happens, Jesus teaches us that we are to prefer love to justice. And when loving a person agapically does not lead one to treat him unjustly, justice adds nothing that agapic love does not already secure. Agapic love renders the order of justice "obsolete and invalidated," to quote Nygren.

What I shall argue first is that there are two points at which, in spite of his best efforts, justice intrudes into Nygren's agapism. Justice is not superseded. The first point of intrusion pertains to one of the idiosyncratic points in Nygren's version of modern day agapism and can be presented rather briefly; the second pertains to modern day agapism in general, and will take more time to present.

There are, in principle, two quite different ways of understanding how Nygren was thinking when he argued that agapic love renders justice obsolete and invalid. One interpretation is that the concept of justice does not have, and never did have, application to reality; there is not and never was any such thing as treating someone justly or any such thing as treating someone unjustly. It was a mistake ever to have thought otherwise; that's what we learn from Jesus' teaching. The concept of justice is like the concept of phlogiston in early modern physics; the concept never had any application. There is not and never was any such thing as phlogiston. The other possible interpretation of Nygren's thought is that though the concepts of justice and injustice do apply to reality, agapic love renders the concepts useless — worse than useless, distracting. If we love our neighbors agapically, there's no point in asking what justice requires.

Though much of Nygren's rhetoric about justice is open to both interpretations, there are important components of his thought that are incompatible with the former interpretation. In the preceding chapter we took note of his insistence that the only worth possessed by human beings is the worth created in them by God's agapic love. We surmised that his reason for holding this position was that, if human beings had worth antecedent to God's love of them, it would be required of God that God treat them with due respect for that worth — that is, treat them as justice requires. But if that were the case, then, even if God treated them as he did out of sheer generosity and not *because* justice required it, God would still be doing what was in fact required of God; and that would sully the pure spontaneous generosity of God's love. Nothing is required of God.

But now notice that even if Nygren were right in claiming that you and I have no worth antecedent to God's love of us, his view implies that we do have worth *consequent on* God's love of us.[1] Thus the neighbor has worth antecedent to my love of her — consequent to God's love but antecedent to mine. So there are, after all, things that due respect for the worth of the other requires of me; the neighbor comes into my presence bearing the requirements of justice. The concept of justice is not like the concept of phlogiston; there really is justice and there really is injustice, and there have been as long as God has gratuitously loved human beings.

It remains open to Nygren to insist that there is no point in being attentive to justice and injustice; the order of justice has been superseded by agapic love. Be that as it may, however, if God's agapic love for us creates worth in us, then, on the assumption that justice consists of treating a person as befits his or her worth, justice and injustice are there in reality, placing their claims on us whether or not we act out of recognition of those claims.

Now for a second and more consequential point at which justice intrudes unbidden into Nygren's way of thinking and into classical modern day agapism generally. As we saw in the preceding chapter, the modern day agapist regards God's forgiveness of the sinner as paradigmatic of God's love for us and the model for our love of the neighbor. I submit that if we look closely at the nature of forgiveness, we will see that the person who thinks entirely in terms of love and takes no note of injustice cannot forgive. This is irony indeed, that the manifestation of love that the modern day agapist cites as paradigmatic of God's love and the model for ours should undermine his claim that the love Jesus asks of us pays no attention to justice and injustice. I will be saying more about forgiveness in later chapters; here I will say only enough to make the point at hand.

What stands out for Nygren and the other modern day agapists in God's forgiveness of the sinner is that, in forgiving, God is not doing what justice requires; the sinner cannot claim a right to be forgiven. This is not a peculiarity of God's forgiveness. It's true of forgiveness in

---

1. Outka makes this point in his *Agape*, 159; he does not take note of the implication, that justice intrudes into agape.

general that the wrongdoer cannot claim a right to be forgiven; she cannot claim that she would be wronged were she not forgiven. Forgiveness transcends what justice requires.

But there is another aspect of the nature of forgiveness that Nygren and the other agapists ignore. Notice that one cannot dispense forgiveness indiscriminately hither and yon. I can forgive you only if you have wronged someone, and only *for* the wrong you did them.[2] I cannot forgive you for your way of treating me if what you did has not deprived me of something to which I had a right — though I might incorrectly size up the situation and *believe* that I have been wronged by you and hence believe that forgiving you is a possibility.

Let us now go beyond the condition that must be satisfied for forgiveness to occur and take a brief look at its nature. Being deprived by someone of something to which one had a right generates in one the right to treat the wrongdoer in certain ways that were impermissible before — the right to be angry at him, the right to punish him or support the imposition of punishment, and so forth. The rights so generated have traditionally been called *retributive* rights. I will save for Chapter Seventeen a discussion of whether such rights really are rights to retribution. So let me give them the neutral name of *corrective* rights. And let me call those rights whose violation generates corrective rights *primary* rights.

Given this distinction between primary rights and corrective rights, we can identify an essential component of forgiveness. Forgiveness requires that one forego exercising some or all of one's corrective rights. John has wronged Martha, deprived her of certain of her primary rights. On account of being wronged by John, Martha now has certain corrective rights against him. For Martha to forgive John is, among other things, for her to forego exercising some or all of those corrective rights. Now suppose that Martha never thinks in terms of justice and injustice — never thinks in terms of someone being wronged, never thinks in terms of what is due someone, never thinks in terms of what someone has a right to. Justice is not part of her conceptual repertoire. She can still be wronged, she can still acquire corrective rights, she can still not exercise her corrective rights. But thoughts to that effect never cross her mind.

Add now that Martha has been wronged but does not exercise her corrective rights. Though John has wronged her, she does not recognize that he has done so and does not recognize that she has any corrective rights to exercise or forego. She feels no anger toward him and makes no effort to have him punished. In this situation, Martha does

2. Whether one can forgive someone only if one is oneself the wronged party is a topic that I will take up in Chapter Fifteen.

not and could not understand herself as forgiving John; she lacks the concepts necessary for that. The concept of forgiveness has the concept of being wronged as a component. Martha does not have the concept of being wronged in her conceptual repertoire; so she cannot understand herself as forgiving John.

A question whose answer is perhaps less obvious is whether Martha has nonetheless in fact forgiven John. One can kick something without having the concept of kicking and thus without understanding oneself as kicking. Is forgiving like kicking in that respect?

I think not. Though Martha's external behavior is just like that of the person who forgives, she would not be forgiving John. Not every case of failing to exercise one's corrective rights is a case of forgiving. The haughty aristocrat who does not exercise his corrective rights toward someone who has wronged him because he cannot be bothered with scum like this is not thereby forgiving the wrongdoer. So too, if one does not realize that one has been wronged and does not realize that one has thereby acquired certain corrective rights against the person who wronged one, one cannot forgive the wrongdoer.

In short, not only can one not *understand* oneself as forgiving someone without employing the concepts of rights and wrongs, justice and injustice. One cannot even *perform the act* of forgiving someone without employing those concepts. If forgiveness is an example of the sort of love that Jesus enjoined us to have for the neighbor, such love cannot be deaf and blind to injustice; it has to be alert to justice and injustice. As I said before, this is irony indeed for the modern day agapists, that close scrutiny of what they regard as the paradigmatic example of agapic love would show that agapic love cannot be practiced if one puts justice and injustice out of mind!

AGAPIC LOVE MAY PERPETRATE INJUSTICE

How might a proponent of classical modern day agapism respond? I think his best response would be to concede that agapic love cannot be deaf and blind to justice and injustice, but then go on to insist that nevertheless it remains the case that we ought always to love every neighbor agapically, it being assumed that treating someone as justice requires is perforce not to love him or her agapically.

Look once more at forgiveness. Be it granted that one can neither understand oneself as forgiving nor actually forgive without employing the concepts of justice and injustice. Nonetheless, when one forgives the wrongdoer, one is not acting as justice requires, since justice does not require forgiveness. In forgiving the wrongdoer, one's sole thought is to promote his good — to bring about the good in his life of being forgiven. The love Jesus asks of us for each neighbor is like forgiveness in that respect: attentive to justice and injustice if need be, but never justice-*motivated*.

Let me now offer an argument against this revision of the original position. When first thinking about these matters, it's tempting to assume that benevolence in general, and agapic love in particular, will automatically do what justice requires; further reflection shows, however, that benevolence, whether or not it takes the form of agapic love, often perpetrates injustice. That was Nygren's interpretation of Jesus' parable of the laborers in the vineyard and his parable of the prodigal son. It's important for us to engage Nygren's interpretation of these parables. But before we do that, let's consider some other examples of agapic love perpetrating injustice.

Sometimes justice requires that one distribute some good to a certain group of people; not to do so would be to treat them unjustly. But it's easy to think of cases, both real and imagined, in which some distribution of goods is unjust even though it was out of pure generosity that the distributor made the distribution, not because justice required it.

Imagine a good-hearted man, call him Sam, who likes to distribute small gifts to the children in the neighborhood every now and then. Today he is distributing candy. Justice does not require that he do this; none of the children would be wronged were he not to do it. He just likes to do it. But Sam has taken a dislike to one of the neighborhood children, Roger. So in his distribution of candy he sees to it that Roger doesn't get any. Surely Roger has been wronged by Sam — wronged by Sam's excluding him from his gratuitous distribution of candy, perhaps also wronged by Sam's dislike of him.

The modern day agapist has a response. Though it was benevolence that Sam was exhibiting, he violated the equal-regard rule of application. He excluded Roger from the scope of his love. Correct. So let me offer an example of benevolence perpetrating injustice in which the issue of partiality does not arise.

The *New York Times* of January 16, 2006, announced that the 2006 Gilmore Artist Award of $300,000 had been awarded to the Argentinian pianist, Ingrid Fliter. The Gilmore Award is unusual in that it does not involve an open competition; nobody under consideration knows that he or she is under consideration. The members of the jury work secretly. They receive nominations, listen to CDs, and when they have narrowed the list down to manageable size, travel the world to listen incognito to live performances.

I feel sure that, in making the award, the members of the jury for the 2006 Gilmore Award gave no consideration whatsoever to the flourishing of the nominees. They simply followed the explicit and implicit rules of the award and gave the prize to the nominee who, in their judgment, had given the best performances. Had they judged that Ms. Fliter had performed best but, for whatever reason, given the award to someone else, they would have wronged her, deprived her of that to which she had a right. She might never have discovered this injustice; it would have been an injustice nonetheless.

Now let's do some imagining. Imagine that each of the members of the Gilmore jury has been reading Kierkegaard, Nygren, Barth, Niebuhr, Ramsey, and the like, and has become a convinced agapist of the modern classical sort. None of them has ever discussed this with the others, nor has any of them ever done or said anything that revealed his new-found agapism to the others. They are closet agapists.

Now they are down to the final choice between Ms. Fliter and her last competitor. They all know the explicit and implicit rules for the award; they know what justice requires. But being agapists, that does not move them. What moves them is their commitment to treat these two candidates with equal-regarding agapic love. Add that none of them has any prior attachment to either of the candidates.

Will they give the award to Ms. Fliter and thus do what justice requires? They might or they might not; it all depends. Suppose they have each arrived at the judgment that the award would do the runner-up a great deal more good than it does Ms. Fliter. Neither the honor nor the money would mean all that much to her; she already has plenty of both. He, on the other hand, has little of either. So what will these equal-regarding agapists do? Will they give the award to Ms. Fliter on the ground that while that does not advance the good of her competitor, it also does not advance her good very much, and hence comes closer to treating the two with equal regard than would giving the award to him? So far as I can see, that is what they will do. So in that circumstance, the agapist judges will do what justice requires even though they are not motivated thereby.

But suppose the life-situation of the two competitors is the other way around. The honor and the money would mean very little to the runner-up but a great deal to Ms. Fliter; giving them to her would advance her good a lot more than giving them to him would advance his good. But as convinced agapists of the classical modern day sort, they treat the good of these two people with equal regard. So they give the honor and the money to the loser in the competition. Though this will not advance the good of the winner, it will also do very little to advance the good of her competitor; hence this comes as close to treating them with equal regard as is possible in the situation. But the winner would then be wronged. Agapic love perpetrates injustice.

The examples of unjust love that I have presented are examples of unjust distributions. Cases of benevolent paternalism provide us with another large set of examples of unjust agapic love. Suppose that a student has written a top-notch paper in a course that I am teaching. Justice demands that I give him an A; not to do so would be to wrong him. But suppose that he is not only a very good student but cocky, arrogant, and full of himself. I reflect that his life over the long haul will go much better if he is less cocky, and I make the judgment that giving him a B-minus will contribute to bringing about that desired change of character. So I give him a B-minus and write some comments highlighting the flaws in his paper; professors can find flaws in even the best student papers. Agapic love has perpetrated injustice.

This example of unjust benevolent paternalism pales before examples that can be culled from the history of Christendom. The task of the state was traditionally thought to include cultivating virtue and true religion in the citizenry. The means adopted for achieving that end often included a good deal of coercion and hard treatment, reaching all the way to torture. The justification offered was that when a great good is at stake, a good deal of coercion and hard treatment are justified, perhaps even required. If a person's eternal welfare is in the balance, then even torture is justified. It's an argument that, so far as I can see, the modern day agapist cannot reject; hard treatment of one and another sort is often the only means available for promoting some aspect of the neighbor's good. All by itself, the hard treatment would be a flagrant violation of agapism; but if the good of the end outweighs the evil of the means, then it is justified — perhaps required.[3] I am reminded of a comment that I once heard attributed to Hannah Arendt: the problem with Christians in politics is that they love too much.

A common response to this point nowadays is that the medieval torturers were mistaken in one or another, or both, of two assumptions they were making. They were mistaken in assuming that hard treatment can induce religious and moral reform, and/or they were mistaken in assuming that the reform they sought to induce was in fact for that person's good. Either way, the idea is that torture did not in fact enhance the victim's good; it is not an example of benevolence that wreaks injustice because it is not an example of (successful) benevolence.

This response poses an issue for the interpretation of agapism that I

3. Another version of agapism would be that it is never acceptable to impose a life-evil of any sort whatsoever on anyone, no matter how much good one anticipates would come from it. It is even more obvious that such agapism will often abet injustice than the form I consider in the text. Yet a different version of agapism would be that though life-evils of some sorts may be imposed if one anticipates that life-goods will result, life-evils of other sorts must never be imposed. The usual suggestion is *violence;* one must never use violence.

have skipped over thus far — an issue not only for the interpretation of agapism but for the interpretation of egoism, eudaimonism, and utilitarianism as well, and for any other ethical system that there may be. An ethical system offers a rule specifying whose good we may or should seek to promote as an end in itself, in what way, and under what circumstances. When we apply the rule we are, of course, employing our beliefs on these matters along with our belief as to whether the projected action will in fact enhance the person's good. Along the way it was incumbent on us to monitor the formation of our beliefs on these matters and to employ such practices of inquiry as make us entitled to them. But that's the best we human beings can do: apply the rule by employing beliefs to which we are entitled. Those entitled beliefs may be false; but nothing more can be asked of us.[4]

The historical evidence seems to me to indicate that at least some of the medieval torturers believed that by torturing heretics they could bring about their moral and religious reform, and that this would be a great good in their lives. I surmise that at least some of the torturers were entitled to these beliefs; they were not to be blamed for holding them. If so, they did what modern day agapism says they should have done; they aimed at promoting the good of the person as an end in itself. Nonetheless they wronged him, perpetrated a gross injustice.

WHY ONE SHOULD NOT PERPETRATE INJUSTICE IN THE NAME OF LOVE

Nygren would agree with the point I've been making, that benevolence in general, and agapic love in particular, sometimes perpetrate injustice; he interpreted Jesus' parables as making exactly that point. But he would not concede that this constitutes an objection to his position that every neighbor is always to be loved agapically. That is the upshot of his interpretation of the two parables of Jesus. The generosity of the landlord toward the workers who came late led him to treat the early workers unjustly; so be it, Jesus tells us. The generosity of the father toward the younger son led him to treat the elder son unjustly; so be it, Jesus tells us. Love trumps injustice.

So let me now complete the argument by showing why the fact that agapic love sometimes perpetrates injustice is a reason for rejecting clas-

---

4. The theory of entitlement that I am alluding to here is developed in detail in my essay, "Entitlement to Believe and Practices of Inquiry," in Nicholas Wolterstorff, *Practices of Belief: Selected Essays, Volume 2*, ed. Terence Cuneo (Cambridge: Cambridge University Press, 2010).

sical modern day agapism. If agapic love sometimes perpetrates injustice, then it cannot be true that we must always love every neighbor agapically. Before we get to that, however, I want to challenge Nygren's claim that what Jesus teaches in these two parables is that, when agapic love perpetrates injustice, we must remain faithful to love and say farewell to justice.

Nygren's interpretation of the parables seems to me an almost-willful misinterpretation. He interprets the landowner, in the parable of the laborers in the vineyard, as saying to the early workers, "Suppose it's true that in being generous to the late-comers I am treating you unjustly; am I not permitted to exercise my generosity in whatever way I wish?" What the landowner actually says is rather, and I quote, "Friend, I am not treating you unjustly *(adikos)*; did you not agree with me for a denarius? Take what belongs to you, and go; I choose to give to this last as I give to you. Am I not allowed to do what I choose with what belongs to me? Or do you begrudge my generosity?" The grumblers are mistaken in thinking they have been treated unjustly; they have to rethink their understanding of justice. Whether the landowner is right about this is a topic that I will take up in Chapter Eighteen, in the context of a comprehensive discussion of just and unjust generosity.

Nygren interprets the father in the parable of the prodigal son as saying to the elder son, "From the point of view of justice you are entirely right; I have wronged you. But your brother who was lost has been found; and that calls for a party even if it does wrong you." What the father actually says is rather, and I quote, "You are always with me, and all that is mine is yours. But we have to celebrate and rejoice, because this brother of yours was dead and has come to life, he was lost and has been found." In short, the elder son is mistaken in thinking that he is being treated unjustly. He has to rethink his understanding of justice.

Even without a comprehensive discussion of just and unjust generosity, we can see that the father was right about this. Not only has the elder son always been included in the father's household; what remains of the inheritance is entirely his. So how is he wronged? It's likely that the son was thinking in terms of the reciprocity code: good is to be answered with good and evil with evil. What his dissolute brother deserves is punishment; it's he, the upright elder son, who deserves a banquet. The father rejects the code. Yes, the behavior of the younger son was bad; but he has returned penitent, so now is the time for a feast of forgiveness. Justice does not require that he be punished.

The landowner and the father neither concede the charge of injustice nor wave it away as irrelevant; they contest it. Nygren thinks he sees in these parables the affirmation by Jesus of love trumping injustice. That's not there to be seen. And not only is it not there. Let me now go on to argue that, on Nygren's interpretation, the remarks of the land-owner and of the father cannot be true. It's necessarily false that perpe-trating injustice is permissible.

The landowner says that he is allowed to do what he has done. Sup-pose he has done what Nygren says he has done, namely, treat the early workers unjustly, deprive them of what they had a right to. But if they did indeed have a right against the landowner to better pay, then he, the landowner, had the correlative obligation toward them to pay them better.[5] He *ought to* have paid them better. Thus on Nygren's interpreta-tion, the landowner says that he is permitted to do that which in fact he ought not to do. That is necessarily false.[6] The same point holds for Nygren's interpretation of the father in the parable of the prodigal son.

The classical version of modern day agapism says that we should al-ways treat each neighbor with agapic love; and it understands agapic love in such a way that treating someone as one does because justice re-quires it is not an instance of agapic love. In this world of ours we must expect that agapic love, so understood, will sometimes work injustice. That confronts the agapist with a conundrum. If in loving someone agapically I treat him unjustly, then I violate his right not to be so treated. And if he has a right not to be so treated by me, then I ought not to treat him that way. In general it's true that if someone has a right against me to my not treating him that way, then I have a correlative ob-ligation toward him not to treat him thus. The position of the agapist implies that I am sometimes permitted to do what I ought not to do; sometimes it is even the case that I *should* do what I ought not to do. That cannot be right. Something has to give in the classical version of modern day agapism.

5. I defend this principle of correlatives at some length in *Justice: Rights and Wrongs.*
6. If Nygren's thought had been that the all-day workers had a *prima facie* right, but not an *all-things-considered* right, to be paid more, then there would be no problem, since then, correlatively, the landowner would have had only a prima facie obligation, but not an all-things-considered obligation, to pay them more. But nothing in what Nygren says suggests that that is how he was thinking. His thought is that, since agapic love pays no attention to what justice requires, it will sometimes do what is unjust, all things considered — and that that is a consequence that the followers of Jesus, if not everybody, should accept.

Chapter Five

NIEBUHR'S NON-CLASSICAL AGAPISM

AFTER NYGREN, the modern day agapist who reflected most extensively on the relation between love and justice was Reinhold Niebuhr. Along with the other modern day agapists, Niebuhr held that when Jesus enjoined us to love our neighbors as ourselves, he was not enjoining us to love each neighbor with some kind of love or other; he was enjoining us to love our neighbors with that special kind of love which is neighbor-love, agapic love. And he shared with all the modern day agapists the view that agapic love is that species of benevolence which consists of loving someone *because* she is one's neighbor. He agreed with Nygren that agapic love cannot have oneself as recipient; he often speaks of agapic love as *self-sacrificial* and as characterized by "pure disinterestedness."[1] But he appears to agree with Kierkegaard that one can seek to promote the good of someone out of agapic love and also seek to promote that same good of that same person out of some other motive — though I know of no passage in which he systematically discusses the issue.

It was on the rule of application for agapic love that Niebuhr decisively departed from the classical representatives of the modern day agapist movement. He held that there are conditions in which one should not treat a neighbor with agapic love. If one's neighbor is a participant in a conflict situation and treating him with agapic love would wreak injustice on someone, then one should do what justice requires and not what love requires. This is the direct opposite of Nygren's position.

Along with the other members of the modern day agapist movement, Niebuhr presented his line of thought as a plausible interpretation of, and extrapolation from, the New Testament texts. His reason for developing a distinctly non-classical interpretation of those texts was his conviction that what the classical interpretation led its proponents to say about the relation of love to justice was indefensible systematically.

In the preceding chapter I argued that the proposal that one should prefer love to justice when the two conflict is necessarily false. If I treat you unjustly, you are wronged by what I do; if you are wronged by what I

---

1. D. B. Robertson, *Love and Justice: Selections from the Shorter Writings of Reinhold Niebuhr* (Philadelphia: Westminster Press, 1957), 31. Cf. 28: "In so far as justice admits the claims of the self, it is something less than love."

do, I ought not to do it; and if I ought not to do it, then I am not permitted to do it. Niebuhr's argument was different but similar. Holding up before the reader examples of agapic love either perpetrating injustice or inviting victimization, he appeals to our sense that it is morally impermissible to say, "So be it." It was not hermeneutical considerations but this conviction that it is morally impermissible to perpetrate injustice or invite victimization that led him to his own distinct interpretation of the New Testament texts; he took remarkably little notice, for example, of the theme of justice in the New Testament.

It should not escape our attention, however, that underlying the moves Niebuhr made was the conviction he shared with the other agapists, that Jesus spoke with authority and that the gospels are a reliable witness to what he said. Conceding that the classical modern day agapists had rightly interpreted Jesus, and then going on to say that what Jesus said was mistaken was not, for Niebuhr, an option.

JUSTICE IS FOR OUR CONFLICT-RIDDEN CONDITION

The systematic impulse so strong in Nygren was markedly weak in Niebuhr. Nonetheless, a distinct line of thought comes through. The exercise of agapic love in any and all situations is not for this present age but for the age to come; justice is for this present age. "The ethical demands made by Jesus," he says, "are incapable of fulfillment in the present existence of man. They proceed from a transcendent and divine unity of essential reality, and their final fulfillment is possible only when God transmutes the present chaos of this world into its final unity."[2]

The fact that the ethical demands made by Jesus cannot be fulfilled in this present age is, of course, not sufficient by itself to establish that there are situations in which we should not even try to meet those demands; Niebuhr concedes that we will also never fully succeed in fulfilling the demands of justice.[3] What needs to be added is that Jesus' ethic of love is incapable of being fulfilled in this present age *without perpetrating or abetting injustice or inviting victimization*. The impossibility of fulfilling the ethic without violating justice is what shows that it was never meant as a universal ethic for life in this present age.

We human beings are pervasively self-interested and incapable of curing ourselves thereof to any significant degree. Human life is an

2. Reinhold Niebuhr, *An Interpretation of Christian Ethics* (New York: Harper & Brothers, 1935), 56-57.

3. See, for example, *Interpretation*, 108.

arena of "claims and counterclaims," of "competing wills and interests."[4] We do not live in harmony. "The ethic of Jesus does not deal at all with the immediate moral problem of every human life — the problem of arranging some kind of armistice between various contending factions and forces. It has nothing to say about the relativities of politics and economics, nor of the necessary balances of power which exist and must exist in even the most intimate social relationships. The absolutism and perfectionism of Jesus' love ethic sets itself uncompromisingly not only against the natural self-regarding impulses, but against the necessary prudent defenses of the self, required because of the egoism of others" (*Interpretation*, 39).

It was characteristic of liberal Protestants in the early decades of the twentieth century to argue that love *of* the neighbor will evoke love *from* the neighbor. If Christians were only more loving, God's kingdom of love and justice would appear on earth. Liberal Protestants, said Niebuhr, "approached the injustices and conflicts of this world with a gay and easy confidence. Men had been ignorantly selfish. They would now be taught the law of love. . . . Once . . . obscurantist theology had been brushed aside, the Church would be free to preach salvation to the world. Its word of salvation would be that all men ought to love one another. It was as simple as that."[5]

Niebuhr's response was impatient dismissal. The law of love is not a prudential strategy for creating a community of loving people. Self-interest is too deeply entrenched in human beings for that. Only God's eschatological triumph will loosen the grip of sin on human beings; it is naïve to think that Christians loving their neighbors will remake those neighbors into loving human beings. This is the core of Niebuhr's so-called "realism." "Emulation of the character of God is advanced [in the New Testament] as the only motive of forgiving enemies. Nothing is said about the possibility of transmuting their enmity to friendship through the practice of forgiveness. That social and prudential possibility has been read into the admonition of Jesus by liberal Christianity" (*Interpretation*, 40-41).[6]

---

4. Reinhold Niebuhr, *The Nature and Destiny of Man: A Christian Interpretation* (New York: Charles Scribner's Sons, 1949), vol. 2, 72.

5. *Interpretation*, 169-70. Cf. 177: "Liberal Christian literature abounds in the monotonous reiteration of the pious hope that people might be good and loving, in which case all the nasty business of politics could be dispensed with." The whole sixth chapter of *Interpretation* is devoted to a biting attack on the naivete of liberal Protestantism.

6. Cf. *Nature and Destiny of Man*, vol. 2, 87-88: "The Christian faith in its profoundest versions has never believed that the Cross would so change the very nature of historical existence that a more and more universal achievement of sacrificial love would finally transmute sacrificial love into successful mutual love, perfectly validated . . . by historical

What drew Niebuhr's attention was not only that agapic love will sometimes perpetrate or abet injustice but that, when a person tries to live her entire life by "the law of love," the result is far more likely to be that she herself is victimized than that the recipients of her love are transformed into loving human beings. The life and death of Jesus stand as stark testimony to this tragic truth. As Niebuhr puts it in an oft-quoted passage:

> The divine love can have a counterpart in history only in a life which ends tragically, because it refuses to participate in the claims and counterclaims of historical existence. It portrays a love "which seeketh not its own." But a love which seeketh not its own is not able to maintain itself in historical society. Not only may it fall victim to excessive forms of the self-assertion of others; but even the most perfectly balanced system of justice in history is a balance of competing wills and interests, and must therefore worst anyone who does not participate in the balance. (*Nature and Destiny of Man*, vol. 2, 72)

Niebuhr appears to imply in this passage that one should never sacrifice one's life for the sake of the neighbor. This has been a persistent point of objection to Niebuhr's interpretation of the New Testament: where does Jesus say that we should love the neighbor only so long as it doesn't require anything drastic by the way of self-sacrifice? Jesus himself sacrificed his life out of love. Are we not to do likewise?

It cannot be denied that in this passage and a number of others Niebuhr leaves himself open to this objection. But when these passages are set in the context of his discussion as a whole, it becomes clear that he is not saying that one's promotion of the good of the other should never be self-sacrificial. He is talking about the *law* of love, what I have called *the rule of application;* and he is disagreeing with those who interpret that law as saying that we should all always be ready to promote the good of the neighbor as an end in itself whether or not doing so comes at the cost of our own victimization. Niebuhr agrees with the other modern day agapists that agapic love is self-sacrificial benevolence; what he never tires of emphasizing is that agapic love invites victimization. But human society could not continue if we all always allowed ourselves to

---

social consequences. The New Testament never guarantees the historical success of the 'strategy' of the Cross. Jesus warns his disciples against a too sanguine historical hope: 'In this rejoice not, that the spirits are subject unto you; but rather rejoice because your names are written in heaven.' In that warning we have a telling refutation of the utopian corruptions of Christianity."

be victimized. And it is implausible to interpret Jesus as enjoining us to act in such a way that human society would come to an end.

In the following passage, Niebuhr blends this point about victimization with the point that benevolence often perpetrates or abets injustice.

> In the collective relationships of mankind ruthless aggression must be countered by resolute defense; and the impulse of dominion must be resisted, if slavery is to be avoided. A sacrificial submission to a ruthless antagonist may mean a noble martyrdom if the interests of the self alone are considered. But if interests other than those of the self are sacrificed, this nobility becomes ignoble "appeasement." This fact our Christian perfectionists learned (and sometimes failed to learn) in the tragic decades of recent history. . . . A saintly abnegation of interest may encourage the ruthless aggrandizement of the strong and the unscrupulous. These facts are so plain that every effort to introduce suffering love as a simple alternative to the complexities and ambiguities of social justice must degenerate into sentimentality.[7]

Only when human beings have been purged of their sinfulness by the "impossible possibility"[8] of God's eschatological triumph will benevolence that stands ready to be self-sacrificial no longer perpetrate and abet injustice and no longer invite victimization; only in the "frictionless harmony"[9] of the eschaton can the law of love be the universal basis of an enduring human community.

What's called for in cases of conflict is justice, not agapic love. "Every definition of justice . . . presupposes sin as a given reality. It is only because life is in conflict with life, because of sinful self-interest, that we are required carefully to define schemes of justice which prevent one life from taking advantage of another" (*Love and Justice*, 49). "The problem of politics and economics is [thus] the problem of justice. The question of politics is how to coerce the anarchy of conflicting human interests into some kind of order, offering human beings the greatest possible opportunity for mutual support. In the field of collective behavior the force of egoistic passion is so strong that the only harmonies possible are those which manage to neutralize this force through balances of power, through mutual defenses against its inordinate expression, and through techniques for harnessing its energy to social ends.

---

7. Reinhold Niebuhr, *Faith and History: A Comparison of Christian and Modern Views of History* (New York: Charles Scribner's Sons, 1949), 184.

8. The phrase comes from the fourth chapter, "The Relevance of an Impossible Ethical Ideal," of Niebuhr's *Interpretation*.

9. The phrase is to be found in *Nature and Destiny of Man*, vol. 2, 78.

All these possibilities represent something less than the ideal of love" (*Interpretation,* 140).

Justice is relevant where the self-interest of different parties is in conflict; it consists of the just resolution of those conflicts.[10] Such a resolution "involves the assertion of rights, the rights of the disinherited"; very often it requires "the use of coercion" (*Love and Justice,* 34). Those who deprive others of their rights do not cease doing so upon being loved by their victims. "The necessity of . . . coercion, based upon the assertion of interest on the part of the less privileged, is such a clear lesson of history that one hesitates to belabor the point and would refrain from doing so were it not for the fact that half of the academic treatises on social ethics and Christian ethics were written as if no such necessity existed" (36).

But the assertion of rights required by justice is "incompatible with the pure love ethic found in the Gospels" (*Love and Justice,* 34), as is the employment of coercion. In the assertion of rights and in the unavoidable use of coercion, "the social struggle involves a violation of a pure ethic of love" (35). In Nygren's view, we must act out of agapic love whether or not we perpetrate injustice; in Niebuhr's view, we must in each case discern whether agapic love is called for or justice, and act accordingly. For Nygren, agapic love has no constraints, not even if it perpetrates injustice; for Niebuhr, agapic love is constrained by the requirements of justice.

The reader may have noticed the reference, in the last passage quoted, to "the social struggle." Whereas Niebuhr thought that agapic love could almost never be applied to relations within and among social entities — states, business enterprises, etc. — without perpetrating or abetting injustice or inviting victimization, he held that this was not true for relations among individuals. The reason for the difference is that in our personal relationships the "forces of natural sympathy" (*Love and Justice,* 125) sometimes overcome our self-interest, thus enabling us to treat the other with genuine love. When we feel sympathy for the other, we imagine ourselves in her situation and see the situation from her perspective. Such sympathetic imagination is next to impossible for social entities to achieve. Thus it is that "the full evil of human finitude and sin is most vividly revealed in conflicts between national communities. . . . They present a tragic revelation of the impossibility of the law of love because no party to the conflict has a perspective high enough to judge the merits of the opponent's position. Every appeal to moral standards thus degenerates into a moral justification of the self against the enemy" (125-26).[11]

10. "Justice requires discriminate judgments between conflicting claims" (*Love and Justice,* 28).

11. Cf. *Love and Justice,* 35: "The relations between groups are so indirect that the con-

Though the contrast between what is possible in relations among individuals and what is possible in relations among social entities is a staple in Niebuhr's thought from early to late, he warns against exaggerating the difference. "Even in the most intimate community, the family, parental, conjugal, and filial affection is no perfect guarantee of justice and harmony. All these forces of natural sympathy may become facades behind which the will-to-power operates. Even when it is less pronounced than the imperialism of groups it may be more deadly for operating at such close range" (*Love and Justice*, 125).

The universal application of agapic love is incompatible with the need to secure justice among parties whose self-interest brings them into conflict with each other: that is the dominant theme in all of Niebuhr's writing on ethics. It is not the whole of what he has to say about the relation between love and justice, however. He also says that justice is an "approximation" to the ideal of love (*Love and Justice*, 111) and, using a different metaphor, that it is an "echo" of the ideal.[12] For "equality is . . . the regulative principle of justice; and in the ideal of equality there is an echo of the law of love, 'Thou shalt love thy neighbor AS THYSELF'" (108).

In the development of civilized communities across history we can discern ever closer approximations to the ideal of equal-regarding benevolent love. "The basic rights to life and property in the early community, the legal minima of rights and obligations of more advanced communities, the moral rights and obligations recognized in these communities beyond those which are legally enforced, the further refinement of standards in the family beyond those recognized in the general community — all these stand in an ascending scale of moral possibilities in which each succeeding step is a closer approximation of the law of love" (*Love and Justice*, 110). Yet "every achievement [remains] in the realm of approximation. The ideal in its perfect form lies beyond the capacities of human nature" (111).

What must be added is a point made earlier: that not only does love transcend the possibilities of our present existence but so also does justice. Thus "the ideal of love and the ideal of equality" can be thought of as together standing "in an ascending scale of transcendence to the facts of existence. The ideal of equality is a part of the natural law which

---

sequences of our actions in the life of another group are not easily discerned, and we therefore continue in unethical conduct without the restraint upon our conscience that intimate personal relations create. Very few white men have any conception of the havoc that is wrought in the souls and upon the bodies of Negroes by prevailing race prejudices." The point is also developed in *Moral Man and Immoral Society* (New York: Charles Scribner's Sons, 1932), xi-xii, and xxiii-xxiv.

12. In another passage he speaks of love as "the fulfillment and highest form of the *spirit* of justice" (*Love and Justice*, 25; italics added).

transcends existence, but is more immediately relevant to social and economic problems because it is an ideal *law*,[13] and as law presupposes a recalcitrant nature which must be brought into submission to it. The ideal of love, on the other hand, transcends all law. It knows nothing of the recalcitrance of nature in historical existence. It is the fulfillment of the law. It is impossible to construct a social ethic out of the ideal of love in its pure form, because the ideal presupposes the resolution of the conflict of life with life, which it is the concern of law to mitigate and restrain. For this reason Christianity really had no social ethic until it appropriated the Stoic ethic" (*Love and Justice,* 149-50).

The fact that the just resolution of conflicts among self-interested parties is an echo of the ideal of love, an approximation to the ideal but never more than that, is seen by Niebuhr as carrying the implication that the ideal of love stands to even our finest achievements as a spotlight on their failings. Confronted with conflicting self-interest, "humanity always faces a double task. The one is to reduce the anarchy of the world to some kind of immediately sufferable order and unity; and the other is to set these tentative and insecure unities and achievements under the criticism of the ultimate ideal. When they are not thus challenged, what is good in them becomes evil and each tentative harmony becomes the cause of a new anarchy. With Augustine we must realize that the peace of the world is gained by strife. That does not justify us either in rejecting such a tentative peace or in accepting it as final. The peace of the city of God can use and transmute the lesser and insecure peace of the city of the world; but that can be done only if the peace of the world is not confused with the ultimate peace of God" (*Love and Justice,* 60-61).[14]

---

13. Italics added.

14. Cf. *Love and Justice,* 32-33: "Whether we view the ethical teachings of Jesus from the perspective of the individual or of society we discover an unattainable ideal, but a very useful one. It is an ideal never attained in history or in life, but one that gives us an absolute standard by which to judge both personal and social righteousness. . . . Perhaps it ought to be added that an attempt to follow this ideal in a world that is, particularly in its group relationships, hardly human and certainly not divine, will inevitably lead us to where it led Jesus, to the cross.

"Valuable as this kind of perfectionism is, it certainly offers no basis for a social ethic that deals responsibly with a growing society. Those of us who believe in the complete reorganization of modern society are not wrong in using the ideal of Jesus as a vantage point from which to condemn the present social order, but I think we are in error when we try to draw from the teachings of Jesus any warrant for the social policies which we find necessary to attain to any modicum of justice. . . . Those of us who dissociate ourselves from the easy optimism of modern liberalism and who believe that a just society is not going to be built by a little more education and a few more sermons on love have particular reason to reorient our thinking in this matter so that we will not come forward with a social ethic involving the use of force and coercion and political pressure of every kind and claim the authority of Jesus for it."

I submit that whatever may be said about this as an interpretation of Jesus' ethic of love, there is something perplexing about it as a systematic position. If "the ideal of love" can serve as a critique of our endeavors to secure justice, why is it incapable of giving us even the outlines of a social ethic? The ideal pronounces a "No" on all our endeavors to secure social justice. But it does not only pronounce a "No." Discerning, as it does, degrees of approximation to love, it also pronounces a "Better" and a "Worse." And in that "Better" and "Worse," pronounced by the ideal of love, do we not have the outlines of a social ethic? In short, how can Niebuhr contend that "the ethic of Jesus may offer valuable insights to and sources of criticism for a prudential social ethic which deals with present realities; but no such social ethic can be directly derived from a pure religious ethic" (*Interpretation*, 51)?

I know of no passage in which Niebuhr takes note of this objection. But I think we can surmise how he would answer. Doing justice requires that we take note of the rights of persons and social entities; often it also requires that coercion be employed if they are to enjoy their rights. Agapic love, by contrast, takes no note of rights and renounces all use of coercion. Thus it is impossible to get justice out of love; agapic love does not deal in the coinage of justice. And it makes no difference whether we are talking about social justice or about justice in personal relationships; Niebuhr's rhetoric is misleading on this point.

All true; agapic love does not deal in the coinage of justice. Nonetheless there is, on Niebuhr's view, a certain structural affinity between justice and the ideal of love. True justice requires that everybody's rights be honored equally; "the simplest of all moral principles [is] that of equal justice" (*Interpretation*, 131). And the rule for agapic love is that each of one's neighbors is equally a candidate for agapic love. So when we look, from the standpoint of the ideal of love, at our endeavors to secure justice, we not only see that the whole endeavor deals in a coinage that the ideal of agapic love has nothing to do with; we also discern, within those endeavors, points where equality of treatment is secured and points where equality is violated. Love takes note of those points. And whereas Niebuhr highlights the points where love discerns the violation of equal treatment and pronounces a "No," implicit in his argument, but never acknowledged, is the fact that love pronounces a "Yes" on those points where it discerns the presence of equality of treatment.[15]

---

15. In ch. 3 of the second volume of *Nature and Destiny of Man*, a chapter that he titles "The Possibilities and Limits of History," Niebuhr offers a typology of the ways in which the ideal of love can serve as a source of critique of the successes and failures of justice. Along the way he repeatedly reminds the reader that we must expect of a straightforward attempt to put agape into practice here in this world of conflicting self-interests that the result is likely to be one's death or the perpetuation of injustice on others or both.

PARADOX IN NIEBUHR'S INTERPRETATION

Niebuhr agreed with the other modern day agapists that the person who acts out of agapic love will not act as he does because justice requires it, and conversely, that the person who acts as he does because justice requires it is not acting out of agapic love. The line of thought that led him to this conclusion was different, however, from that which led Nygren to the same conclusion. Nygren located a fundamental conceptual incompatibility between agapic love and seeking justice in the fact that whereas agapic love is intrinsically spontaneous, to seek justice is to do what is required of one. Niebuhr agreed. But what he emphasized more than this conceptual incompatibility was the incompatibility that shows up when we take note of what must actually be done to secure justice.

As we have seen, conflict among self-interested parties was always up front in Niebuhr's mind when he thought about justice. Securing justice requires determining what is due whom in such situations, and then rendering that to him or her, this often requiring coercion. It was especially in love's renunciation of coercion that Niebuhr located the conflict between love and justice. By refusing to employ coercion, including coercion aimed at rendering to someone what is due him or her, agapic love over and over perpetrates and abets injustice and invites victimization.

Prominent in Niebuhr's multifaceted attack on the liberal tradition of Christianity was his charge that it watered down the radical quality of agapic love in order to make it seem plausible that such love could serve as the basis of social order. A good many critics have argued that Niebuhr himself engaged in such watering down. The charge misses the target. If Niebuhr is guilty of the charge of watering down the New Testament ethic of love, it is not because he watered down the nature of love but because he restricted the scope of its application.

In situations of conflict, go with justice rather than love, says Niebuhr. Love is relevant when conflict is absent. But it was about the need for love in situations of conflict that Jesus was most emphatic. Love your neighbor, he said, even if that neighbor is your enemy — even if he has wronged you and remains unrepentant. Do not return evil for evil; return good for evil. Practice love not only in non-conflictual situations but also in situations of conflict. Clearly there is something seriously askew about Niebuhr's position as an interpretation of what Jesus taught.

And not only is there a serious discrepancy between the situations in which Jesus enjoins love and those in which Niebuhr recommends love. There is also a serious discrepancy between Niebuhr's understanding of justice and the understanding of justice that Jesus employed when he identified himself as anointed by God to bring justice. When first one hears Niebuhr's affirmation of the importance of justice, one concludes that there is here a sensitivity to the theme of justice in the biblical literature that is completely missing in Nygren. But when one learns that the coming of the eschaton represents for Niebuhr the withering away of justice, one realizes that here too we are confronted with an interpretation that has gone wrong. The coming of the eschaton represented, for Jesus, not the withering away of justice but its full rule. The relevance of justice is not confined to situations of conflict.

Niebuhr was right to want both love and justice. But rather than having both by assigning justice to this present age of sinful self-interest and love to the coming age of frictionless harmony, with a bit of seepage from the latter into the former, we need a way of having both in this present age and both in the age to come. We need a way of understanding love and a way of understanding justice that does not polarize them. Better said: we need an understanding of love and an understanding of justice such that love incorporates justice.

A fundamental assumption in both Nygren and Niebuhr is that love may conflict with justice and nonetheless be *well-formed*. Nygren instructs us to remain faithful to love in such situations of conflict at the cost of perpetrating injustice; Niebuhr instructs us to remain faithful to justice in situations of conflict at the cost of love. Both positions prove untenable. In the chapters that follow I will question the assumption. Love that perpetrates injustice is malformed love. And *contra* Niebuhr, absence of conflict does not render justice irrelevant. As I have argued elsewhere, there is justice in the Trinity.[16]

16. "Is There Justice in the Trinity?" in Miroslav Volf and Michael Welker, eds., *God's Life in Trinity* (Minneapolis: Fortress, 2006).

PART TWO

Care-Agapism

Chapter Six

JUSTICE AS LOVE

Reviewing Where We Are

Before I set out to develop my own version of agapism, let me rehearse a few of the points made in the Introduction. Every ethical system employs the idea of things that are good *for* one, these being states and events, actions and activities, in one's life. I call such goods *wellbeing-goods,* on the ground that it is the presence and absence of such goods in one's life that determine the degree of one's wellbeing.

In addition to employing the idea of wellbeing-goods, every ethical system employs the idea of seeking to promote the wellbeing-goods of someone as an end in itself; and every system has a rule specifying whose wellbeing-goods one may or should seek to promote as an end in itself and under what circumstances. Some systems also have things to say about the manner in which one may or should seek to promote someone's wellbeing as an end in itself. And some offer an account of what it is for some state or event, some action or activity in one's life, to be good *for* one. I observed that seeking to promote someone's wellbeing as an end in itself is one form that love takes. Thus every ethical system has a position on whom one may or should love, and under what conditions.

A point I did not make in the Introduction is that it is commonly assumed by writers on these matters that something is intrinsically good *for* one only if one enjoys it, only if one finds it satisfying. Robert Adams call this "the enjoyment criterion," James Griffin calls it "the experience requirement."[1] Usually no argument is offered for the thesis "that something can be noninstrumentally good for a human being only if it is enjoyed by him."[2] When an argument is offered, it is always cursory; the thesis is treated as more or less self-evident. Here, for example, is the full extent of what Kraut says in support of the thesis:

Swimming may certainly be a good way for us to get across the lake, it may burn calories, it may maintain muscle tone; these are all good

---

1. Robert Adams, *Finite and Infinite Goods,* 100; James Griffin, *Well-Being* (Oxford: Clarendon, 1986), 317-18, n. 5.
2. Richard Kraut, *What Is Good and Why,* 128.

reasons for thinking that it is good for the swimmer as a means to further ends. But can it be good for him apart from these results? If we
have some temptation to answer affirmatively, that temptation will
certainly be strongest when we think of someone who loves swimming — who, in other words, enjoys it. For when we think of someone swimming but deriving not the least bit of pleasure from doing
so, it is difficult to believe that this could be good for him for any reason other than the good consequences of his activity. (127-28)

The enjoyment criterion for wellbeing seems to me mistaken. Consider a person in a coma. There are states and events in her life that are
good *for* her. Many of those are, of course, only instrumentally good for
her. But something can be instrumentally good for someone only if it
brings about something that is intrinsically good for her. But a person in
a coma isn't having any experiences, so of course she isn't having any
satisfying or enjoyable experiences.

In the Introduction I went on to argue that there are states and
events, actions and activities, in the life of a person that are goods *of* that
person but not goods *for* him or her; they make the person's life more estimable than it would be otherwise even though they do not enhance the
person's wellbeing. Anything that is a good *for* someone will be a good *of*
him, but the converse is not the case. The example I gave to make the
point was this: suppose that a hacker succeeds in tapping into my email
correspondence but never reveals to me or anyone else that he has done
so and never does anything with what he learns other than enjoy it in private. I think that having my privacy invaded in this way is an evil in my
life. But since it has no effect on my wellbeing, it's not an evil *for* me.

Though there are some philosophical topics for which the concept of
wellbeing-goods would be the appropriate concept, I observed that it is
the broader concept of *life-goods* that we need for our purposes. The reason I gave is that our topic is justice and love. And not only is it a good in
one's life that one's privacy not be invaded for prurient reasons; one has
a *right* to that good. Justice requires that one not be so treated by one's
fellow human beings. To generalize: a moral right is always a morally legitimate claim to the life-good of being treated a certain way. But some of
the life-goods to which one has a right are not goods *for* one; being deprived of them has no impact whatsoever on one's wellbeing.

Let me now add that an adequate understanding of the scope of love
also requires the broader concept of life-goods. The point can be introduced by referring to some remarks C. S. Lewis makes in *The Problem of
Pain.*[3] Lewis is arguing against a common understanding of love as con-

3. I am using the sixth impression (London: Collins/Fontana, 1965).

sisting of being nice to people, being kind. "Kindness . . . cares not whether its object becomes good or bad, provided only that it escapes suffering" (29). Lewis maintains that this is in fact "the opposite pole from Love" (34). Love "demands the perfecting of the beloved" (34). "It is for people whom we care nothing about that we demand happiness on any terms: with our friends, our lovers, our children, we are exacting and would rather see them suffer much than be happy in contemptible and estranging moods" (29). "Love may forgive all infirmities and love still in spite of them; but Love cannot cease to will their removal" (34).

The sort of love Lewis has in mind is love as benevolence, love that seeks to promote the good of a person as an end in itself. And the particular sort of life-good he has in view is that of acting morally. He assumes it to be a good in a person's life that she does the right thing rather than the wrong thing, the thing she ought to do rather than the thing she ought not to do; and he assumes that love will sometimes, perhaps often, take the form of aiding and prodding her to do the right thing.

I think Lewis is right on both counts. The prominence of the ideal of autonomy in the culture of our day produces in many people a discernible skittishness when it comes to aiding and prodding others to do what one thinks they ought to do; there is a discernible preference for being nice, as Lewis calls it, for letting others act as they wish. No one treats children that way, however, nor does the state treat its citizens that way.

Now for the application of the point to the issue at hand. Doing what one ought to do is an intrinsic good in one's life. And sometimes love for our fellows requires that we seek to promote the life-good of their doing what they ought to do — provided, of course, that we do so in such a way that we don't wrong them. But often it proves to be the case that a person's doing what he ought to do is not a good *for* him. Coming to the aid of the mugged man in the ditch was a good deed on the part of the Samaritan in Jesus' parable; it was an intrinsic good in his life. But it was scarcely good *for* him. He had to go out of his way to carry the man to the nearest inn, and he was out of pocket the money he paid for the man's lodging.

I can imagine a rejoinder. My argument assumes that one's moral condition is not, as such, an aspect of one's wellbeing. It assumes that doing what one ought to do sometimes enhances one's wellbeing and sometimes diminishes one's wellbeing, but that, as such, it is irrelevant to one's wellbeing. The assumption is common in discussions about wellbeing. But is it correct? Whether one does or does not do what one ought to do determines one's moral condition. But isn't one's moral condition, "the state of one's soul," an aspect of one's well-being? Doesn't understanding the scope of love along the lines that Lewis suggests point not to the need for the broader concept of life-goods but instead to the need for a more expansive understanding of wellbeing-goods? Given that the Samaritan did what he ought to do, he did not diminish his wellbeing. He diminished his wellbeing in certain respects, but not overall.

Well, suppose that the Samaritan seriously injured his back while carrying the wounded man to the inn and that, for the rest of his life, he lived in intractable pain. Would it then be the case that doing what he did diminished his wellbeing? If we regard doing what one ought to do as one among other wellbeing-goods, how do we assess the contribution of such an action to one's overall wellbeing? Can the moral goodness of an action be outweighed by non-moral evils that accompany or result from it, so that the total package diminishes one's overall wellbeing? Or does the moral goodness of an action always and necessarily outweigh whatever non-moral evils accompany and result from it, so that it is impossible to diminish one's overall wellbeing by doing the right thing?

These are conundra that it seems to me best to avoid. I hold that there is a concept of wellbeing such that we are saying something true when we say that the Samaritan did what was right and good even though it diminished his wellbeing, even though it was not good *for* him. It would be even more obviously true had he injured his back and spent the rest of his life in severe pain. It's that concept of wellbeing that I have been employing in our discussion. And it is that concept of wellbeing that is employed in the cry that comes down to us through the ages, "Why do the wicked prosper and the righteous suffer?" And as to the point made when someone says that the state of one's soul is an aspect of one's wellbeing, I think the point is better made by saying that the state of one's soul is an aspect of one's *flourishing*. Though doing what one ought to do may prove not to be good *for* one, it is a good *of* one.

As I noted in the Introduction, the ethical systems most commonly discussed by philosophers — strictly speaking, *types* of systems — are egoism, eudaimonism, and utilitarianism. The reasons I gave for rejecting those systems left us in the position of looking for a rule of application that says or implies that one should sometimes promote the good of someone other than oneself as an end in itself, but which rejects both the agent-wellbeing condition proposed by the eudaimonists and the maximizing condition proposed by the utilitarians. Agapism — seldom discussed by philosophers but discussed often and at length by theologians and religious ethicists — is such a (type of) system.

Agapism is less well defined as a systematic type than are the other three. Its origins lie in Hebrew and Christian scripture; and such systematic unity as the type possesses emerges from the tradition of engaging those somewhat cryptic prophetic texts. In the late nineteenth century and the twentieth there emerged, within the tradition of agapism, a highly articulate movement that I have called *modern day agapism*. For several chapters now we have been exploring that version of agapism, partly because of its popularity and intrinsic interest, partly because uncovering where and why it fails in relating love to justice proves instructive for our own attempt to work out a defensible version of agapism.

It is time now to turn to that. My discussion will be located within the tradition of agapism in that I too will present my position as a plausible and systematically defensible interpretation of, and extrapolation from, the founding texts of the tradition. I will not stop there, however. I will present the position I develop as plausible in its own right.

The Episode of Jesus Giving the Two Love Commands

All three synoptic gospels report the episode in which Jesus presented the two love commands (Matthew 22:34-40; Mark 12:28-34; Luke 10:25-37). They all assume or report that various parties had been trying to trap Jesus in his words; they differ somewhat in the details of their descriptions of the episode.

Matthew says that when the Pharisees learned that the Sadducees had been unsuccessful in trapping Jesus, they resolved to see what they could do. A lawyer from among them asked Jesus the test question, "Teacher, which commandment in the law is the greatest?" Presumably there was consensus on the matter among the members of the Pharisee party, and presumably the lawyer thought that either Jesus did not know about this consensus or did know about it but rejected it. Either way, the lawyer could pounce on Jesus' answer and say, "Gotcha; that's not the greatest commandment." But Jesus got it right. Matthew records no response on the part of the lawyer or his Pharisee colleagues. Presumably the answer Jesus gave was the one they had anticipated using to trump his answer.

Mark reports a scribe as asking the question rather than a lawyer from the Pharisee party. Though Mark does not say that the scribe asked the question to test Jesus, it's clear from how Mark concludes his description of the episode that that was in fact what the scribe was doing. No one dared ask Jesus any further questions, says Mark. In Mark's narration, Jesus introduces the first commandment with the *Shema*, "Hear, O Israel, the Lord our God, the Lord is one." And the scribe, rather than walking away defeated, expresses his approval of Jesus' reply. You are right, he says; these two commandments are "much more important than all whole burnt offerings and sacrifices." The response of Jesus to this comment by the scribe is that "You are not far from the kingdom of God." Given the querulous attitude of the interrogator, it is not implausible to construe this response as ironic.

In Luke, as in Matthew, it's a lawyer who puts the test question to Jesus. The question is a bit different, however, from that which Matthew reports. "What must I do to inherit eternal life?" the lawyer asks. Jesus turns the tables on his interrogator by getting him to answer his own question: "What is written in the law? What do you read there?" The lawyer cites the two love commandments, whereupon Jesus praises him. "You have given the right answer," he says, and then tells the lawyer to "do this and you will live." The lawyer sees that he has been bested. But he is not yet ready to give up. In order to "justify himself," as Luke puts it, he tries again and asks, "Who is my neighbor?" Jesus then tells the parable of the good Samaritan. At the conclusion of the parable, Jesus again puts the lawyer on the spot by asking him to declare which of the three travelers was a neighbor to the man who was mugged. "The one who showed him mercy," says the lawyer. "Go and do likewise," says Jesus.

More important for our purposes than any of the differences in how the episode is reported are two points of similarity. First, when it comes to the commandments themselves, the differences in formulation are entirely minor. The only significant difference is that Matthew reports Jesus as making a comment about the relation of the second commandment to the first; it is "like" the first, he says: "You shall love the Lord your God with all your heart, and with all your soul, and with all your mind. This is the great and first commandment. And a second is like it. You shall love your neighbor as yourself. On these two commandments depend all the law and the prophets." Jesus does not explain in what way the second commandment is like the first; but even the most casual reader will pick up that it is at least like the first in that it gives centrality to love.

Second, in all three reports the interlocutor tacitly or explicitly concedes or affirms that these are indeed the two great commandments.

JUSTICE IN THE SECOND LOVE COMMAND

Clearly Jesus and his interlocutors hold that the two love commandments capture the essence, the heart, of the Torah. But they are also the greatest and most important *in* the Torah; that is to say, they are to be *found* in the Torah, they are *written in* the Torah. Perhaps looking at the contexts in which they occur in the Torah will help us understand how they would have been understood by the writers or editors of the Torah.[4] From this it does not follow that that is how Jesus and his hearers understood them. But a reasonable rule of procedure is to assume that, absent evidence to the contrary, Jesus and his hearers would have understood them in roughly the same way. Certainly it's more likely that that's how they understood them than that they understood them as you and I understand these sentences all by themselves in present day English.

In a later chapter I will have something to say about the first commandment and its context in the Torah. Here let us focus on the second commandment. The commandment is quoted from Leviticus 19. The situation is Moses delivering God's law-code for Israel. Moses moves back and forth in how he refers to those who are to be treated in accord with the injunctions he delivers: sometimes he refers to them as *kin*, sometimes as *neighbors*, sometimes as *members of the people*. Though the Hebrew terms that these English terms translate may well have had somewhat different meanings, here in this passage they are functionally equivalent. Moses is instructing the Israelites on how they are to treat their fellow Israelites. A bit later he adds that resident aliens are to be treated as members of the people: "When an alien resides with you in your land, you shall not oppress the alien. The alien who resides with you shall be to you as the citizen among you; you shall love the alien as yourself" (19:33-34).

Let us have before us some of the injunctions that lead up to the injunction to love your neighbor as yourself:

> When you reap the harvest of your land, you shall not reap to the very edges of your field, or gather the gleanings of your harvest. You shall not strip your vineyard bare, or gather the fallen grapes of your vineyard; you shall leave them for the poor and the alien: I am the LORD your God.
>
> You shall not steal; you shall not deal falsely; and you shall not lie to one another. And you shall not swear falsely by my name, profaning the name of your God: I am the LORD.
>
> You shall not defraud your neighbor; you shall not steal; and you shall not keep for yourself the wages of a laborer until morning. You shall not revile the deaf or put a stumbling block before the blind; you shall fear your God: I am the LORD.
>
> You shall not render an unjust judgment; you shall not be partial to the poor or defer to the great; with justice you shall judge your

---

4. Cf. Lenn E. Goodman in *Love Thy Neighbor as Thyself* (Oxford: Oxford University Press, 2008), 18: "Biblically, *Love thy neighbor as thyself* is nested in a catena of *mitzvoth* that inform its meaning."

neighbor. You shall not go around as a slanderer among your people, and you shall not profit by the blood of your neighbor: I am the
LORD.[5]

You shall not hate in your heart anyone of your kin; you shall reprove your neighbor, or you will incur guilt yourself. You shall not
take vengeance or bear a grudge against any of your people, but you
shall love your neighbor as yourself: I am the LORD. (9-18)

The Israelites are to treat justly the members of their people. They
are not to oppress or slander them. When a neighbor is in trouble, they
are not to stand idly by. They are to reprove the neighbor when he does
wrong; but they are not to bear grudges against him, hate him, or take
vengeance against him. Moses then says, "you shall love your neighbor
as yourself."

How are we to understand the relation of this last injunction to those
that lead up to it (and to those that follow it)? No doubt we should hear
a contrast between this injunction and the one that precedes it by just a
bit, "You shall not hate in your heart anyone of your own kin." But apart
from hearing that contrast, should we understand it as just one injunction among others, one member of a miscellany of injunctions?

The contrast between the specificity of the preceding injunctions
and the generality of the love command makes that implausible. The
specificity/generality contrast calls for it to be understood as prefaced
with a tacit "in short." "*In short*, love your neighbor as yourself." That is
how Jesus and his interlocutors understood it. They did not understand
it as one among others, nor has the Jewish tradition generally understood it that way. These are the two greatest commandments in the Torah, the thought being not just that these are the most important
among a multitude of independent commands but that together they
capture the essence of the Torah. They sum it up.

Yet there is something unexpected and surprising about the love
command when interpreted as the general principle underlying the
specific injunctions Moses has just delivered. If one were told in advance that the general principle would give centrality to love, one would
expect the command to be, "You shall love your neighbor." That's not
what Moses says. Moses injects the unexpected note of self-love into his
statement of the summary principle. "Love your neighbor as yourself."
On second thought, this note should not come as a surprise. Moses took
for granted that we love ourselves. What he then says is that we are to

---

5. The commentator on Leviticus in the HarperCollins Study Bible, Jacob Milgrom, interprets this last clause as meaning that you shall not "stand by idle when your neighbor is
in danger."

love not only ourselves but our neighbors as well. That's the upshot of all the more detailed injunctions: do not love only yourself, love your neighbor as well.

Lenn Goodman, in his discussion of the command, argues that we should hear in it something more than an injunction to love one's neighbor as well as loving oneself; we should hear in it an injunction as to *how* to love one's neighbor. If I come across someone whose self-preoccupation takes the form of cruelty to his pets, I might say to him, "You should show some love for your pets as well as for yourself." I would not say, "You should love your pets *as* yourself." The little word "as" introduces a distinctive note. This is what Goodman says:

> Leviticus . . . calls on us to focus our concerns and direct our actions toward the interest of our fellow human beings, not merely as useful allies or potential enemies to be won over but as moral counter-parts, deserving a regard commensurate with all that we ask or as-pire to. It thus far outreaches prudential concerns. . . . The love that the Torah commands means accepting the sanctity of each person's capacity to choose and cherish. We need not share each person's goals. . . . But our first obligation to one another is respect for subjecthood. (14)

> The commandment to love our fellows is, I believe, no more nor less than a call to the recognition of their deserts. Persons must be treated as persons. *Love thy neighbor* makes explicit the obligation that the life of another person sets before us; the measure *as thyself* spotlights the existential equality of persons — lest we lose sight of the precious dignity of the other while yet preserving at least some fragment of a presumption of the dignity that is our own. (26)

This seems to me true and important: we are to treat our neighbors as our moral counterparts. I will be developing the point in later chapters.

Reproving your neighbor when he has done wrong is one of the things Moses cites as an example of loving the neighbor. Moses agrees with C. S. Lewis on this; or rather, Lewis agrees with Moses. More impor-tant for my subsequent purposes is the fact that various ways of treating the neighbor justly are cited as examples of loving one's neighbor. Treating the neighbor justly is not viewed as incompatible with loving the neighbor, nor is it viewed as an alternative to loving him. Treating the neighbor justly is an *example* of loving him, a way of loving him.[6] Love is not justice-indifferent benevolence.

6. Cf. Goodman, *Love Thy Neighbor*, 16: "Charity, rabbinically, is of a piece with justice."

Moses

Nygren

Niebuhr

Frankena

Let's allow the import of the point to sink in. Doing justice is an example of love. Moses does not pit love and justice against each other. He does not say that we are to love the neighbor and pay no attention to what justice requires; that was Nygren's position. He does not say that we are to love the neighbor so long as doing so does not abet or perpetrate injustice; that was Niebuhr's position. Nor does he say that we are to love the neighbor in addition to treating him justly; that is the position William K. Frankena develops in his book, *Ethics,* that I referred to earlier. After exploring various ways of interpreting agapism, Frankena concludes that "The clearest and most plausible view . . . is to identify the law of love with . . . the principle of beneficence, that is, of doing good." He then says that, so interpreted, "it is one of the basic principles of ethics but not the only one." It must be "supplemented by the principle of distributive justice or equality" (58). "Only if pure agapism is supplemented by a principle of justice" is it "an adequate morality" (58).

I propose looking for an understanding of love such that the imperative to act justly is not in conflict with the law of love, not a restriction thereon, not even a supplement, but such that doing justice is *an example* of love. First, though, I must explain how I think of justice.

Chapter Seven

WHAT IS JUSTICE?

TREATING THE NEIGHBOR JUSTLY is an example of loving the neighbor. But what is justice?[1] Justinian's great codification of ancient Roman law, *The Digest,* opens with one of the most famous definitions of justice ever offered. The definition comes from the third-century Roman jurist, Ulpian. Justice *(iustitia),* said Ulpian, is a steady and enduring will to render to each his or her *ius (suum ius cuique tribuere).* Though it is the virtue of justice that Ulpian has in mind, it's easy to adapt his formula so that it defines the social condition of justice. A society is just insofar as its members are rendered their *ius.*

Shortly I will consider how *ius* is best translated. But first we should note that underlying Ulpian's formula is the distinction between *possessing* some *ius* and *being rendered* that *ius.* To possess the virtue of justice is to have a steady and enduring will to render to each person the *ius* that he or she possesses, the *ius* that is his or hers; society is just insofar as its members are rendered the *ius* that they possess, the *ius* that is theirs. Ulpian uses the possessive *suum: suum ius* (his *ius*).

This distinction, between possessing some *ius* and being rendered that *ius,* is indispensable for an understanding of justice. One may possess some *ius* without being rendered that *ius,* or, as I shall often say, without *enjoying* that *ius.* If, for example, I deprive you of your *ius,* your right, to a certain prize, you still have a right to that prize; but you are not enjoying the right, it is not being rendered you. Thus it is not strictly accurate to speak, as I just did, of depriving you of your right to the prize; speaking strictly, I don't deprive you of your right to the prize but of your *enjoyment* of that good to which you have a right.

Just above, I translated *ius* as "a right." In the context in which I employed the term, that was the correct translation. But our term "a right" is not an exact synonym of the Latin *ius.* Suppose that one thinks of punishment of wrongdoers not in terms of the good that punishment might do them but purely in terms of retribution. Then one would not

---

1. What I say in this chapter is an extreme condensation of points developed at length in my *Justice: Rights and Wrongs;* qualifications and elaborations are absent, and the detailed argumentation that I develop in the book is missing. As I mentioned in the Preface, this present book is to be seen as a companion volume to *Justice: Rights and Wrongs.* A few brief passages in this chapter are taken over from that earlier work.

speak of punishment as something the wrongdoer has a *right* to but as something he *deserves;* punishment is his *just desert.* The Latin term *ius* referred both to what, in English, we would call a person's rights and to what we would call his just deserts. When Ulpian said that justice is rendering to each his or her *ius,* what he meant is that justice is rendering to each his or her *right or desert.*[2]

The distinction I just drew, between rights and just deserts, reflects the most fundamental distinction within the order of justice, that between what I called, in an earlier chapter, *primary* justice and *corrective* justice. My focus in the remainder of this chapter will be entirely on primary justice.

Primary justice, on Ulpian's formula, is present in society when the members of society enjoy what they have a right to. Be it noted that rights are not some odd sort of entity that we possess and then enjoy or fail to enjoy. One possesses a right *to something;* and one *enjoys* some right when one enjoys, or is rendered, *that to which* one has a right.

To understand what we are talking about when talking about rights it may help to introduce a few paraphrases. Instead of saying that I have a right to the good of someone's treating me a certain way, I could say that their treating me that way is *due* me from them. Or I could say that I have a *legitimate claim* against them to their treating me that way. When using this latter terminology, we must be careful to distinguish between *having* a legitimate claim to being treated a certain way and *engaging in the act of claiming* that treatment. It is one thing to have a legitimate claim to police protection; it is quite a different thing to show up at a meeting of the city council and claim that right — that is, insist that the police protect one as one has a right to be protected by them.

To understand what we are talking about when talking about rights, it also helps to look at rights from the shadow side — that is, from the angle of one's condition when one is not enjoying that to which one has a right. If I have a right against you to your treating me a certain way, then I am *wronged* if you fail to treat me that way. I still have the right against you; that does not change. But I am not enjoying the right; and in not enjoying it, I am wronged by you. Wrongs are the shadow side of rights just as guilt is the shadow side of obligation. If I fail to treat you as I ought to treat you, I am guilty.

And what is it to have a right to something? To have a right to something is to stand in a certain kind of normative social relationship;

2. Actually, our words "desert" and "deserve" can be used to refer both to rights and to just deserts; thus a correct translation of Ulpian's formula would be, justice is rendering to each his or her deserts — alternatively, rendering to each what he or she deserves. It appears that *ius* was also sometimes used to refer to what we would call obligations.

sociality is built into the nature of rights. More specifically: having a right to something is always having it *with respect* to someone, having it *against* someone. In the limiting case, that 'someone' is oneself; one is other to oneself. But usually the other is someone else than oneself. Rights are normative bonds between oneself and the other. In good measure those normative bonds of oneself to the other are not generated by any exercise of will on the part of either party. The bond is there already, antecedent to will, binding oneself and the other together. The other comes into my presence already standing in this normative bond of her to me and me to her. Already she has a right to my not insulting her.

That to which I have a right against the other is that she treat me a certain way, a way that would be a good in my life — *treating me a certain way* being understood as including refraining from doing something to me. A right is a legitimate claim to the life-good of being treated a certain way by the other — or in the limiting case, by oneself.

By no means, however, does one have a right to all those ways of being treated by others that would be a good in one's life. I rather think it would be a good in my life were I to own a Rembrandt etching; but I do not have a right to that good. A common apothegm in present day political liberalism is that "the right has priority over the good." Whatever may be meant by that, in the order of concepts it's the other way around: the good has priority over the right. One has rights to only a subset of all the good ways of being treated by others.

Thus far this has been straightforward, though not, indeed, entirely non-controversial. Now we get to the challenging part. What accounts for the fact that one has a right to certain good ways of being treated by one's fellows and not to others? Or to get at the same issue from a somewhat different angle: I said that a right is always a right to the life-good of being treated a certain way by someone; and I suggested that having a right against someone to the life-good of their treating one a certain way is a *normative bond* between oneself and that person. Normative bonds come in various sorts. What sort of normative bond is this, of having a right against the other to the life-good of their treating one a certain way?

It is, for one thing, a normative bond that is intimately connected to the normative bond of obligation. I hold that entities of certain sorts do not have rights because they do not have lives that can go better and worse — mountains, for example. Let us set such entities off to the side. Then I hold that the following principle obtains:

Principle of Correlatives: A has a right against B to B's doing X just in case B has an obligation toward A to do X.

For example, Mary has a right against me to my not insulting her just in case I have an obligation toward Mary not to insult her.

Some writers hold that this Principle of Correlatives is analytically true; that is to say, they hold that to say that A has a right against B to B's doing X is to make the same claim as when one says that B has an obligation toward A to do X. Same claim, different words. It's like saying that A is to the south of B just in case B is to the north of A. Same claim, different words. If someone denied the principle just enunciated about north and south, we would conclude either that he was either extremely obtuse or didn't understand the meaning of either "south of" or "north of."

Some writers deny the Principle of Correlatives; they hold that even if something is of the sort of entity that can have rights, one might have an obligation toward that entity without that entity having a correlative right. Such writers are neither obtuse nor ignorant of the meaning of the words "right" and "obligation." So the Principle of Correlatives, if true, is not analytically true — not true by virtue of the meanings of the words plus the principle of non-contradiction.[3] (I should make clear that all along we are talking about _moral_ rights and _moral_ obligations.) The relevant comparison is not to *A is to the north of B if and only if B is to the south of A*, but rather to *a triangle is equilateral if and only if it is equiangular*. Though there is a necessary connection between equilaterality and equiangularity, they are not the same thing in different words.

And now for an exceedingly important feature of rights that most writers, if not all, agree on. Rights possess what some call *trumping* force, what others, with the same thought in mind, call *peremptory*. Let me explain. If I have a right to the life-good of being treated a certain way by you — not a prima facie right but an all-things-considered right — then, no matter how many goods may be brought about in my life and the lives of other people by depriving me of that good, you should not deprive me of it. Indeed, by the Principle of Correlatives you are *obligated* not to do so. Because I have a right to the life-good of being treated that way by you, that life-good *trumps* all those other life-goods. If I have an all-things-considered right not to be tortured by you, then no matter

---

3. In the Introduction to *Justice: Rights and Wrongs*, I argued for the non-analyticity of the Principle of Correlatives by observing that if someone were to be absolved of his guilt for wronging someone, the moral condition of the other person would still be that she had been wronged. But this was just confusion on my part. If the Principle of Correlatives is necessarily true, as I hold that it is, then any alteration in the moral condition of the one party has to be accompanied by an alteration of the moral condition of the other party. Since it seems to me that the moral condition of the one party, of having been wronged, cannot be altered, this is an argument for the conclusion that absolution of guilt is impossible. Whatever so-called absolution may be, it's not the removal of guilt.

how many goods may be brought about in my life and the lives of others by torturing me, you ought not to torture me.

So once again our question. What accounts for the fact that one has a right to certain of the ways of being treated by one's fellows that would be goods in one's life and not to others? Well, given the trumping principle just enunciated, it seems evident that to explain rights we have to bring into the picture some consideration distinct from that of the good of being treated in certain ways. No matter how many life-goods some action of yours may pile up, if bringing about those goods requires depriving someone of that to which he has an all-things-considered right — and requires of you that you violate an all-things-considered obligation of yours toward him — then you should not do it.

What might that other consideration be? I see only one possible answer to this question. The additional consideration is the *worth of human beings.* Understanding the import of this claim means taking note that the life of a human being is not to be identified with that human being whose life it is, nor, consequently, is the relative excellence or disexcellence of her life to be identified with her own greater or lesser worth. Admirable people sometimes live wretched lives; despicable people sometimes live rather good lives. At the very foundation of the idea of a right, so I suggest, is this distinction between the relative excellence of some human being's life and the relative excellence of that human being herself.

Underlying the idea of a right are the following two phenomena. On the one hand, we all have worth on account of features we possess, accomplishments we have attained, relationships in which we stand, and so forth. One person has the worth of one who has written a superb novel, another has the worth of one who has courageously devoted herself to combating poverty, another has the worth of one who has won the 100 meter dash in the Olympics, and so forth. On the other hand, certain ways of treating a human being bear the significance of befitting or not befitting the worth of that human being. Should the organizers of the Olympics refuse to give the gold medal to the person who won the 100 meter dash, they would not be treating him as befits his worth. They would not be showing him due respect for his worth. They would be demeaning him.

I can now say what it is for a person to have a right to the life-good of being treated a certain way. One has a right against someone to the life-good of their treating one a certain way just in case, were they to deprive one of that life-good, they would be treating one with less respect than befits one's worth. They would be treating one with under-respect. They would be demeaning one. Someone's rights are what respect for his or her worth requires. Or to put it from the shadow side: to wrong some-

[margin note: human worth]

[margin note: respect]

one is to treat her with less respect than befits her worth — to treat her with under-respect, to treat her as would only befit someone of less worth.

It follows that any system of ethics that tries to make do only with life-goods and does not also bring the worth of human beings into the picture cannot give an account of rights. And if it cannot give an account of rights, it cannot give an account of justice. For justice, as we saw, prevails in human relationships insofar as persons render to each other what they have a right to.

Justice

WHERE NIEBUHR WENT WRONG

It is now easy to see where Niebuhr went seriously wrong in his way of thinking about justice. He held that justice is relevant in conflict situations. Justice for him consists of rendering just judgment in situations of conflict and of meting out justice in case the conflict involves an infraction of justice. Niebuhr was, and still is, far from alone in thinking of justice this way, as consisting of *rendering just judgment* and of *meting out justice*.

(Yes, but Niebuhr seemed to address large social group rights & natural rights)

But this cannot be correct. Justice includes rendering just judgment in conflict situations and includes meting out corrective justice when there has been an infraction of primary justice. But this cannot be the whole of justice. I may treat you justly even though there is no conflict between the two of us and even though neither of us has wronged the other. I may treat you justly in a situation of "frictionless harmony." I do so if I treat you in such a way as befits your worth.

SPEAKING UP FOR RIGHTS-TALK

Talk about rights enjoys a bad press in many quarters. Though the charges are multiple, there is one charge that sounds out above all others. Rights-talk, so it is said, expresses and abets one of the most pervasive and malignant diseases of modern society, viz., possessive individualism. In using rights-talk one places oneself at the center of the moral universe, focusing on one's own entitlements to the neglect of one's obligations toward others and the cultivation of those other-directed virtues that are indispensable to the flourishing of our lives together. The prevalence of rights-talk, so it is said, obscures from us the singular importance of love, care, friendship, and the like. It demotes the giving self and promotes the grasping self, demotes the humble self and promotes the haughty self. It both encourages and is encouraged by the

Rights talk (possessive individualism)

does it have to be so?

possessive atomism of the capitalist economy and the liberal polity. It invites us to think of ourselves as sovereign individuals.

Rights-talk, so the charge goes, is for the purpose of *me* claiming *my possessions, you* claiming *your possessions, him* claiming *his possessions.* That's what it's for: claiming one's possessions, giving vent to one's possessiveness, each over against the other. Possessive individualists are not abusing a neutral language by wresting it to their own malign purposes. They are using it as it's meant to be used. Rights-talk is inherently individualistic and possessive.

This charge is commonly supported by a narrative concerning the origin of the idea of rights — especially the idea of natural rights. The idea of natural rights, so it is said, was an invention either of nominalist philosophers of the fourteenth century or Enlightenment philosophers of the late seventeenth and eighteenth century. Either way, the moral to be drawn is the same: possessive individualistic ways of thinking spawned the idea of natural rights and only within such ways of thinking does the idea have a home.

But if rights are what I said they are, normative social bonds of a certain sort, why would anyone lodge against rights-talk the charge of expressing and abetting possessive individualism? There is a normative social bond between me and the other whereby the other bears legitimate claims on me as to how I treat her. What connection could there possibly be between, on the one hand, possessive individualism and, on the other hand, talking about those social bonds, bringing them to speech?

The clue lies not in rights themselves but in how they are all-too-often understood by theorists, viz., not as what respect for worth requires but as safeguards for personal autonomy. And it lies in confusing rights themselves with the honoring and dishonoring of rights and with the claiming of rights. As noted earlier, it is one thing for the other to have a legitimate claim against me; it is another thing for me to *honor* that legitimate claim, and yet a third thing for her to *claim* that legitimate claim, that is, to engage in the action of insisting that I honor it. Now imagine a society inhabited by possessive individualists. What will they do? Each will claim his own rights while neglecting or refusing to honor the rights of others. In no way does this alter the structure of the rights themselves; that structure remains intact and symmetrical. The other comes into my presence bearing legitimate claims against me and I come into her presence bearing legitimate claims against her. It is the *practice of honoring* rights and the *practice of claiming* rights that have been distorted.

Before we leap to the conclusion that because of misunderstandings in theory and abuses in practice, rights-talk should be abolished, let it be noted that the language of love, service, responsibility, and the like is also misunderstood and abused, used to express appalling attitudes of domination on the one hand and servility on the other. And while we are on the topic of individualism, it should be noted that rights-talk scarcely has a monopoly on the language of choice for self-preoccupied individuals. We have all known self-preoccupied persons who thought and spoke not at all in terms of rights but entirely in terms of charity or obligation; their souls were filled to overflowing with their own virtue and rectitude — or with their own failings and guilt. Self-preoccupation comes in many forms. Sometimes it employs the language of rights; sometimes it employs the language of duty; sometimes it employs the language of love, charity, and benevolence.

But what then of the narrative which says that the idea of natural rights was born of individualistic habits of thought in either the fourteenth or seventeenth centuries and carries possessive individualism in its DNA? That narrative has now been decisively refuted, most notably by the eminent medievalist Brian Tierney in *The Idea of Natural Rights*.[4] Tierney shows beyond the shadow of a doubt that the canon lawyers of the twelfth century were working with the explicitly formulated concept of natural rights; and no one would accuse the canon lawyers of being possessive individualists. In the second chapter of my *Justice: Rights and Wrongs*, I go farther back yet. Though the twelfth-century canon lawyers were apparently the first to work systematically and explicitly with the concept of natural rights, the existence of natural rights was unmistakably taken for granted by the church fathers and, back behind them, by the writers of the Old Testament/Hebrew Bible. The recognition of natural rights is a precious gift of the Hebrew Bible to all of humankind.

4. (Atlanta: Scholars Press, 1997).

Chapter Eight

BEGINNING TO RETHINK LOVE

A LOVE THAT INCORPORATES JUSTICE

With this way of understanding justice in hand, we are ready to begin re-thinking love. All along we have taken for granted that to seek to promote the good in someone's life as an end in itself is to love that person. We are now in a position to see that there is something else that love seeks as an end in itself. Love for another seeks to secure that she be treated justly by oneself and others— that her rights be honored, that she be treated in a way that befits her worth. The understanding of love that we need, if agapism is to be plausible as an ethical system, is an understanding of love as seeking both to promote the good in a person's life and to secure that she be treated as befits her worth. To treat her as one does because justice requires it is to love her. Of course, that to which she has a right is itself a good in her life, not something in addition, and so too for being treated as befits her worth. So the more precise way of putting the point is that we need an understanding of love such that seeking to secure for someone the good of being treated as befits her worth is an example of love for her.

It is this sort of love that Jesus had in mind, and Moses before him. New Testament agape joins seeking to promote a person's good with seeking to secure due respect for her worth; it seeks both as ends in themselves.

Love thus understood incorporates eros, or something closely akin thereto. Eros is attraction-love, the love of being drawn to something on account of its worth, attracted to it, sometimes even mesmerized by it. As such, eros is a mode of acknowledgment of worth. Though not every instance of acknowledging something's worth would be called *love* in present day idiomatic English, every instance of eros is an instance of acknowledgment of worth. Treating someone as one does because justice requires it is a way of acknowledging her worth. Thereby it is eros or a near kin of eros. Nygren polarized agape and eros. Agape incorporates eros.

Is Self-Love Legitimate?

But before we engage in the re-thinking of love that these comments point towards, we must address an issue that I left open when, in the Introduction, I rejected egoism, eudaimonism, and utilitarianism and set out in search of a defensible version of agapism. I left open whether one may or should sometimes seek one's own good as an end in itself. The egoist holds that one should seek *only* one's own good as an end in itself. I agreed with the eudaimonist and the utilitarian that this is mistaken. Not only *may* one sometimes seek the good of another as an end in itself; often one *should*. But what about one's own good? May or should one sometimes seek one's own good as an end in itself? And may or should one sometimes seek to secure as an end in itself that one is oneself treated with due respect for one's worth?

In the course of our discussion of modern day agapism we discovered sharp disagreement between Nygren and Kierkegaard on the legitimacy of self-love. Nygren rejected out of hand all forms of self-love. Kierkegaard allowed self-love in two forms. The rule of application for agapic love includes oneself in its scope; each of us is a neighbor to himself. And natural forms of self-love are legitimate if so shaped and formed as to become expressions and manifestations of agapic love for oneself. In my discussion of modern day agapism I did not take a position in this dispute. I must now do so.

Many, both within and without the Christian tradition, believe that Christian scripture teaches the illegitimacy of self-love. And of those who do not take Christian scripture as authoritative, some have their own reasons for holding that self-love is wrong. Let me quote what Harry G. Frankfurt says on the matter in his fine book, *The Reasons of Love:*

> It is widely presumed that for a person to love himself is so natural as to be more or less unavoidable; but it is also widely presumed that this is not such a good thing. Many people — especially when they imagine that the propensity to self-love is both ubiquitous and essentially ineradicable — believe that this headlong tendency of most of us to love ourselves is a grievously injurious defect of human nature. In their view, it is largely self-love that makes it impossible for us to devote ourselves sufficiently and in a suitable way — that is, selflessly — to other things that we love or that it would be good for us to love. Loving oneself is, they think, a serious and often crippling impediment to caring appropriately not only about the requirements of morality but also about important nonmoral goods and ideals. The allegation that we are too deeply immersed in self-

love is frequently offered, indeed, as identifying an almost insurmountable obstacle to our living as we should.[1]

In the course of discussing this common repudiation of self-love, Frankfurt makes the point that those who attack what they call "self-love" often have something quite different in mind than self-love; it's self-indulgence that they are thinking of. Kant, for example, describes those who love themselves as "motivated predominantly by an interest in satisfying their own inclinations and desires, and who on any particular occasion will naturally be moved to act by whichever of those inclinations and desires happens to be the strongest" (*Reasons of Love*, 78). This is not self-love but self-indulgence, says Frankfurt. And not only is self-indulgence different from self-love; often the two are opposed. "Parents who love their children take great care, if they are sensible, to avoid being indulgent. Their love does not motivate them to give their children whatever the children happen to want. Rather, they show their love by being concerned about what is genuinely important to their children — in other words, by aiming to protect and to advance their children's true interests. . . . Precisely because they do love their children, they decline to do many things that their children would very much like them to do" (78-79). "In just the same way, a person shows that he loves himself. That is, he shows it by protecting and advancing what he takes to be his own true interests, even when doing so frustrates desires by which he is powerfully moved but that threaten to divert him from that goal. . . . It is not by self-indulgence . . . that a person manifests his self-love. Genuine love for ourselves, like genuine love for our children, requires conscientious attention of a different kind" (79).

With this important distinction between self-love and self-indulgence in mind, imagine for a moment a person who really does not have any love for herself. She seeks to promote her own good only as a means to promoting the good of someone else or as a means to securing due respect for their worth. Her love is through and through self-sacrificial. She spends herself for others. She is totally self-giving, totally selfless. Or if she is not and discerns that she is not, she chastises herself, tells herself that she should be doing better, laments that the cancer of self-love is still gnawing away within. She does not locate her own intrinsic worth in being self-giving. She thinks she has no intrinsic worth.

Should we all be like her? I daresay most of us would say that we should not; most of us would say that *none* of us should be like her. Such a person is morally disoriented, malformed, the root of her malformation being that she is morally obtuse about her own worth.

1. (Princeton: Princeton University Press, 2004), 71.

I argued in the preceding chapter that not to be treated with due respect for one's worth is to be wronged, deprived of that to which one has a right, treated unjustly. Add, now, that to be indifferent to someone's being wronged is itself a way of wronging them, itself a way of failing to treat them with due respect for their worth. Being indifferent to the demeaning of someone is itself a way of demeaning them. And that is something one ought never to do, whether the person is another or oneself. The self-sacrificial person we imagined is indifferent to people not treating her with due respect for her intrinsic worth, since she thinks she doesn't have any such worth. Such indifference to being wronged by others is a way of wronging herself. And that she ought not do.

Furthermore, if one is indifferent to being wronged, then one will of course not take steps to stop or prevent the wronging. Now, given the Principle of Correlatives, if a person is wronged by someone, then the person who wronged her has treated her as he ought not to have treated her; he has failed in his moral obligations. It follows that, in failing to take steps to stop or prevent the wrongdoing, the victim perforce fails to take steps to encourage the moral reformation of the wrongdoer. But as we learned from the passages quoted from C. S. Lewis in Chapter Six, failure to take appropriate steps to encourage the moral reformation of a wrongdoer is sometimes, maybe often, a failure of love. Total selflessness proves to be a failure of love for others. The totally selfless person is to be lovingly chastised, not admired. A tenable version of agapism will have to hold that we should love not only others but ourselves as well.

Approach the issue from yet a different angle. If my neighbors may or should love me, why would it be unacceptable in principle for me to love that same person, namely, myself? Whether it is my neighbors who seek to advance my good as an end in itself or I who do so, it amounts to the same thing — namely, seeking to advance my good as an end in itself. So the reason why others may or should seek to advance my good as an end in itself, whereas I should not, cannot lie in a difference between what they may or should do and what I should supposedly not do, since it is identical in both cases, viz., seeking to advance my good as an end in itself. The reason must lie in the fact that in one case it is *they* who do this whereas in the other case it is *I* who do it. But what is it about them and about me that brings it about they may or should sometimes do the very thing that I should never do? I fail to see any plausible answer to this question. Self-love does of course contain pitfalls unique to itself; what is called for is avoiding those pitfalls, not rooting out all self-love.

In *The Reasons of Love,* Frankfurt adds one more consideration. He argues that "people cannot avoid loving themselves . . . as long as they love anything at all. If a person loves anything, he necessarily loves himself" (86). The argument is interesting and, to my mind, compelling. But since it is somewhat intricate and would take considerable time to lay out in sufficient detail to be intelligible and persuasive, I will forego doing so.[2] I remind the reader that mine is not a book on love in general but on the relation between love and justice.

JESUS AND SELF-LOVE

The proscription of self-love is no more plausible as an interpretation of the founding texts of agapism than it is as a systematic position. Do not love only yourself, said Moses; love your neighbor as well. Treat your neighbor as your moral counterpart. The command does not enjoin us to love ourselves; it assumes that we do. It enjoins us to love the neighbor as well as loving ourselves. Had Moses or Jesus thought that self-love was illegitimate, they would have said that we are to love the neighbor *instead of* loving ourselves. That is not what they said; they said that we are to love the neighbor *as* we love ourselves. The legitimacy of self-love is presupposed.[3]

I know of no passages in which Nygren explain how his insistence that Christianity is opposed to all forms of self-love is to be harmonized with the second love command. Perhaps he thought that Jesus, in issuing the second love command, was doing no more than taking note of the fact that we do love ourselves, presupposing nothing one way or the other as to the permissibility of self-love. But from other passages in the gospels we learn — so the thought continues — that Jesus enjoined the eradication of self-love.[4]

Given the stories of healings that Jesus performed, there is no plausibility whatsoever in the idea that Jesus was of the view that self-love should be eradicated. Here is the story, chosen more or less at random, of the healing of the blind man, Bartimaeus, as we find it in Mark 10:46-52:

As [Jesus] and his disciples and a large crowd were leaving Jericho, Bartimaeus son of Timaeus, a blind beggar, was sitting by the road-

2. Frankfurt also argues (88-90) that if I did not love myself, others could not love me. I find this argument also cogent, but again, too complex to present without distracting us from our purpose.

3. Contrary to the interpretation of the texts that I am offering here, namely, that it is presupposed that self-love is permissible, Augustine appears to have held the stronger view that we are implicitly *enjoined* to love ourselves. In *The City of God*, 19.14, he says: "Now God, our Master, teaches two chief precepts: that is, love of God and love of neighbour. In these precepts, a man finds three things which he is to love: God, himself, and his neighbour; for a man who loves God does not err in loving himself." I am quoting from the translation by R. W. Dyson (Cambridge: Cambridge University Press, 1998), 941.

4. Chris Eberle suggested to me that this may have been how Nygren was thinking.

side. When he heard that it was Jesus of Nazareth, he began to shout out and say, "Jesus, Son of David, have mercy on me!" Many sternly ordered him to be quiet, but he cried out even more loudly, "Son of David, have mercy on me!" Jesus stood still and said, "Call him here." And they called the blind man, saying to him, "Take heart; get up, he is calling you." So throwing off his cloak, he sprang up and came to Jesus. Then Jesus said to him, "What do you want me to do for you?" The blind man said to him, "My teacher, let me see again." Jesus said to him, "Go, your faith has made you well." Immediately he regained his sight and followed him on the way.

It was his own wellbeing that Bartimaeus desired; he passionately wanted to be healed of his blindness. Rather than chastising him for his self-love, Jesus granted him what he desired.

The Love Command and the Golden Rule

The Aristotelian tradition holds that human beings are like all other living organisms in having a nature with a built-in orientation and tendency toward what is good for them, toward their own wellbeing. Suppose we accept this thesis, with the important qualification that this orientation and tendency toward one's own wellbeing can become malformed in various ways, seriously so. What the love command then assumes, in its reference to self-love, is that in persons this orientation and tendency toward one's own wellbeing takes the reflexive form of loving oneself. One does not just focus on and pursue the various life-goods that one takes to be constitutive of, and contributory to, one's wellbeing. One introduces oneself into the picture, along with a certain stance toward oneself, viz., that of loving oneself. Not loving those life-goods. Loving *oneself.*

There is a duality in the self. Each of us is a Thou to himself or herself. We not only think about others; we think about ourselves. We not only speak about others; we speak about ourselves. We not only grieve over the failings and rejoice over the successes of others; we grieve over the failings and rejoice over the successes of ourselves. We not only love and hate others; we love and sometimes hate ourselves. Remarkable and mysterious, this ability one has, by virtue of being a person, to be a Thou to oneself — one among other Thous. The I-Thou relation is interior to the self.

The second love command, assuming this reflexive ability to treat oneself as a Thou to oneself, identifies a certain stance of oneself toward the Thou that is oneself, the stance, namely, of loving that Thou;

and it then says that that is the stance one is to take toward all those Thous who are one's neighbors.

The command assumes, so it appears, that this stance of loving oneself is not an incidental but a fundamental aspect of what it is to be a properly functioning human person who has emerged from infancy. To be a properly functioning person is to love the Thou that is oneself. The Alzheimer's patient does not love herself; she is no longer capable of functioning as a person. Many of those who commit suicide do not love themselves; they are <u>malfunctioning</u> in a profound way.

Luke reports that Jesus, immediately after delivering the Beatitudes, enjoined his followers to obey what has come to be called the Golden Rule: "Do to others as you would have them do to you" (Luke 6:31). Before one can apply the Golden Rule one must ask how one wants to be treated by others; that question answered, one then treats them that way.

Note the differences between these two commands, the second love command and the Golden Rule. Unlike the Golden Rule, the second love command assumes our mysterious ability as persons to be a Thou to ourselves. Then, rather than saying that our treatment of others is to accord with a certain treatment of us by them, it says that our treatment of others is to accord with a certain way of treating ourselves. And whereas the Golden Rule is formal, in that it leaves it up to us to figure out what treatment of ourselves by others we desire, the second command is anything but formal; the treatment of oneself by oneself that one is to replicate in one's treatment of others is that of *loving* oneself. Notice, however, that loving oneself will surely include wanting others to treat one in certain ways. The love command *incorporates* the Golden Rule.

DID JESUS ABROGATE THE LOVE COMMAND?

In the course of his farewell address to his disciples, as reported in the Gospel of John, Jesus said, "A new commandment I give to you, that you love one another; even as I have loved you, that you also love one another" (13:34).[5] To this we should add the following from the same speech: "If you love me, you will keep my commandments" (John 14:15).[6]

The fact that Jesus calls this a "new" commandment has sometimes been interpreted as implying that he intended this commandment to

5. The command is repeated at 15:12: "This is my commandment, that you love one another as I have loved you." A truncated version is found at 15:17: "This I command you, to love one another."

6. Cf. John 14:21: "He who has my commandments and keeps them, he it is who loves me." And 14:23: "If a man loves me, he will keep my word."

replace the second of the two that are the greatest in the Torah. That old commandment is superseded by this new one. If this interpretation were correct, a large question mark would be placed over our conclusions in this chapter.

I think it most unlikely that by calling it a "new" commandment, Jesus meant to suggest that it was to supplant the second of the two greatest commandments in the Torah. Nowhere in his lengthy farewell discourse does he even mention those two commandments; nothing that he says suggests that in calling this one "new," he meant to contrast it with those two as old. And even if he did have that contrast in mind, that would not imply that either of those was superseded. The thought might rather be that this "new" commandment is to be added to the "old" one or ones.

The clue to what Jesus had in mind by "new" is contained in a passage that comes just a bit later in the same discourse: "I did not say these things to you from the beginning, because I was with you." The implicit contrast is not between this commandment and the one from the Torah; the implicit contrast is between this commandment and what Jesus said to his disciples previously. Throughout his farewell discourse Jesus is giving instructions to his disciples on how to continue living as his disciples after his departure. In the course of doing so he says things he had not previously said, or had not said in quite the same way. The new commandment is the most fundamental and comprehensive of his instructions to his disciples for life after his departure.

It would be completely implausible to interpret the second love commandment as meaning that one's love of self is to be the paradigm for one's love of neighbor. This is an interpretation that I did not even consider; our love of self is far too defective to serve as paradigm. But in the case of the new commandment, this is exactly its force. The disciples are to love each other *in the same way* that Jesus loved them; Jesus' love of them is to serve as paradigm for their love of each other. In turn, it is because of their love for him that they are to model their love of each other on his love of them. There is no conflict whatsoever between this new commandment and the second of those from the Torah; Jesus' disciples can obey this new commandment and simultaneously obey the old one.

Chapter Nine

LOVE AS CARE

INTRODUCING THE IDEA OF LOVE AS CARE

Now and then we say about a person that she does not love herself; on occasion, people say this about themselves. Sometimes the point being made is that the person has become indifferent to her own wellbeing. More often the point is that the person is indifferent to whether or not she is treated with due respect for her worth — usually because she thinks of herself as having no intrinsic worth.

Is there a term in present day idiomatic English, in addition to the term "love," for the union of these two kinds of love, love that seeks to enhance a person's wellbeing or flourishing and love that seeks to secure that a person's rights are honored, that she be treated with due respect for her worth? I think there is. It's the term "care," understood not as caring *for* someone who needs aid or assistance but as caring *about* someone.[1] Frankfurt remarks that "as with every type of love, the heart of [self-love] is that the lover *cares* [my italics] about the good of his beloved for its own sake. He is disinterestedly concerned to protect and to pursue the true interests of the person whom he loves" (*Reasons of Love*, 85). Correct. But the lover's care may also take the form of seeing to it that the *worth* of the beloved be respected, that she not be demeaned, not be wronged, not be treated unjustly. Care combines seeking to enhance someone's flourishing with seeking to secure their just treatment.[2]

Given the fact that care combines these two, the possibility arises of care seeking to bring about some good in a person's life and, in the course of so doing, treating that person or some other person unjustly. Cases of unjust paternalism come to mind. What are we to say about such cases? Is unjust paternalism care or is it not?

---

1. It's likely that some readers will reply that "benevolence" is the term we want. All we have to do is remind people that being treated in accord with one's rights is itself a good in one's life. I judge this to be a mistake. I think "benevolence" in present day idiomatic English carries the strong connotation that when one treats someone benevolently, one is paying no attention to what justice may or may not require.

2. Strictly speaking, seeing to it that someone is treated with due respect for her worth is a special case of seeking to promote the good in her life; for my purposes, however, it is important to single out this special case for special attention.

One way to go here would be to declare that if in the course of seeking to promote someone's good one wrongs someone, one's care falls short of the ideal. I think that that is not the right way to go. The fact that one has treated someone unjustly is not a regrettable falling short of the ideal; it's a case of doing what one ought not to have done. Better to describe it as *malformed* care. The fact that one has sought to promote the good of the other makes one's action an example of care. But when we look at the action in its totality, we see that the care is malformed. Well-formed care does not wrong a person in the course of seeking to promote her good. Well-formed care incorporates reverence, respect for the recipient of one's care.[3]

Nor does well-formed care wrong anyone else. When thinking and speaking about love or care it's easy to focus all one's attention on the recipient. But that's a mistake. Seeking to promote the good of someone or to secure that her rights be honored almost always involves treating not just the recipient in a certain way but others as well. Care about someone is malformed if it wrongs anyone, not only if it wrongs the recipient.

For care to be well-formed it is not required that one have in mind all those who might be affected by one's action and consciously aim at not wronging them; that's impossible. All that's required is that one not in fact wrong them. That's true even for the one who is the recipient of one's care; well-formed care does not require that one consciously aim at not wronging the recipient. Care as seeking to promote the good of someone may or may not be combined with seeking to treat that person justly. But if it is well-formed care, it will in fact treat her and everyone else justly.

Care aimed at enhancing someone's life-goods presupposes that one have beliefs as to which states and events, actions and activities, in the life of that person are in fact goods; so too, care aimed at securing that someone be treated as befits her worth presupposes that one have beliefs about that person's worth and about which actions do and which do not befit her worth. And both forms of care presuppose that one have beliefs as to which actions on one's part are likely to bring about what one is seeking.

Fully *responsible* care requires that one be *entitled* to one's beliefs on these matters.[4] The fact that one is entitled to a belief does not entail

---

3. In *The Purpose of the Church and Its Ministry* (New York: Harper & Brothers, 1956), H. Richard Niebuhr remarks that "Love is reverence." It incorporates "deep respect for the otherness of the beloved and the profound unwillingness to violate his integrity" (35). Exactly. (I thank Jack Roeda for this reference.)

4. I develop an account of belief entitlement in my essay "Entitlement to Believe and Practices of Inquiry," in Nicholas Wolterstorff, *Practices of Belief*, ed. Terence Cuneo (Cambridge: Cambridge University Press, 2010).

that it is true; for each of us, there are false beliefs scattered among those to which we are entitled. A consequence of the possible discrepancy between truth and entitlement in one's beliefs is that one's attempt to promote the good of someone or to secure their just treatment may fail even though one acts on the basis of beliefs to which one is entitled. One may bring about the opposite of what one intended, impairing their good rather than enhancing it, demeaning them rather than treating them with due respect. But one has done the best that can rightly be expected of one.

One's attempt may fail in either or both of two ways: one may succeed in promoting what one *believes* to be the good or the right of the other when that is not in fact their good or right, or one may be correct in thinking that such-and-such is their good or right but fail in one's attempt to bring it about. The term "care," as I have been using it and will continue to use it, is not a success term. If one seeks to promote what one believes to be the good or the right of someone, then one is caring about that person whether or not what one is seeking to promote is in fact their good or right and whether or not one succeeds in bringing about what is in fact, or what one believes to be, their good or right. Care may be malformed on account of wronging someone, it may be less than fully responsible on account of employing beliefs to which one is not entitled, and it may be unsuccessful on account of failing to achieve what it aims at; but if one seeks to promote what one believes to be someone's good or to secure what one believes to be their right, one is caring about them.

On the other hand, if all a person ever does is *desire* that the good of someone be enhanced or *desire* that her worth be respected, I will not describe her as caring about that person. Care is *seeking to promote* what one believes to be that person's good or right. Seeking to promote what one believes to be a person's good or right comes in many forms; but only if one actually *seeks* her good or *seeks* her right is one caring about the person. I recognize that I am departing from idiomatic English on this point; idiomatic English allows us to say that a person cares about someone even if all he ever does is desire the good or the right of the person.

Some readers will wonder whether, in arguing that love as care is the understanding of love that agapism requires, I am reflecting the influence of the currently popular *ethics of care*.[5] It might have gone that way; but it did not. My suggestion that the concept of love that we need for

---

5. The best articulations of an ethic of care seem to me to be Virginia Held, *The Ethics of Care: Personal, Political, Global* (Oxford: Oxford University Press, 2006); and Michael Slote, *The Ethics of Care and Empathy* (London and New York: Routledge, 2007).

our purposes is love as care rather than love as benevolence did not emerge from reading around in the current literature on the ethics of care; it emerged from engaging the agapist tradition and its founding documents and discovering that modern day agapism is incapable of giving a satisfactory account of how justice fits into an agapist framework. As we shall see in the next chapter, the version of agapism that I propose does not give centrality to empathy; in that way it differs from several versions of the ethics of care currently on offer. I will leave it to others to draw additional contrasts and comparisons.

REQUIREMENTS FOR LOVE AS CARE TO BE ACCEPTABLE ON HERMENEUTIC GROUNDS

Understanding love as care holds out the promise of enabling us to develop a systematically defensible version of agapism. Whether that promise is realized depends, in good measure, on whether we can formulate a systematically defensible rule of application for care. I will take up that topic in Chapter Eleven. In the remainder of this chapter I shall consider whether construing love as care is defensible as an interpretation of the meaning of *agapē* in the New Testament. From our discussion in the preceding chapter it's clear that it is defensible as an interpretation of what Jesus and Moses meant when they said that we are to love our neighbors as ourselves. But Jesus also used the term *agapē* when he attributed love for us to God and enjoined love for God on us. Can these also be understood as care?

It was Nygren's view, as we saw, that when Jesus enjoined love for God on us, he meant something different by *agapē* from what he meant when he enjoined love for the neighbor on us — this in spite of the fact that, in Matthew's narration, Jesus said that the second commandment is *like* the first. I suggest that such a position should be adopted only as a last resort. The declaration by Jesus that the second commandment is like the first places the burden of proof on those who hold that *agapē* in the second commandment means something quite different from what it means in the first commandment. It may turn out that the burden of proof can be borne; but, other things being equal, an interpretation that yields a unified understanding of the love that we should have for God and the love that we should have for the neighbor is to be preferred.

Given the structure of the second commandment, "Love your neighbor as yourself," it is also a desideratum that we achieve a unified account of the love that we typically have for ourselves and the love that we should have for the neighbor. Such a unified account is implicit in what has already been said; the love referred to in both cases is love as care.

Finally, the declaration at various points in the New Testament[6] that we are to love each other as God has loved us implies that, other things being equal, an understanding of love that unifies God's love for us with the love that we should have for the neighbor is to be preferred.

In short, an interpretation of New Testament agape would ideally satisfy the following two conditions: it would understand love in such a way that treating someone as one does because justice requires it is an example of love; and it would offer a unified understanding of God's love for us, the love that we should have for God, the love that we typically have for ourselves, and the love that we should have for the neighbor. Good reasons may turn up for concluding that an understanding of love that satisfies all of these criteria is impossible; but other things being equal, an interpretation that does satisfy them is to be preferred.

We have already gone a considerable way toward achieving such an understanding. Love as care incorporates doing what justice requires. And the love that we typically have of ourselves and should have of the neighbor is love as care. What remains to consider is whether the love that we should have for God can be understood as care, and whether the love that God has for us can also be so understood.

CAN WE CARE ABOUT GOD?

Begin with the first of these. Can we care about God? Many in the Christian and Islamic traditions would say that we cannot. And among those who concede that it is possible to care about God, many would say that it is profoundly inappropriate to do so, and worse than inappropriate, wrong.

Caring about someone presupposes that one regard the recipient of one's care as vulnerable. We human beings are vulnerable with respect both to our flourishing and to the honoring of our rights. In Plato's *Symposium,* the lover advances from love of beautiful things in space and time to love of the form, the Beautiful itself. The Beautiful itself is invulnerable, as are all the Platonic forms. They have no life, so they have no life-goods; and since they have no life-goods, one cannot seek to promote their life-goods. Their invulnerability makes them the sort of thing that one cannot care about. Love of the Beautiful itself is love as eros, not love as care.

A doctrine prominent in the Christian and Islamic traditions, less so in the Jewish tradition, is the doctrine that God is invulnerable. My guess is that resistance to saying that we can care about God is almost al-

6. E.g., 1 John 4.

ways grounded in the combination of sensing that care presupposes vulnerability and believing that God is invulnerable. But is it true that God is invulnerable in the relevant way? Is it true that we human beings can neither increase nor decrease the good in God's life? Is God like the Platonic forms in being invulnerable?

Here is not the place to engage the theologico-philosophical tradition on this point; I have done that elsewhere.[7] Let me confine myself to observing that the Hebrew and Christian scriptures unmistakably present God as vulnerable. If one holds that God is not vulnerable, it will have to be systematic considerations that one appeals to, not hermeneutic considerations.

Earlier we looked at the context in which the second of the two love commandments occurs in the Torah; let us now look at the context in which the first occurs. The commandment is to be found in Deuteronomy 6:5. The situation is the same as that in Leviticus: Moses is presenting to the Israelites the commandments that God charged him to deliver "so that you and your children and your children's children may fear the LORD your God all the days of your life, and keep all his decrees and commandments, . . . so that your days may be long . . . [and] so that it may go well with you" (6:2-3). The One issuing these commandments, says Moses, is the God "who brought you out of the land of Egypt, out of the house of slavery. The LORD your God you shall fear; him you shall serve, and by his name alone you shall swear" (6:12-13). It is in this context that Moses says, "Hear, O Israel: the LORD is our God, the LORD alone. You shall love the LORD your God with all your heart, and with all your soul, and with all your might" (6:4-5).

When read out of context, the totalism of the command seems puzzling and problematic. The Israelites are to love Yahweh with *all* their heart and *all* their soul and *all* their might. Are they then to love nothing other than Yahweh? What about loving their neighbors? When read in context, the import of the totalism is clear. The One who delivered Israel from slavery in Egypt is to be Israel's *only God;* Israel's religious devotion is to be focused entirely and exclusively on Yahweh. "Do not follow other gods," says Moses, "because the LORD your God . . . is a jealous God" (6:14-15). Loving Yahweh with all one's heart, soul, and might is fully compatible with also loving one's neighbor.

What do we learn from the passage about what it is to love God? Well, from the structure of the passage it's clear that obeying God's com-

7. In my essays "Suffering Love" and "Is God Disturbed by What Transpires in Human Affairs?" I defend, in detail, the claim made above that God is susceptible to being wronged. These essays can now be found in Nicholas Wolterstorff, *Inquiring about God: Essays in Philosophy of Religion,* ed. Terence Cuneo (Cambridge: Cambridge University Press, 2009), 182-222; 223-38.

mandments is not something *other than* loving God but an *instance* of loving God. Loving God is constituted, in part, of obeying God.

And why should Israel obey, and thereby love, *this* God rather than being indifferent to this God or loving other gods? The NRSV says that Israel is to *fear* God; I think a better translation would be *revere.* The word "fear" suggests that the Israelites are to obey Yahweh because if they don't they are in big trouble; they had better be afraid of this God. Moses neither says nor suggests this. What he suggests is that they are to obey, and thereby love, Yahweh because Yahweh has delivered them from slavery, led them to a fertile land, and is now offering them a law-code that will enable them to flourish. Moses is here identifying the normative standing of Yahweh vis-à-vis Israel that gives Yahweh the *right* to issue commands to Israel as distinct from having the *power* to compel conformity. It happens all the time that people issue commands, or try to issue commands, that they have no right to issue. Yahweh has the right to issue commands to Israel because of what Yahweh has done for Israel.

Given that Yahweh has the standing right to issue commands to Israel, when Yahweh does in fact issue commands, Israel is under obligation to obey those commands. Correlatively, Yahweh has a right to their obeying those commands; obedience is due Yahweh. If obedience is not forthcoming, Yahweh is wronged, treated unjustly. In general it's the case that in issuing legitimate commands, one makes oneself vulnerable to being wronged by having one's commands disobeyed. God is vulnerable to being wronged by being disobeyed. The claim that we cannot care about God because God is in no way vulnerable is not tenable as an interpretation of the text.

Let me add a consideration that emerges from our discussion of modern day agapism. In Chapter Three we took note of the fact that forgiving someone presupposes that one has been wronged by that person; one has not been treated as one had a right to be treated. Fundamental to the biblical presentation of God is the declaration that God forgives. That declaration presupposes that God is vulnerable to being wronged by us — and not just *vulnerable* to being wronged, but in fact wronged.

CAN GOD CARE ABOUT US?

What remains to consider is God's love of us. When the biblical writers declare that God loves us, is this love plausibly understood as care? Hebrew and Christian scriptures pervasively use family language in speaking about God's relation to human beings: God is our parent, father or mother; we are God's children. In the prayer guide Jesus gave his followers, he instructed them to address God as *Father*. The suggestion that God's love of us takes the form of caring about us is unmistakable. In the course of his conversation with a member of the Pharisee party named Nicodemus, Jesus is reported in the Gospel of John as saying that "God so loved the world that he gave his only Son." Loving the world is surely caring about the world!

We know how Nygren would reply — and on this point Nygren is giving expression to the conviction of many in the Christian tradition. In God's love of us there is no tinge of treating us as justice requires because there is nothing that justice requires of God. It is out of pure grace that God promotes our good; God's love for us is pure benevolence, gratuitous generosity all the way down. So though it would not be a mistake to say that God cares about us, it would nonetheless be seriously misleading. Care, as the term is used in present day English and as I am using it here, includes seeing to it that a person is treated justly; care that treats someone unjustly is malformed care. Thus, to speak of God as caring about us is to suggest that God sees to it that we are treated justly. And that, so the objector says, is false. God's forgiveness of the sinner is paradigmatic of all God's love. Forgiveness is not required by justice; forgiveness is pure grace.

My reply is twofold. A point made over and over in the divine law code that Moses delivers to Israel is that the members of the people are to treat each other justly;[8] we saw a few examples of this when we looked at the context in Leviticus of the command to love one's neighbor as oneself. The claim that God's care about human beings does not incorporate God's concern that we be treated justly is patently false as an interpretation of the text.[9]

Second, in our final two chapters I will articulate and defend the thesis that Paul's overarching argument in his letter to the Romans is that there is no partiality in God's offer of justification to human beings; God's generosity is a just generosity. Thus, not only is God concerned that we treat each other justly; God's care about us is itself just.

---

8. I develop the point at length in the third chapter of *Justice: Rights and Wrongs*.

9. There are, as everybody knows, rather many other passages in the Old Testament/ Hebrew Bible in which God appears to command people to do what seems to us patently unjust. In my essay "Reading Joshua" I discuss some of the most egregious examples. The essay is published in *Divine Evil? The Moral Character of the God of Abraham*, ed. Michael Bergmann, Michael Murray, and Michael Rea (New York: Oxford University Press, 2011), 236-56.

In Conclusion

Love as care satisfies the criteria proposed for an adequate understanding of *agapē* in the New Testament. Care includes seeking that the beloved be treated justly. And care is the sort of love that is typical of love for oneself, that Jesus attributes to God for us, and that Jesus enjoins on us for God and for neighbor. Understanding love as care gives us a unified understanding of these four manifestations of love.

Let me try to forestall a misunderstanding of the upshot of my argument. It is not my contention that care is the only sort of love God has for us, nor that it is the only sort of love that we typically do or should have for ourselves; neither is it my contention that love as care is the only sort of love that we should have for God and for neighbor. God's love for us is not only love as care but also love as eros, attraction-love. So too, the love that we should have for God and that is appropriate to have for self and neighbor is not only love as care but love as eros. Where there is worth, it is appropriate to be drawn to it, attracted.

Chapter Ten

DO MOTIVATIONS MATTER?

MANY DIFFERENT REASONS and many different motivations lead us to care about others — or so it seems. Sometimes we care about someone because we are attached to her, bonded. Sometimes we care about someone because we find ourselves attracted to him. Sometimes we care out of compassion: our heart has been touched by the plight of the other. Sometimes out of solidarity: we discover that someone whom we have never met before graduated from the same college, grew up in the same small town, is a member of the same church, and we feel a special affinity that leads us to care about him.

Does it matter what motivates care? We are at the point in our discussion where we are ready to set about formulating rules of application for care. Must the rules declare that some reasons and some motivations are inherently unacceptable? No doubt reasons and motivations of the sorts mentioned do often yield care that is unacceptable in one way or another; the care motivated by my attachment to someone may take a bad turn. But are reasons and motivations of the sorts mentioned unacceptable in principle?

A striking feature of modern day agapism is its insistence that in the second love command, Jesus was not enjoining us to love each neighbor with some form or other of love but enjoining us to love each neighbor with that special form of love that most members of the movement called *neighbor-love,* that Kierkegaard called *Christian love,* that I have been calling *agapic love.* Neighbor-love is that species of benevolence in which one loves someone *because* he is one's neighbor.

Acknowledging that someone is one's neighbor is, of course, not sufficient, all by itself, to motivate love for her; one can acknowledge that someone is one's neighbor (in Jesus' sense) and do nothing. Kierkegaard held that what has to be added is recognition of duty: Jesus' second love command makes it one's duty to love everyone who is one's neighbor because he is one's neighbor. Nygren held that what has to be added is the infusion into us of God's love, which then flows outward toward everyone who is one's neighbor.

Were the modern day agapists right in their claim or assumption that New Testament agape is love of someone just because she is one's neighbor? If they were, then none of those examples of care that I mentioned in the opening paragraph of this chapter counts as an instance of New Testament agape. None of them has the right sort of motivation.

KIERKEGAARD'S CLAIM THAT ALL LOVE OTHER THAN AGAPIC LOVE IS SELF-LOVE

Why did the members of the movement adopt such an extraordinary position? Why did they interpret Jesus as enjoining us to love every neighbor with neighbor-love rather than enjoining us to love every neighbor out of some motive or other? Kierkegaard was more forthcoming on the point than anyone else in the movement; so let's look at what he had to say.

Kierkegaard held that reflection on the various dynamics of benevolence-love reveals it to be an implication of Jesus' second love command that it is our duty to love every neighbor out of duty — specifically, out of the duty to love everyone who is one's neighbor just because he is one's neighbor. Kierkegaard's reason for making this claim was his conviction that every motive for benevolence-love other than duty is some dynamic that belongs to our nature as human beings, that every such natural dynamic is preferential as among one's neighbors, and that all preferential love is not only incompatible with the injunction to love everyone who is one's neighbor but that it is, at bottom, a form of self-love. "Self-love and passionate preferential love are essentially the same" (*Works of Love*, 53).

M. Jamie Ferreira remarks that when Kierkegaard says that "erotic love and friendship *as such* are only enhanced and augmented self-love" (*Works of Love*, 267), he is "not saying anything particularly novel. Aristotle's discussion of friendship in the *Nicomachean Ethics* affirms that 'friendship is based on self-love.' Why? — because a friend is a good for us" (*Love's Grateful Striving*, 44). I hold, to the contrary, that Kierkegaard is saying something extremely novel. Aristotle's argument is that friendship is a mixture of love for oneself and love for the other (on the latter, see 1156b 6-11; 1159a 7-10); nowhere does he suggest that, at bottom, all naturally motivated love is love for oneself. That radical claim is Kierkegaard's.

As we saw in Chapter Two, it was not Kierkegaard's view that every manifestation of self-love is wrong; he differs on this point from Nygren. After remarking that "erotic love and friendship *as such* are only enhanced and augmented self-love,"[1] he immediately adds that "erotic love is undeniably life's most beautiful happiness, and friendship the greatest

---

1. What he means by "enhanced and augmented" self-love is that, in friendship at its best, things are no long *mine* and *thine* but *ours*.

temporal good" (*Works of Love*, 267). Thus, from the claim that every naturally motivated form of love is preferential and that all preferential love
is a form of self-love, he does not draw the conclusion that every natural
form of love is wrong and should be rooted out. The conclusion he
draws is rather that no form of naturally motivated preferential love is
Christian love, the love that Christ enjoined. Jesus was not enjoining us to
love ourselves. We already do that. "Wherever the essentially Christian is,
there also is self-denial, which is Christianity's essential form. In order to
relate oneself to the essentially Christian, one must first and foremost become sober; but self-denial is the very transformation by which a person
becomes sober in the sense of eternity" (*Works of Love*, 56).

From our earlier discussion we know how such a passage is to be interpreted. The topic under discussion is not the permissibility or
impermissibility of self-love; the topic is the nature of "the essentially
Christian" form of love. The essentially Christian form of love is not a
form of self-love. It loves one's neighbor for the sake of the neighbor,
not for the sake of oneself; and it does so out of the duty to love her in
that way just because she is one's neighbor — though let's not forget
that, in Kierkegaard's view, one is neighbor to oneself.

Kierkegaard employed his claim, that every form of naturally motivated love is at bottom a form of self-love, to argue that Jesus enjoined
us to love every neighbor with a form of love distinct from all naturally
motivated forms of love; we are to love the neighbor out of duty. For us,
quite obviously, his claim is not only hermeneutically but systematically
important.

Genuine care about the other consists of seeking *as an end in itself* to
promote her good or to secure that she be treated justly. Now suppose it
is the case, as Kierkegaard insists, that every motive for care that I mentioned in the opening paragraph of this chapter evokes only care about
oneself, not about the other. Then none of those would be motives for
seeking *as an end in itself* the good or the right of *another*; the care they
evoke as an end in itself would be exclusively care about *oneself*. Suppose
Kierkegaard is also right in his claim that only if one seeks someone's
good out of duty is one's love not a form of self-love. Then our rules for
the application of care will have to specify that care about the other
must be done out of duty; otherwise it isn't really care about the other
but care about oneself.

KIERKEGAARD'S ARGUMENT FOR HIS POSITION

Earlier in this chapter I reminded the reader that when discussing
Kierkegaard, we have to remember that he uses "neighbor" in such a

way that one is neighbor to oneself. As a corollary to this idiosyncratic usage, let us, in the remainder of this chapter, include, under "benevolence-love," seeking the good of oneself.

When speaking about natural love, Kierkegaard usually has in mind either attachment- or attraction-love, or benevolence-love evoked by these two forms of love. In discussing his view I will follow him in this regard and set benevolence-love grounded in compassion or solidarity off to the side. Everything that he says about the sorts of love he has in mind can easily be applied to these others.

Let me highlight the distinction I just now employed between, on the one hand, attachment or attraction to someone, and, on the other hand, benevolence-love for someone *because* one is attached or attracted to her. The former I call attachment-love or attraction-love; the latter I call attachment-*grounded* benevolence-love or attraction-*grounded* benevolence-love. Attachment-love and attraction-love are not, as such, love that seeks to advance the good of someone. They are the love that *consists of* being attached to someone or something and the love that *consists of* being attracted to someone or something. They do, however, typically evoke or motivate benevolence-love for the object of the attachment or attraction.

Kierkegaard is correct in claiming that attachment and attraction are preferential; the benevolence-love they motivate is thus also preferential. One finds oneself attached only to some people; one finds only some people attractive. But why does he hold that all benevolence-love so motivated is, at bottom, a form of self-love?

After declaring that "preferential love in passion or passionate preference is actually another form of self-love," he says that "it will now be shown" that this is the case (53). What then follows is this argument:

> Just as self-love selfishly embraces this one and only *self* that makes it self-love, so also erotic love's passionate preference selfishly encircles this one and only beloved, and friendship's passionate preference encircles this one and only friend. For this reason the beloved and the friend are called, remarkably and profoundly, to be sure, the *other self,* the *other I. . . .* But where does self-love reside? It resides in the I, the *self.* Would not self-love then also start loving the *other I,* the *other self?* (53)[2]

Kierkegaard's claim is that attachments and attractions are preferential, as is the benevolence-love that they motivate, that this makes benevolence-love so motivated at bottom selfish, and that selfish love is

---

2. The idea that one's friend is "the other I," "the other self," originates in Aristotle. See *Nicomachean Ethics,* 1166a 32, 1169b 6, and 1170b 6-7.

self-love. Let's grant that, insofar as one's love is selfish, it contains a note of self-love. But how does the fact that some form of benevolence-love is limited in its scope establish that it is selfish? I act selfishly when I save the biggest piece of pie for myself. Why am I acting selfishly when I give a piece of pie to each of my friends and none to anybody else? Suppose that out of generosity I give a piece to each of my friends *and none to myself.* Since I am still being preferential, I am still, on Kierkegaard's argument, being selfish. Why is that?

Kierkegaard realizes that he has to say something more if his case is to be convincing. This is what he adds:

> Even if passionate preference has no other selfishness in it, it would still have this, that consciously or unconsciously there is self-willfulness in it — unconsciously insofar as it is in the power of natural predispositions, consciously insofar as it utterly gives itself to that power and assents to it. However hidden, however unconscious the self-willfulness is in this passionate giving of oneself to its "one and only object," the arbitrariness is still there. The one and only object was certainly not found by obedience to the royal Law, "You shall love," but by choosing, yes, by unconditionally selecting one single individual. . . . When the lover or friend is able to love only this one single person in the whole world . . . there is an enormous self-willfulness in this enormous devotion, and in his impetuous, unlimited devotion the lover is actually relating himself to himself in self-love. Self-denial wants to root out this self-love, this self-willfulness, by means of eternity's *you shall.* (55)

The passage is only slightly less cryptic than the one it was meant to explain: it's the self-willfulness of preferential love that makes it selfish, and hence a form of self-love. Let me offer a speculative suggestion as to how Kierkegaard was thinking.

In attachment-grounded benevolence, my natural self plays a role that it does not play when I extend benevolence to someone out of duty. My attachments are a manifestation of the workings of my human nature; it's natural for human beings to form attachments. And the attachments themselves constitute part of my character, part of who I am. So when I extend benevolence-love to someone because I am attached to him or her, I allow my nature as manifested in this aspect of my character to motivate my benevolence-love. But when my benevolence-love is motivated by duty, it's my recognition of duty that shapes my love, not my natural dynamics and the personal character those dynamics have produced. Perhaps this is how Kierkegaard was thinking. If so, it's a very Kantian line of thought.

Now add this: if my natural dynamics and the character they have produced motivate my benevolence-love for someone, that's because, to use Kierkegaard's word, I "assent" to their doing so. And this implies, in turn, that I find my attachments and the natural dynamics that produced them *good;* otherwise I would have struggled to get rid of them. It must be that I *like* this aspect of myself, that I approve of it, that I find it of worth, that I am attracted to myself in this respect. It must be that I *love* myself in this regard, the form of the love being love as attraction. The conclusion Kierkegaard draws is that all natural loves are at bottom a form of self-love.

If this is indeed how Kierkegaard was thinking, the central point in the analysis seems to me acute and important. Sometimes people find themselves acting benevolently toward someone because they are attached to them but wishing they could get rid of the attachment; their love is deeply conflicted. Normally, however, implicit in attachment-grounded love is approval of the attachment; implicit is love of oneself with respect to the attachment. It's a point Harry Frankfurt makes in *Reasons of Love,* as I remarked in our discussion of self-love in Chapter Eight.[3]

But note two things. First, the form of self-love claimed to be implicit in my attachments is love as attraction, not love as benevolence. It's a case of acknowledging one's worth, not a case of seeking to advance one's good or right. It's one thing for attachment-grounded benevolence-love for the other to be accompanied, in the normal case, by approval of one's attachment; it's quite another thing for the *benevolence-love itself* that the attachment evokes to be really benevolence for oneself and not for the other. Kierkegaard's argument, as I have reconstructed it, is a reason to conclude that the former is the case; it is not a reason to conclude that the latter is the case. The argument does nothing whatsoever to show that the following is not the situation: the benevolence-love that my attachment to you evokes in me is benevolence *toward you* even though implicit in the entire package is my approval of the attachment.

Second, if the argument were a good one, it would undermine Kierkegaard's own position. Suppose that I seek the good of the other out of my conviction that it is my duty to do so. Perhaps there are conflicted cases in which a person strongly wishes that he did not regard it as his duty to seek the good of some particular person but finds himself incapable of shaking the conviction that it is; he feels guilty when he imagines himself not seeking that person's good. In the normal case, however, one's seeking the good of someone out of the conviction that

3. This is what he says: "People cannot avoid loving themselves, it appears, as long as they love anything at all. If a person loves anything, he necessarily loves himself" (86).

it is one's duty to do so will be accompanied by approval of this conviction. One approves of oneself in this regard; one loves oneself with that
mode of love which is acknowledgment of worth. But if that were sufficient to establish that what appears to be benevolence-love for the other
done out of duty is in fact nothing but self-love, then what Kierkegaard
calls Christian love would also be a form of self-love.

Though he doesn't make much of it, Kierkegaard also had a hermeneutical reason for his insistence that benevolence grounded in attachment or attraction is not an instance of the love that Jesus asks of us. "Is
it not remarkable," he says, "that in the whole New Testament there is
not a single verse about friendship in the sense in which the poet cele-
brates it . . . ? Let the poet search the New Testament for a word about
friendship that could please him, and he will vainly seek to the point of
despair" (45-46). Coming from someone who knew the New Testament
as well as Kierkegaard knew it, this claim is astonishing. It's true that in
the New Testament there are no hymns in praise of *eros* or *philia;* St.
Paul's hymn of praise to love in 1 Corinthians 13 is a hymn of praise to
agapē. Nonetheless, the gospels are full of stories about Jesus' friend-
ships. In his farewell speech to his disciples, as recorded in the Gospel
of John, Jesus explicitly calls them friends, using the standard Greek
term for a friend, *philos* (John 15:14-15).

Jesus Is Silent about Motives for Love

If one first reads around in the writings of the modern day agapists and
only thereafter reads the reports in the three synoptic gospels of the episode in which Jesus enunciated the two love commands, what strikes
one immediately is that Jesus says nothing at all about reasons or motives for loving the neighbor; all he says is that one should love one's
neighbor as oneself. He nowhere rejects caring about some people because one is attached to them, caring about others because one feels
compassion for them, caring about yet others because one finds oneself
attracted to them, and so forth. In all such cases one is doing what Jesus
commanded, caring about the other, seeking to promote her good and
to secure her rights as ends in themselves.

All of us find that there are "neighbors" who fall outside the orbit of
the care evoked by our natural dynamics of attachment, attraction, compassion, identification, and the like. Our natural dynamics leave us indifferent to their good. In such cases, our care about them will have to
be out of duty. Duty is the fall-back position. Jesus does not say what
Kierkegaard interprets him as saying, namely, love your neighbor out of
duty. He says simply, love your neighbor. If no natural dynamics moti-

vate you to care about your neighbor, then care about him out of duty. But it is not your duty to care about every neighbor out of duty.

The parable of the good Samaritan is instructive in this regard. Recall the context. In Luke's narration of the presentation of the two love commands (Luke 10), a lawyer poses to Jesus the test question, "Teacher, what must I do to inherit eternal life?" Jesus turns the question back on him: "What is written in the law?" The lawyer then cites the two commandments from the Torah. Jesus replies, "You have given the right answer; do this, and you will live." Wanting to justify himself, as Luke puts it, the lawyer then asks, "And who is my neighbor?" It is in response to this question that Jesus tells the parable.

In the New Revised Standard Version, Jesus describes the Samaritan in the parable as "moved with pity" when he saw the mugged man beside the road. "Pity" is surely not the best rendering of the Greek into contemporary English. "Pity" connotes an attitude of superiority on the part of the one who pities. There was no attitude of superiority on the part of the Samaritan. He responded as he did because the plight of the mugged man evoked compassion in him. Be it noted that he did not respond as he did because he saw it as his duty to do so.

Running throughout Hebrew and Christian scripture is the assumption that there is in human beings a disposition to compassion, empathy, sympathy, fellow-feeling, a disposition that leads us to rejoice with the rejoicing and to grieve with the grieving. It's one of the dispositions that the eighteenth-century Scottish moral theorists called moral sentiments. The suffering of the other becomes, in some mysterious way, my suffering; the happiness of the other becomes, in some mysterious way, my happiness. The disposition works independently of attachment, of attraction, of social solidarity. The Samaritan was neither attached to the wounded man nor did he feel any social solidarity with him. There is no reason to think that he found something about the man that attracted him. Yet he was moved by compassion. Caring about the neighbor has many springs of action, compassion being one of the most important.[4]

Often in Scripture one finds the injunction, "harden not your heart." Our disposition to compassion is easily inhibited, among the most powerful inhibitors being the stories we tell about the members of some out-group. They are no better than animals, we say, undermining our way of life, one and all evil. When a person's heart has been hardened by an inhibiting story, confrontation with suffering evokes no compassion. The story that hardened his heart has to be contested.

---

4. Michael Slote, in *Ethics of Care and Empathy*, explores the possibility of basing an entire ethic on empathy. He acknowledges that, in so doing, he is standing in the tradition of the eighteenth-century Scottish moral theorists.

Rather than dismissing care about the other grounded in compassion as not measuring up to what he is calling for, Jesus offers such care as an example of what he is calling for. The natural dynamics that lead us to care about the other are often malformed in their workings. But when they are not malformed, it makes no difference whether we care about the other because we are attached to her, because we are attracted to her, because we feel solidarity with her, because we are moved by compassion, or because we see it as our duty to care about her. Just see to it that you not care only about yourself but also about your neighbor.

Chapter Eleven

RULES OF APPLICATION FOR CARE

TWO RULES OF APPLICATION for care have been implicit in our discussion for quite some time now; all we have to do is bring them into the light of day. Arriving at the point where we can formulate a third rule will take some work. The three rules together should be thought of as replacing the agent-happiness principle of the eudaimonist and the maximizing principle of the utilitarian.

An important point to keep in mind, as we formulate and appraise these rules of application, is that without seeking or intending to do so one may enhance or diminish someone's good in the course of intending something else; one may do so without even being aware of doing so. Likewise, without seeking or intending to do so one may treat someone justly or unjustly in the course of intending something else; one may do so without being aware of doing so.

TWO RULES OF APPLICATION

Suppose one accepts the Principle of Correlatives between rights and duties that we formulated in Chapter Seven. Suppose one also accepts the principle that if, in doing something, one would treat someone as one ought not to treat them, that by itself is a decisive reason for not doing it — a decisive reason for it's being something one should not do. Then the first rule of application is obvious:

> Rule 1: *Seeking to promote someone's good or secure someone's rights as ends in themselves should never be done at the cost of wronging someone.*

Using the concept of malformed care that I introduced earlier, this rule declares that one's care about someone should never be malformed.

Given the prominence in the modern day agapist movement of the claim that New Testament agape is self-sacrificial, the second rule may seem surprising coming from someone who locates himself in the agapist tradition, as I do. But it too was implicit in our earlier discussion.

> Rule 2: *One should seek to promote one's own good and secure justice for oneself as ends in themselves, though never at the cost of wronging someone.*

119

Note that this second rule does not merely say that it is acceptable to care about oneself; it says that one *should* care about oneself. What we saw in our discussion of self-love in Chapter Eight is that the person who does not care about herself thereby wrongs herself.

To these two rules of application for care it's worth adding an epistemological principle that surfaced in our discussion of care:

> Epistemological principle: *When caring about someone, the beliefs one employs concerning their life-goods and rights, and concerning causal efficacy, should be beliefs to which one is entitled.*

Using the concept of responsible care that I introduced earlier, this rule declares that one's care should be responsible.

Jesus' Sermon on the Mount

I propose arriving at the point where we can formulate a third rule of application for care by once again engaging the founding texts of the agapist tradition, attending to an important part of Jesus' teaching about which I have thus far said nothing.

I have articulated my version of agapism in the context of comparing and contrasting it to egoism, eudaimonism, and utilitarianism. That was not the context within which Jesus presented his ethic of love. Jesus knew nothing of eudaimonism and utilitarianism. And though the second love command is a rejection of egoism, Jesus nowhere formulates egoism as a position that he opposes. The polemical context for the second love command was instead Jesus' emphatic rejection of what I shall call the *reciprocity code*. It was in the so-called Sermon on the Mount that Jesus most sharply contrasted the ethic of love with the reciprocity code. So let's consider how he formulated the contrast. The relevant part of the sermon is reported in Matthew 5:17-48 and in Luke 6:27-36.

These are among the most provocative and controversial passages in the entire New Testament; even the claim that Jesus' main point here is repudiation of the reciprocity code in favor of the ethic of love will be contested. But if we read with care the passages as a whole, and do not merely snatch at golden nuggets and run with them, I think the conclusion is inescapable that this is exactly what Jesus was doing, commending his ethic of love in the context of launching a biting attack on the reciprocity code.

"Do not resist an evildoer," says Jesus in Matthew's narration. "If anyone strikes you on the right cheek, turn the other also" (5:39). The saying is often cited by pacifists in defense of their position of non-violent resistance. But what the sentence says is not that we should be non-violent in our resistance to evildoers; it says that we should not resist evildoers. Few pacifists go that far. In the same passage Jesus says, "Give to everyone who begs from you, and do not refuse anyone who wants to borrow from you" (5:42). I know of no one who is as generous as this sentence says he should be. And I know of no one who has done what the following words of Jesus in the same passage say we should do: "If your right eye causes you to sin, tear it out and throw it away. . . . And if your right hand causes you to sin, cut it off and throw it away" (5:29).

I have spoken thus far of what *the sentences say* — alternatively expressed, of what *the sentences mean*. But the relevant question of interpretation is not what the sentences say or mean; in this case, that's clear. The relevant question of interpretation is *what Jesus was saying* with these sentences. What a speaker or writer says by using a sentence may or may not be the same as what the sentence says or means. When someone speaks ironically, what he says is (more or less) the opposite of what his sentence means in the language.

In the narrations of both Matthew and Luke, Jesus was using the sentences I just quoted, and others like them, to contrast his ethic of love with the reciprocity code. In Matthew's narration, that contrast was preceded by a contrast between the ethic of love and what Israel's law required, this contrast then flowing seamlessly into the contrast with the reciprocity code. So let us begin by looking at the contrast in Matthew between the ethic of love and the requirements of the law; then, at the point where Matthew segues into the contrast between the ethic of love and the reciprocity code, let us bring Luke's narration into the picture.

"Do not think that I have come to abolish the law or the prophets," says Jesus. "I have come not to abolish but to fulfill" (5:17). What then follows is a series of five paragraphs, each introduced with the formula, "You have heard that it was said, . . . but I say to you." The point in each case is that what one finds in the law and the prophets is the bare minimum of what the ethic of love requires. The ethic of love does not repudiate Israel's law; it catches it up into a more challenging ideal. Though love underlies the law, its expression there is often minimalist.

"You have heard that it was said to those of ancient times, 'You shall not murder'; and 'whoever murders shall be liable to judgment.' But I say to you that if you are angry with a brother or sister, you will be liable to judgment; and if you insult a brother or sister, you will be liable to the council" (5:21-22). Of course you should not murder. But when you discern that underlying the injunction not to murder is the command to love, then you will realize that not only should you not murder; you should not even get angry with your fellows or insult them.

"You have heard that it was said, 'You shall not commit adultery.' But

I say to you that everyone who looks at a woman with lust has already committed adultery with her in his heart. If your right eye causes you to sin, tear it out and throw it away" (5:27-29). Of course you should not commit adultery. But when you discern that underlying the injunction not to commit adultery is the command to love, then you will realize that not only should you not commit adultery; you should not even lust after a woman. Get rid of your lust. Tear it out.[1]

"You have heard that it was said to those of ancient times, 'You shall not swear falsely, but carry out the vows you have made to the Lord.' But I say to you, Do not swear at all. . . . Let your word be 'Yes, Yes' or 'No, No'" (5:33-37). Of course you should not commit perjury or make insincere pledges. But when you discern what underlies these injunctions, then you will realize that not only should you not commit perjury or make insincere pledges; you should speak truthfully whether or not you have sworn or pledged to do so.

"You have heard that it was said, 'An eye for an eye and a tooth for a tooth.' But I say to you, Do not resist an evildoer" (5:38-39). We have now moved seamlessly into the rejection of the reciprocity code.

Many commentators suggest that "an eye for an eye and a tooth for a tooth" should be heard as a repudiation of blind vengeance and an affirmation, instead, of the reciprocity code. The point of Israel's law, they suggest, is that one is to exact *no more* than an eye for an eye and *no more* than a tooth for a tooth. The commentators may well be right about this; and it may well be that that is how Jesus understood the force of the eye-for-an-eye rule. If so, then what he is saying is that of course you should not engage in blind vengeance. But when you discern that underlying the prohibition of blind vengeance is the command to love, then you will realize that not only should you refrain from blind vengeance; you should also refrain from paying back evil with proportionate evil. You should return good for evil. You should reject not only blind vengeance but reciprocity as well.

And now let's have before us the entire passage from Matthew in which Jesus segues from urging a deepened understanding of the law to rejection of the reciprocity code:

> You have heard that it was said, "An eye for an eye and a tooth for a tooth." But I say to you, Do not resist an evildoer. But if anyone strikes you on the right cheek, turn the other also; and if anyone

---

1. I skip the third paragraph: "It was also said, 'Whoever divorces his wife, let him give her a certificate of divorce.' But I say to you that anyone who divorces his wife, except on the ground of unchastity, causes her to commit adultery; and whoever marries a divorced woman commits adultery."

wants to sue you and take your coat, give your cloak as well; and if anyone forces you to go one mile, go also the second mile. Give to everyone who begs from you, and do not refuse anyone who wants to borrow from you.

You have heard that it was said, "You shall love your neighbor and hate your enemy." But I say to you, Love your enemies and pray for those who persecute you, so that you may be children of your Father in heaven. For he makes his sun rise on the evil and on the good, and sends rain on the just and the unjust.[2] For if you love those who love you, what reward do you have? Do not even the tax collectors do the same? And if you greet only your brothers and sisters, what more are you doing than others? Do not even the Gentiles do the same? Be perfect, therefore, as your heavenly Father is perfect. (Matthew 5:38-48)

Here is the corresponding passage from Luke:

Love your enemies, do good to those who hate you, bless those who curse you, pray for those who abuse you. If anyone strikes you on the cheek, offer the other also; and from anyone who takes away your coat do not withhold even your shirt. Give to everyone who begs from you, and if anyone takes away your goods, do not ask for them again. Do to others as you would have them do to you.

If you love those who love you, what credit is that to you? For even sinners love those who love them. If you do good to those who do good to you, what credit is that to you? For even sinners do the same. If you lend to those from whom you hope to receive, what credit is that to you? Even sinners lend to sinners, to receive as much again. But love your enemies, do good, and lend expecting nothing in return. Your reward will be great, and you will be children of the Most High; for he is kind to the ungrateful and the wicked. Be merciful, just as your Father is merciful. (Luke 6:27-36)

The reciprocity code had two aspects. If someone does you a favor, you owe them an equal favor in return. If someone does you an evil, an equal evil is due them.[3] "Evil" must be understood as deprivation of

2. The translation I am using, NRSV, has "righteous" and "unrighteous" where I have "just" and "unjust." The Greek words are *dikaios* and *adikos*.

3. In his essay, "Evil in Person," Jean-Luc Marion calls the negative side of the code "the logic of evil." He does not note that this is just one side of the complete code — that the logic of evil has as its counterpart the logic of the favor or the gift. The essay is to be found in his book, *Prolegomena to Charity*, trans. Stephen E. Lewis (New York: Fordham University Press, 2002).

some life-good. In both cases, the positive and the negative, the code says that the balance that existed before the engagement took place must be restored. Things have to be evened up. From Jesus' comments one can infer that this code was prominent in Jewish society of the time. From the texts of pagan antiquity we know that it was also prominent in ancient Greek and Roman society.

Jesus' attitude toward the positive side of the code, that if someone does you a favor, you should do them a favor in return, is deflationary acceptance. Though we should not feel bound in general to return good for good, for the most part it's not a bad thing to do, especially among friends. By and large it's not a good thing among friends for generosity to go entirely in one direction. But there's no point in issuing exhortations on the matter, says Jesus; everybody accepts the principle, sinners, tax collectors, gentiles, they all return favors for favors. "If you do good to those who do good to you, what credit is that to you? For even sinners do the same."

Jesus' attitude toward the negative side of the reciprocity code, that if someone does evil to you, then an equal evil is due them, is flat-out rejection. Returning evil for evil, redressing harm with harm, paying back injury with injury, is out. In all cases one is to do good; one is to love the other — even when the other is one's enemy and has treated one maliciously. "Love your enemies, do good to those who hate you." In so doing you are like God, who is kind even to the ungrateful and the wicked.

These injunctions of Jesus, so puzzling to so many readers over the centuries, are vivid metaphorical and hyperbolic repudiations of the negative side of the reciprocity code and injunctions to put in its place the ethic of love. To interpret them with unimaginative literal-mindedness is to miss the point. If someone strikes you on the cheek, don't try to get even; offer him your other cheek. If someone steals your coat, don't pay him back; offer him your shirt. If someone conscripts you to carry his load for one mile, don't repay harm with harm; offer to carry his load a second mile. These are vivid metaphorical and hyperbolic ways of making the point that we are to repudiate the code of repaying evil with evil and are instead to seek the good even of those who do us evil.

It's easy to carry on with contemporary metaphorical and hyperbolic examples of the same point. If someone steals your bicycle, don't try to get even; offer him your car. If someone discovers your social security number, don't pay him back; offer him your credit card. If someone steals your CD player, don't try to get even; offer him your computer. And so forth.

Jesus is not enjoining non-resistance to evil in these passages, though that is what the sentence "Do not resist an evildoer" means, literally. And certainly he is not saying that though resistance is acceptable, it has to be non-violent. No one interprets everything in these passages literally. But if one nonetheless singles out the sentence "Do not resist an evildoer" and insists on a literal interpretation of that sentence, then what Jesus is saying is not, do not resist an evildoer *with violence,* but, *do not resist an evildoer, period.*[4]

I have elsewhere[5] expressed my admiration for Richard Hays's book, *The Moral Vision of the New Testament.*[6] But on this point, Hays's formidable hermeneutical skills abandon him. He describes the sayings of Jesus in the passage from Matthew that I have quoted as "illustrations of the peaceloving and generous character that the teaching of Jesus seeks to inculcate. Jesus' disciples are to relinquish the tit-for-tat of the *lex talionis*" (326). This seems to me correct but misleadingly incomplete. What Jesus repudiates is not only the *lex talionis* but the reciprocity code as a whole of which the *lex talionis* is the negative side. But when Hays goes on to say that Matthew 5:38-48 teaches "nonviolent enemy-love" (323), and that the "teaching of Matthew 5:39 is about nonviolence" (326), he is allowing his pacifist convictions to distort his interpretation.

Hays interprets Matthew 5:39 as saying, "Do not resist an evildoer with violence." But, to repeat, what the text says is "Do not resist an evildoer." Hays does not accept the literal interpretation of this saying; he remarks that the posture of the new community that Jesus is forming "is not to be one of supine passivity" (326). But if we accept that this saying is not to be taken literally, then, among the considerations to be employed in determining what Jesus was saying, is the larger context within which the saying occurs. And that larger context is not the affirmation of pacifism but the rejection of the reciprocity code.

Hays, along with other pacifists, cites in support of his pacifist interpretation Jesus' own behavior when he was arrested (322). But if Jesus' behavior at his arrest is employed to support an interpretation of the text, then what his behavior supports is not the pacifist interpretation but the literal, non-resistance, interpretation. For what is striking about

---

4. Glen Stassen — in "The Fourteen Triads of the Sermon on the Mount (Matthew 5:21–7:12)," *Journal of Biblical Literature* 122.2 (2003): 267-308 — interprets "do not resist an evildoer" as meaning, "do not retaliate by evil means." But that seems to me untenable in the light of the "you have heard it said . . . but I say . . ." structure of the pericope. No one was saying that we may or should retaliate by evil means. Stassen gives an intellectually imaginative unified interpretation of the fourteen pericopes in Matthew 5–7, and helpfully summarizes a variety of other interpretations. Oddly, Jesus' opening statement, that he has come not to abolish but to fulfill the law plays no role in Stassen's interpretation; I judge that he also does not give sufficient recognition to Jesus' repudiation of the reciprocity code, and that this contributes to his interpreting literally passages that I judge should be interpreted as metaphor and hyperbole.

5. In *Justice: Rights and Wrongs.*

6. (San Francisco: Harper Collins, 1996).

Jesus' behavior upon being arrested is not that he resisted non-violently but that he did not resist.

The person looking for advice on the morality of violent versus non-violent resistance to evil, of coercive versus non-coercive resistance, has to look elsewhere. May it be that coercing the evildoer is sometimes the most loving thing one can do? Jesus doesn't tell us here, one way or the other. What he says is simply, do not return evil for evil. Impose on the evildoer some diminution of his wellbeing only if that serves the good. Reject vengeance. Do not try to get even. Repudiate the reciprocity code.

Though Jesus' most vivid and extensive rejection of the reciprocity code in favor of the ethic of love occurred in the episode reported in the two passages from Matthew and Luke, he rejected the code on other occasions as well. One Sabbath day Jesus was invited for dinner to the home of one of the leaders of the Pharisee party. It soon became clear to him that, apart from himself, the invited guests were friends and relatives of the host. That led him to remark to the host,

> When you give a luncheon or a dinner, do not invite your friends or your brothers or your relatives or rich neighbors, in case they may invite you in return, and you would be repaid. But when you give a banquet, invite the poor, the crippled, the lame, and the blind. And you will be blessed, because they cannot repay you, for you will be repaid at the resurrection of the just. (Luke 14:12-14)[7]

This is a barbed rejection of that aspect of the reciprocity code which says that favors must be answered with favors.

The epistolary literature of the New Testament carries forward Jesus' rejection of the reciprocity code. In 1 Peter 3:9 we read, "Do not repay evil for evil or abuse for abuse; but, on the contrary, repay with a blessing." In his first letter to the Thessalonians Paul says, "See that none of you repays evil for evil, but always seek to do good to one another and to all" (5:15). And in his letter to the Romans Paul says, "Do not repay anyone evil for evil, but take thought for what is noble in the sight of all. . . . Never avenge yourselves, but leave room for the wrath of God; for it is written, 'Vengeance (ekdikēsis) is mine, I will repay, says the Lord'" (Romans 12:17-19).[8]

---

7. Where I have "just," the NRSV has "righteous." The Greek has *dikaioi*.
8. The quotation is from Deuteronomy 32:35.

An Ethic Meant for Everyone

Christian writers rather often describe Jesus' teaching in the Sermon on the Mount as an ethic for Christians.[9] Matthew's description of the situation in which Jesus delivered the sermon would seem to make this interpretation plausible: "Seeing the crowd, Jesus went up on the mountain, and when he sat down, his disciples came to him. And he opened his mouth and taught them" (5:1). What then follows is the sermon addressed to the disciples. The relevant question, however, is not whether the sermon was originally addressed only to the disciples but whether its content was *intended* only for them; the former does not imply the latter.

Luke's description of the situation in which the sermon was delivered is significantly different from Matthew's. "Jesus came down with [his twelve apostles] and stood on a level place, with a great crowd of his disciples and a great multitude of people. . . . And he lifted up his eyes on his disciples, and said . . . (6:17-19).[10] What then follows is the sermon, perhaps addressed to the disciples, but clearly meant for the entire crowd. In Luke's narration, the ethic Jesus preaches is an ethic for everybody.

We could ask whether there are other passages in the gospels in which Jesus clearly indicates that he intends the ethic of love for everybody or only for his followers; we could ask whether it even makes sense to interpret him as intending the ethic only for his disciples, leaving the crowd free to take it or leave it. But the fact that in Luke's narration the ethic is meant for everybody, and that this is compatible with Matthew's narration, is sufficient by itself to tilt our interpretation in that direction. Everybody should reject the reciprocity code. Nobody should feel bound by the positive side of the code and everybody should reject the negative side — not reject it in the weak sense of not regarding it as obligatory but reject it in the strong sense of acknowledging that one *should* not, or *ought* not conform to the negative side.

We should not answer evil with evil, harm with harm, injury with injury. Our response to harm and injury should be seeking to bring about good. It would be implausible to interpret Jesus as meaning that not even as a means to bringing about a greater good in someone's life should one impose an "evil" on that person — a diminution in his or her flourishing. What he means is that we are to impose an evil (harm, injury) on someone *only* as a means to, or constituent of, a greater good.

9. That is how Richard Hays speaks of it, in *Moral Vision of the New Testament.*

10. In Luke's report, Jesus' discourse was not the Sermon on the Mount but the Sermon on the Plain.

THE REJECTION OF RETRIBUTION

The idea of retribution is the idea of redressing the harm done to some victim by the imposition of an equivalent harm on the victimizer. We can infer from what Jesus says that it was commonly believed in Jewish society of his day that retribution is not only permissible but something we should do, perhaps ought to do. We know from other sources that this belief was also common in ancient pagan society.

The rejection by Jesus of the negative side of the reciprocity code implies the rejection of retribution. Not only is there no obligation to redress harm by harm, injury by injury, evil by evil. Jesus forbids retribution. Injury imposed on the wrongdoer must be justified by some greater good that it brings about, not by the fact that the wrongdoer imposed an injury. If redressing injury (harm, evil) has any place at all in the moral order, God will do it. Leave it to God. Often we cannot even imagine what it would be like to redress the injury; what would it be like to redress the evils of the Holocaust?[11] When we can imagine what it would be like, often we cannot do it.

I realize that this interpretation of what Jesus said will prove controversial in many quarters; the idea that retribution is obligatory has been, I would guess, the majority opinion in the Christian tradition. But if Jesus was not rejecting retribution in rejecting the negative side of the reciprocity code, what was he doing? I see no plausible answer to this question.

To assuage some worries, let me add immediately that punishment is not to be equated with retribution. Retribution is one, but only one, rationale for punishment. In the chapter in Romans immediately following the chapter in which Paul instructed his readers not to repay evil with evil, he describes rulers as God's servants. They encourage those who do good; and by imposing punishment on wrongdoers, they express anger *(orgē)* against wrongdoing and serve as a terror *(phobos)* to such conduct. Nothing is said about retribution, about getting even, about reciprocating evil with evil, about redress, about vengeance. Punishment as a condemnation of the wrongdoer is a good in his life[12] and

cf.
Punishment

11. In commenting on the sentence, "'Vengeance is mine,' says the Lord," Jeffrie Murphy suggests that we human beings are not good enough to be trusted with evening things up, and don't know enough about the hearts of human beings. ("Hatred: A Qualified Defense," in Jeffrie Murphy and Jean Hampton, *Forgiveness and Mercy* [Cambridge: Cambridge University Press, 1988], 98-102). Both points are correct. But I think that even if I did understand Hitler's heart and was myself a very good person, I would still have no idea whatsoever as to what it would be like to even things up in Hitler's case.

12. Recall what Moses says in Leviticus, as he leads up to the love command: "You shall reprove your neighbor, or you will incur guilt yourself. You shall not take vengeance . . . against any of your people."

serves the social good of deterring such wrongdoing. I will have more to say about this understanding of punishment in Chapter Seventeen.

Jesus' injunction to forgive the repentant wrongdoer was of a piece with his rejection of retribution. To forgive someone for the wrong he did me is to bestow on him the good of not holding it against him — so I will argue in Chapters Fifteen and Sixteen. If I do not hold against a person the wrong he did me, then obviously I will not seek to have that wrong redressed; conversely, if I do seek to have that wrong redressed, I hold it against him. Jesus' injunction to forgive the repentant wrong-doer implies opposition to retributive punishment of repentant wrong-doers; his rejection of the negative side of the reciprocity code implies opposition to retributive punishment in general.

In formulating a third rule of application for care, I will assume that nobody should ever choose as an end in itself anything other than enhancing the good of persons and securing justice. We should care about our enemies as well as our friends.

A THIRD RULE OF APPLICATION

It is sometimes acceptable for me to impose some evil (harm, injury) on you when doing so is required for promoting a greater good in your life. But what about imposing some evil on you when doing so is required for promoting someone else's greater good? Is that ever acceptable?

I know of no passage in any of the modern day agapists in which they directly address the issue. But if I understand the spirit of their thought, they all held that this is unacceptable. They talked about *equal regard* and *no preference*.

They may have meant by this that one is to seek with equal commitment to *promote* the flourishing of everyone who is one's neighbor. But surely that is impossible to bring off, given the scarcity of time and resources available to us. And it would be wrong to try. I ought to give the flourishing of my own children more attention than I do the flourishing of children who live five blocks over.

Alternatively, they may have meant that one is never to seek to *diminish* the flourishing of one person in order to enhance the flourishing of another. Perhaps it is possible to follow the no-partiality principle on this interpretation thereof; but it too is a principle that we should not try to follow. If someone is about to inflict serious evil on another person and I am in a position to prevent him from doing so, then, even if my preventing him from doing so requires diminishing his flourishing, it is often not only acceptable that I do so but sometimes morally required.

We arrive, then, at a third rule of application for care:

> Rule 3: *One should never seek to impose some evil on someone (i.e., diminish the person's flourishing) as an end in itself; one should seek to impose some evil only if doing so is an indispensable means to promoting greater goods in the life of that person and/or others, only if one should be promoting those greater life-goods, and never at the cost of wronging someone.*

Possible ?

One can be a eudaimonist and reject this rule; there is nothing inconsistent in combining eudaimonism with the reciprocity code. The relation of the rule to the maximizing principle of the utilitarian is more complex. Note that the rule says that one may trade off life-evils for greater life-goods only if one *should* promote those life-goods; the fact that it is *acceptable* to promote those goods is not enough. The utilitarian says that I may diminish the good of anyone whatsoever just provided that, in so doing, I maximize overall life-goods. It need not be the case that I *should* bring about that particular complex of overall life-goods; it's enough that it is acceptable for me to do so. I think one needs a stronger justification than that for inflicting evil on someone. Doing so has to be <u>indispensable</u> to promoting life-goods that one *should* promote. And sometimes one should or ought to promote *particular* life-goods of *particular* human beings even if some alternative action would achieve greater *overall* life-goods — for example, when the particular human beings are one's children.

I suppose it would be possible to take delight in inflicting evil (diminution of flourishing) on someone while nonetheless acting in conformity to Rule 3; though one is inflicting evil on this person only because it is necessary for achieving some life-goods that one should promote, one nonetheless does so with pleasure. If so, then the "spirit" of agapism requires that we add to Rule 3 an attitudinal corollary, to this effect:

> Attitudinal corollary: *One is never to take delight in imposing evil (diminution in flourishing) on someone; when necessary to do so, one is to do so with regret.*

Universality Within the Three Rules

Each of our three rules of application for care has universality built into it by the final clause, "but never at the cost of wronging someone." If some human being would be wronged were I to promote these life-goods in this way, then I should not do that.

Application of the rule requires attentiveness to the effects of one's action on the rights of one's fellow human beings — anything but the justice-blindness that Nygren urged! In that way, one is to care about everyone; no one is to fall outside the circle of one's care. It is impossible actively to seek to promote the flourishing of everyone, let alone trying to do so equally; and sometimes we should seek to diminish the good of one person for the sake of enhancing the good of another. What is always possible, however, and what one should always do, is care about everyone by seeing to it that one treats no one unjustly. Understanding love as care rather than benevolence enables us to honor the universality implicit in Jesus' second love command.

WHOSE FLOURISHING SHOULD ONE CARE ABOUT?

The rules for the application of care that I have proposed do not tell us whose flourishing one should care about, other than one's own; they only tell us what we should *not* do in caring about someone. This may seem a deficiency in the rules; in order to act, we need to know not only what we should *not* do but what we *should* do.

I submit that it is not a deficiency in the rules. What each of us should do, and more narrowly, what each of us ought to do, depends crucially on our abilities, our resources, our circumstances, our opportunities, even our convictions. It is for that reason impossible to offer informative general rules as to what any person should do in any situation. To try to formulate rules as to what a human being as such should do is to exhibit a serious misunderstanding of the nature of the moral life. It is to fail to recognize the particularized character of the contours of prudence and obligation.

This is not quite the end of the matter, however. Let's return once more to Jesus' parable of the good Samaritan. Recall that Jesus told the parable in response to the question that a lawyer of the Pharisee party put to him, "And who is my neighbor?" Jesus had just enunciated the Mosaic command, "Love your neighbor as yourself." One surmises that the lawyer now wanted to hear from Jesus that it was permissible to exclude certain people from the scope of his love — the Roman occupiers, for example, perhaps Samaritans.

Upon concluding his story about the mugged man, the priest, the Levite, and the Samaritan, Jesus put a question to the lawyer. It was not the lawyer's question rephrased in the light of the story. Jesus did not ask, "To which of the three passersby was the wounded man a neighbor?" Instead he asked, "Which of the three passersby was a neighbor to the wounded man?" Rather than employing the traditional category that the lawyer had employed, that of *being a neighbor of* someone, Jesus employed the related but different category, *being a neighbor to someone.*

Apparently the Jews of the time despised the Samaritans. So had the mugged man been a Samaritan, it would already have been difficult for the lawyer to concede that whoever came to the aid of the Samaritan was the one who was a neighbor to him. But the parable Jesus told was far more biting than that. We can assume that the mugged man was a Jew; many more Jews than foreigners would have been "going down from Jerusalem to Jericho." It was a Samaritan who came to the aid of a Jew after the Jew's fellow countrymen had passed him by. The lawyer is trapped. He cannot bring himself to say straightforwardly that it was the Samaritan who was a neighbor to the wounded man. So he says, "it was the one who showed mercy on him."[13]

What are we to make of this? Is Jesus implicitly offering a definition of "neighbor" different from the one Moses employed in Leviticus, a definition that includes not just one's kinsmen but all human beings? That's the way the parable is often interpreted. But Jesus does not offer a definition. He does not answer the lawyer's question by offering an expanded concept of neighbor. Instead he tells the story and then asks the question, "Which of the three passersby was a neighbor to the wounded man?" So once again, what are we to make of this?

I take Jesus to be enjoining us to be alert to the obligations placed upon us by the needs of whomever we happen on, and to pay no attention to the fact, if it be a fact, that the needy person belongs to a group that is a disdained or disdaining out-group with respect to oneself. Every society has derogatory terms for members of one and another out-group: wop, dago, Hun, Jap, nigger, "Dutchman belly full o' straw." Whether we ourselves employ such terms or they are applied to us, they prevent us from recognizing our obligations to aid those in need. Discard them all, says Jesus. Do not let them deafen your ear to the cry for help or harden your heart.

What the parable prescribes, says Jeremy Waldron, "is openness and responsiveness to actual human need in whatever form it confronts us. And what it prohibits is the action of those (like the priest and the Levite) who would come where the man and his need is, and look on him, and then pass by on the other side."[14] "Never mind ethnicity, community, or traditional categories of neighbor-ness. . . . To pass by and do

---

13. It may well have been an act of piety on the part of the priest and the Levite to pass by the wounded man; the holiness code forbade touching corpses. If so, then the story has an additional bite.

14. Jeremy Waldron, "Who Is My Neighbor?: Humanity and Proximity," *The Monist* 86.3 (2003): 333-55, here 343. This article was called to my attention by Chris Eberle.

nothing to help a person whose need is so immediately present seems plainly wrong; even the lawyer" sees this.[15]

In short, though there is no general rule of application specifying to whom one should devote one's care, in what way and to what degree, the parable of the good Samaritan teaches an *ethical corollary* to the three rules of application.

> Ethical corollary: *Be open to recognizing the obligations that the needs of the other place upon one, and do not allow any in-group/out-group classifications to deafen one's ear or harden one's heart.*

It is important, however, that we not draw from the parable the conclusion that it is *only* to the needs of those immediately present to us that we are called to respond. Though most of us are aware of the fact that there are millions of people who lack the food and medicine necessary for survival, the plight of most of them is not evident to us. In *Living High and Letting Die: Our Illusion of Innocence*, Peter Unger argues that this is morally irrelevant.[16] He notes that there are a number of agencies with a fine track record of delivering food and medicine to such people, he makes a powerful case for the thesis that the well-to-do among us are morally obligated to do far more than most of us do to support these agencies financially, and he calls attention to some of the psychological factors that lead us to ignore or deny this obligation.

15. Waldron, "Who Is My Neighbor?" 348.
16. (Oxford: Oxford University Press, 1996).

Chapter Twelve

CORRECTING TWO IMPRESSIONS

CORRECTING THE IMPRESSION OF INDIVIDUALISM

My discussion thus far has an individualistic cast to it. I have emphasized that rights are normative social relations. They are legitimate claims to the good of being treated a certain way by someone; only in the limiting case is that "someone" oneself. And one is to care not only about oneself but about one's neighbor. So our discussion has not had an a-social cast. But it has had an individualistic cast in that, in the examples I have given of care, the recipients have all been individual persons and human beings. It seemed to me that when working out my version of agapism, it would be easiest to focus on persons and human beings as the recipients of care. But that's finished; it's time now to expand our field of vision.

Seeking to promote the flourishing of one's fellow human beings requires that one also seek to promote the flourishing of a wide variety of social entities of which those individuals are members or by which they are affected — families, clans, neighborhoods, cities, churches, synagogues, clubs, groups, peoples, states, agencies, institutions, enterprises, organizations. Impairment in the worth and the flourishing of social entities produces impairment in the flourishing of individuals. In a haunting and provocative passage from a letter that the Old Testament prophet Jeremiah sent to his fellow Jews exiled in Babylon, the prophet, speaking in the name of God, instructs his readers to "seek the welfare *(shalom)* of the city" and "pray to the LORD on its behalf, for in its welfare you will find your welfare" (Jeremiah 29:4-7). The same is true for you and me and for our cities: our flourishing is intertwined with the flourishing of our cities — and with the flourishing of very many of the other entities in our social environment. Care about one's neighbor has inescapable civic and political implications. By this I do not mean that care about one's neighbor includes encouraging him or her to take up civic and political responsibilities — though it does indeed include this. I mean that care about one's neighbor requires that one care about the worth and the flourishing of those social entities present in his environment.

To what extent, if at all, can we apply the account of care developed in the preceding pages to care about social entities? Sometimes it's said that social entities of the sorts mentioned are "mere fictions"; they aren't real. Presumably one cannot care about mere fictions. But it's a dark saying. When my bank sends me a letter informing me that it is in the process of closing down one of its branch offices, it's not telling me a story, it's not offering me a brief (unimaginative) piece of fiction. It's making an assertion, true or false. So far as I can see, that is not compatible with the bank itself being a "mere fiction."

Rather more often one hears it said that social entities are "nothing over and above" their members. What's apparently meant by this is that when we appear to be referring to social entities and talking about them, we are really referring to and talking about individuals. We cannot be referring to and talking about social entities since there are no such entities. To the best of my knowledge, most philosophers have given up on the attempt to work out this sort of reductionist view; I do so as well.

So let's agree that there are social entities. If one were of the view that the ontological status of such entities is that they are what logicians call *sets*, that would be a reason for holding that we cannot care about them, cannot promote their flourishing; for sets, obviously, are not the sorts of entities that can wax or wane in wellbeing or flourishing. They have no wellbeing. But I think it is as clear as anything could be that social entities are not sets. Sets have their memberships essentially; a set cannot have more, fewer, or different members from those it does have. But a city remains the identical city amid loss, gain, and change of residents.

We do in fact speak of the wellbeing and the flourishing of social entities, and we do so not only when employing the argot of philosophers but in ordinary discourse. I see no reason to think that, in doing so, we are speaking loosely or metaphorically. When Jeremiah spoke of the *shalom* of the city, he was speaking literally. Some developments in a city are good for the city, some are bad; some developments in a family are good for the family, some are bad; and so forth. And just as there are goods and evils in the life of a person that are not goods and evils *for* that person — they have no impact on his wellbeing — so too there are goods and evils in the career of a social entity that are not goods and evils *for* that entity. Anti-Semitism is an evil in the career of the Jewish people even if, in a given case, it has no adverse impact on the wellbeing of the Jewish people.

Some readers will have noted my use of the word "career" just now when speaking of social entities. Earlier in my discussion, when I was working out my account of agapism, I said that one's degree of flourishing is determined by the worth of states and events in one's life along with the worth of actions and activities that one performs. That explanation, when recalled in the present context, suggests the question, do social entities have lives? If not, does it not then follow that the account of care that we worked out cannot be applied straightforwardly to social entities?

Social entities are unlike human beings in that they are not biologically alive. But God is also unlike human beings in that respect; God is not biologically alive. Yet throughout my discussion I have been assuming that God has life. And as to social entities, it is worth noting that we do sometimes speak of the life of an organization, the life of an agency, etc. When we do so, are we speaking metaphorically? Or are we employing a generic concept of *life*, with biological life then being one species, God's life being another, and the life of social entities yet a third.

So far as I can see, nothing of substance hangs on how we answer this question. What is literally true of social entities is that they have *careers*, or *histories*, and that there are goods and evils in those careers, in those histories. It makes no difference whether one thinks that someone is speaking literally when he refers to the career of some social entity as its life or speaking metaphorically.

Those things that are goods and evils in the career of a social entity will include states and events in its career. Will they also include actions and activities that it performs? Are social entities like persons in this respect? Many of them, perhaps all of them, are indeed like persons in this respect. My city does things, the U.S. Congress does things, my bank does things, my university does things. It's true, of course, that a social entity can do something only by way of one or more persons doing something; Congress can pass a bill only by way of a majority of individual representatives or senators voting for the bill. But then it's Congress that passes the bill and Congress that institutes the legislation which the bill contains.

And social entities have rights; they can be wronged. Many of these rights are legal rights; a striking feature of the American legal system is that crimes in general are construed, for legal purposes, as offences against the state. But not all rights of social entities are legal rights; some are natural rights. And many of those that are legal rights are not the creature of law but the legal recognition of natural rights. We in the contemporary West appear to be less sensitive to the natural rights of social entities than were human beings in other times and places. Down through the ages cities have seen themselves as insulted, families as injured, peoples as demeaned; often they have been right in seeing themselves thus. In our society, agencies and institutions often see themselves as treated unfairly.

This leads to the observation that just as we can, and sometimes must, distinguish between the worth of a person or human being and the quality or worth of his or her life, so too we can and sometimes must distinguish between the worth of a social entity and the degree of its flourishing. A fine city may be undergoing a rough patch in its career due to drought, attacks by enemies, a decline in the economy, or whatever; and a mediocre city may be booming. A city, a family, a people, feels itself insulted when its worth is not recognized, when it is treated as having less worth than it does have.

Let me make one last point here. The relative worth of a social entity and the degree of its flourishing appear to me entirely determined by the contribution those make to the flourishing of human beings. A city is an estimable city insofar as it has in the past enhanced and does presently enhance the flourishing of human beings; a city flourishes insofar as the states and events in its career, the actions and activities it performs, enhance the flourishing of human beings. It follows that one's care about one's city — city here is a synecdoche for social entities in general — should always be instrumental in the structure of one's actions. Since the good of the city is not an intrinsic good, one should not seek to enhance that good as an end in itself

Over and over social entities escape their status of servants; instead of their serving us we serve them. We think of them as having intrinsic worth. We judge that the scope of an empire's conquests and the dazzle of its wealth contribute to its greatness without ever asking whether those conquests and that wealth served to advance the flourishing of persons and justice among them. And once we have taken that step of inscribing intrinsic worth to some social entity, then the flourishing of that entity, or what we regard as its flourishing, becomes for us an end in itself in the structure of our actions. We serve the state, the organization, the club. J. F. Kennedy famously declared in his Inaugural Address, "Ask not what your country can do for you, ask rather what you can do for your country." It was a false disjunction. Of course I am not just to ask what my country can do for me. But the alternative is not to give myself to my country "no questions asked." The alternative is to do what I can to bring it about that my country serves the flourishing of human beings and justice among them, both here and abroad.

We should not draw from these observations the conclusion that attachment and loyalty to one's family, one's country, one's university, one's enterprise, is misplaced. To the contrary: there is something seriously missing in a person's life if she has no attachment and no loyalty to any social entity whatsoever. As with attachments and loyalties in general, one does not become attached to some social entity and loyal to it because one judges it to be the best of its type. One becomes attached to a family and loyal to it because it is the family in which one was reared; one becomes attached to a country and loyal to it because it is the country in which one was born and of which one is a citizen. Attachment to one's family does not lead one to praise it above all others and approve whatever it does; discriminating attachment is what best serves the flourishing of one's family. So too for attachment to one's country and loyalty to it. Loyalty to one's country is fully compatible with lamenting what it does when it acts badly and with being one of its fiercest critics. Indeed, loyalty requires that.

CORRECTING THE IMPRESSION OF ANTHROPOCENTRISM

My discussion thus far has also had an anthropocentric cast; that too must now be corrected. Since I think it's obvious that the account of care I have developed applies to animals and to plants, I will be very brief. Animals and plants are like us in that they have biological life; and in those lives there are states and events, actions and activities, that are good for them and others that are bad for them. They possess wellbeing to one degree or another. And they can be wronged. There is much dispute over which ways of treating them constitutes wronging them; but there can be no disputing that cruelty to animals wrongs them. They are wronged when we torture them for our pleasure. They are wronged when, for our pleasure, we stage cock fights or dog fights in which the cocks or the dogs are provoked into mauling each other.[1]

---

1. In the seventeenth chapter of *Justice: Rights and Wrongs,* I give a much fuller account than I have here of the rights of social entities and of entities that have biological life but are not human.

Chapter Thirteen

IS CARE-AGAPISM TOO EASY?

THE AGAPISM ESPOUSED by classical members of the modern day agapist movement was hard to live by — in fact, impossible. The version of agapism that has emerged from our discussion may seem, by contrast, all too easy. We can keep our attachments to the members of our families, keep our solidarity with our fellow citizens, keep our compassion for the suffering who come within our ken. We can keep the care to which these "special relations" give rise; we do not have to root it out and replace it with the dutiful exercise of pure unsullied "neighbor love." We can continue to care about ourselves; we do not have to become doormats, indifferent to our own good and worth, caring only about others, always sacrificing ourselves. We must care about our enemies. But in some cases that requires no more than seeing to it that their worth is honored; we may not have to go beyond that. And though we may be called to visit prisoners, we will not be called to work to spring them all free; punishment is not intrinsically wrong. A rather easy ethic, so it would seem, certainly easy compared to the truly astringent versions of benevolence-agapism that are on offer.[1]

It is not easy. Egoism and eudaimonism are agent-oriented. The egoist says that the only person whose good one should seek to promote as an end in itself is oneself. Eudaimonism says that one may seek to promote not only one's own good as an end in itself but that of anyone else as well, provided, however, that doing so promises to be a constituent in one's own good. And then there is an ethic that I have not mentioned, popular among lay-people but not among theorists,[2] which says that one should do whatever one's roles require. Members of the army should follow the warrior's creed and do what a good warrior would do in the situation at hand. Businessmen should follow the creed of the

---

1. Easy or not, it is an ethic that is close to, if not perhaps quite identical with, Augustine's summary in *City of God,* 19.14. The order of the concord among human beings that God enjoins, says Augustine, "is first, that a man should harm no one, and, second, that he should do good to all, so far as he can. In the first place, therefore, he must care for his own household; for the order of nature and of human society itself gives him readier access to them, and greater opportunity of caring for them." Dyson translation, 941-42.

2. Though see Francis Herbert Bradley's "My Station and Its Duties," Essay 5 in *Ethical Studies* (London: H. S. King, 1876; repr. Charleston, SC: Nabu, 2010).

businessman and do what a good businessman would do in the situation at hand. And so forth.

Care-agapism is radically different from all of these in that it decenters the self. Believing, as he does, that the other has rights against him as to how he treats her, the care-agapist sets to the side for a time his own preoccupations so as to find out what those rights are; having discovered what they are, he seeks to secure that they are honored. Believing, as he also does, that in each case the good of the other has a unique contour, the care-agapist sets to the side for a time his own preoccupations so as to find out what that contour is; having discovered what it is, he seeks to promote those life-goods that he should. It's not easy, not easy at all, to de-center oneself in this way. Not easy to get out of oneself sufficiently to be able to imagine and think oneself into the rights and the goods of the other, and then to promote and honor those.

The self of the person who seeks to live by the moral law is also decentered. But instead of going out of himself to discover and promote the goods and the rights of others, he goes out of himself to discover what the moral law requires and to act in obedience thereto. For him it is law, and obedience to law, that are fundamental in the deep structure of morality, not the goods and the rights of persons and human beings. Care-agapism listens for and listens to the call of the other.

In trying to discover the goods and the rights of the other, and in seeking to promote the goods that he should promote and secure the rights that he ought to secure, the care-agapist does what he can to prevent his judgment being clouded and his responsiveness inhibited by the membership of the other in some out-group relative to himself. The history of humankind shows how hard this is; it was not easy in the past, it is not easy today. The other is an enemy combatant, we say, a terrorist, a communist, a capitalist, you name it. Thereby we cloud our judgment and harden our hearts.

The care-agapist does what he can to prevent his judgment being clouded and his responsiveness inhibited by his attachments to family, to friends, to colleagues, to neighbors — and by his attachment to himself. We all know how hard it is to liberate oneself from the confining grip of such attachments in order to make even a small financial sacrifice toward alleviating the conditions of those who live in poverty and misery. Again I refer to Peter Unger's book, *Living High and Letting Die*.

But perhaps the hardest teaching of the care-agapist is that retribution is forbidden. One is not to return evil for evil, not to get even, not to seek revenge, not even if one restrains oneself so as not to go beyond getting even. One is to care about one's enemy. Not many present day theorists offer a theoretical defense of the ancient reciprocity code. But the negative side of the code is deeply embedded within the psychological make-up of all of us.

In spite of all the best efforts of prison reformers over the past two centuries to turn prisons into penitentiaries and reformatories, American prisons remain almost totally unsuccessful in that regard. This is true in good measure because most Americans do not think of prisons in these terms; they think of them as places where we pay back the wrongdoer for what he did, where we give him what he's got coming to him, what he deserves. This reflects how difficult it is, when we find ourselves in the presence of evil, not to seek vengeance, not to hate. Here are two examples of the point.[3]

Insurgents strap bombs onto a handicapped girl and send her towards a military checkpoint. The soldiers hesitate to shoot her; when she gets close, the insurgents detonate the bombs. Three soldiers die, two survive. Later those two surviving soldiers are involved in the capture of the insurgents who, so they have learned, engineered the whole sordid affair.

A military convoy is traveling through a small village. An improvised explosive device is exploded under a vehicle full of men. Several of the men die, several are mangled. A crowd gathers around the vehicle chanting "death to the occupiers" and expressing great joy at the destruction. A gunner then trains his weapon on the crowd and gets ready to shoot what are clearly non-combatants. His commanding officer orders him to put down his weapon; the gunner trembles with rage.

It's not easy, not easy at all, for those two soldiers and that gunner to refrain from vengeance; it's hard, very hard, for the soldiers to honor the worth of the captured insurgents and for the gunner to honor the worth of the members of the cheering crowd.

Care-agapism requires that we de-center the self by caring about the other, not only about ourselves. It requires that we discard all those ways of categorizing our fellows that cloud our judgments concerning their goods and rights and that harden our hearts. It requires that we resist our impulse to take revenge. Care-agapism is not easy, not easy at all.

3. Given to me by Chris Eberle in private correspondence.

Chapter Fourteen

LOVE, JUSTICE, AND THE GOOD

IN THE COURSE OF OUR DISCUSSION we identified a number of different sorts of love. It was especially important for our purposes to highlight the difference between love as care and love as benevolence: love as care seeks both to advance someone's good and to honor her worth, and it can have not only the other as object but oneself. But along the way we also found it helpful to identify, as distinct modes of love, attraction-love, attachment-love, and advantage-love (self-love). Had it been important for our purposes we could have identified yet other forms of love — love as friendship, for example.

Much of the vagueness and confusion that one finds in discussions about love has its source in failure to get clear on just which sort of love is under consideration; clarity required drawing distinctions. But now, as we bring Part Two of our discussion to a close, let us reverse course and look beneath the distinctions to the deeper-lying phenomena of which they are examples or manifestations.

ORIENTATIONS TOWARD THE GOOD

Love in all its forms is the manifestation of one or more of three fundamental orientations toward the good. Begin with the orientation that consists of seeking to *bring about* some good. Whether or not the intent succeeds, let us call this orientation *benefaction*.

Benefaction can manifest itself in seeking to create something of worth, that is, in seeking to bring about a new locus of goodness; alternatively, it can manifest itself in seeking to enhance the flourishing or the worth of something already in existence. The latter sort of manifestation can take the form of care, it can take the form of advantage-love, or it can take the form of benevolence, that is, of seeking to advance the good of the other as an end in itself with no consideration of whether or not justice requires that of one.[1] It was this last form of benefaction that

---

1. I should make explicit what the reader will have noticed, that throughout my discussion I have used "benevolence" where the etymologically more precise term would be "beneficence."

the modern day agapist movement mistakenly identified with New Testament agape.[2]

Care differs from benevolence in that one can care about oneself;[3] it differs from advantage-love in that one can care about another; and it differs from both in that the good it seeks to bring about includes not only the flourishing of oneself or the other but due respect for the worth of oneself or the other. It is because of this last feature that care includes seeking justice.

Our human benefaction is consequence and imitation of God's benefaction. God's benefaction comes in the form both of benefaction as creation and benefaction as care. In discussing modern day agapism I observed that the most important clue to understanding the line of thought of the modern day agapists is that they think of all divine love on the model of divine forgiveness. Thus there is in the modern day agapists an unmistakable reluctance to say much about God's creative activity. The picture that emerges from Nygren's *Agape and Eros* is that of human beings somehow already on the scene, lacking all worth, doing wrong, and of God then forgiving them for their wrongdoing and thereby creating in them the worth of being loved by God in the mode of forgiveness. A curious picture indeed!

Escaping from the conundra and paradoxes of modern day agapism required rejecting the assumption that all divine love is to be understood on the model of God's forgiveness of the sinner. God's forgiveness of the sinner is but one manifestation of God's care; God's care is but one manifestation of God's benefaction; and God's benefaction is but one mode of God's orientation toward the good.

Speaking of God's creative activity brings to mind the refrain that occurs six times in the opening chapter of Genesis, "God saw that it was good." The litany culminates with the declaration, upon the creation of human beings, that "God saw everything that God had made, and indeed, it was very good."

Coming to expression here is an orientation toward the good distinct from that of benefaction. Rather than seeking to bring about some good, this orientation consists of *acknowledging* a good already there. In Chapter Three I took note of attraction-love and described it as being drawn to something on account of its worth, relishing it, delighting in it, reveling in it, enjoying it, being gripped by it; I remarked

---

2. Kierkegaard was an exception. Since he thought that agape should extend to oneself, he would not have agreed that agape is a species of benevolence.

3. In Chapter Ten, to make it easier to discuss Kierkegaard's position I used "benevolence" to include seeking one's own good. It is only in that chapter that I used the word in that way. The rest of the time I have used the word in the ordinary way; benevolence is seeking the good *of the other.*

that such love is what Plato called *eros* in his dialogue, *The Symposium.*
Attraction-love is one manifestation of that orientation toward the
good that I call *acknowledgment.* Other manifestations are praise, grati-
tude, and admiration.

Rendering to someone what justice requires because justice requires
it is at one and the same time a manifestation of that orientation toward
the good that is benefaction and that orientation that is acknowledgment. To treat the other justly is to advance her life-good in some respect; that is benefaction. It is also to pay her what due respect for her
worth requires; that is acknowledgment. In doing justice, benefaction
and acknowledgment are united. And because care incorporates acting
justly, care likewise unites benefaction with acknowledgment.

The overarching thesis of Nygren's *Agape and Eros* was that the "motifs" of *agapē, eros,* and *nomos* (justice) are locked in never-ending com-
bat; one has to choose sides. But not only does care incorporate *nomos*
(justice). By incorporating justice, care joins with *eros* as a manifestation
of that orientation toward the good which is acknowledgment.

There remains love as attachment. Given the two orientations toward
the good that we have identified, production of the good and acknowledgment of the good, what space is left for a third orientation? What additional orientation could there be?

The clue to the answer lies in the fact that attachment-love makes
one vulnerable to such emotions as worry, sorrow, and grief. Willing the
good makes one susceptible to the disappointment and regret of failing
to bring about the good one sought to bring about; acknowledgment of
the good makes one susceptible to the disappointment and regret of
watching the good one acknowledges disappear. But neither of these
orientations makes one susceptible to worry, sorrow, grief, and the like
— nor to the kind of elation that is the opposite of sorrow and grief.

To be attached to something is to be emotionally invested in it — specifically, to be emotionally invested in the good of its endurance, in the
good of its flourishing and its being treated with due respect for its
worth, and in the good of one's engagement with it. The mother's attachment to her child is her emotional investment in the good of his
continuing life, in the good of his flourishing and his being treated with
due respect for his worth, and in the good of her own relationship to
the child. The child's attachment to his stuffed animal is his emotional
investment in the good of the animal's not being destroyed, in the good
of its not being mutilated, and in the good of his own relationship to
the animal. In short, the orientation toward the good manifested in attachment is *emotional investment* in the good — or just *investment,* for
short. The emotional investment lying at the heart of attachment is
what makes one susceptible to worry, sorrow, grief, and the like — and

open to elation. When the life of the person to whom one is attached seems threatened, one worries; when he dies, one grieves.

We are each attached to ourselves and susceptible, for that reason, to worry when our own life seems endangered, to sorrow when our flourishing is diminished, to joy when it is enhanced. Nothing remarkable in that. What is remarkable is that we can and do go outside ourselves to invest ourselves in others, thereby de-centering the self. Given my attachment to my child, I now worry not only over threats to my life but over threats to his life, I now sorrow not only over impairments in my flourishing but over impairments in his flourishing, I now get angry not only over insults to myself but over insults to him. We speak of the person whose attachments are few or weak as "pinched" and "narrow." We speak of people in old age whose friends have all died as "pulling back," "withdrawing," "retreating into themselves."

Orientation toward the good in the mode of investment provides some of life's most rewarding experiences. But it's dangerous, dangerous for both lover and loved. The danger for the lover lies in the fact that she has made herself emotionally vulnerable. The danger for the beloved lies in the fact that all too often the love of the lover becomes smothering, domineering, possessive, jealous.

Three fundamental orientations toward the good: benefaction, acknowledgment, and investment. Doing justice blends benefaction with acknowledgment; by virtue of incorporating justice, care does so as well. And investment in the mode of attachment typically calls forth benefaction in the mode of care.

DIVINE LOVE AND HUMAN RIGHTS

In my book, *Justice: Rights and Wrongs,* I argued that the conviction that God loves each and every human being equally and forever provides those who hold that conviction with a distinct way of grounding natural human rights. Since this claim, if true, is obviously an important aspect of the full picture of the relation between love and justice, let me repeat the highlights of my argument while also approaching some points from a somewhat different angle and fleshing out the argument here and there. By "grounding" natural human rights I mean, explaining why we have them.

My understanding of the concept of human rights is the common one. A human right is a right such that the status sufficient for possessing the right is that of being a human being. One does not have to be a *Greek* human being, one does not have to be a *male* human being, one does not have to be an *educated* human being. One does not have to be any particular kind of human being whatsoever. It's enough that one be a human being. And since someone who is a human being cannot cease to be a human being so long as she remains in existence, human rights are ineradicable. The literature on rights in general, and on human rights in particular, reveals that it is easy to confuse *human rights* with *the rights that human beings have*. But the former constitute no more than a species of the latter; we each have many rights that are not human rights.

If animals have rights, as I hold they do, then, since humans are animals of a sort, there will presumably be some among our natural human rights that animals also have. Nonetheless, it would be impossible to read around in the literature on human rights and miss the common assumption that human rights are distinctly *human*. The idea has to be that the *total package* of one's human rights contains rights that no non-human animal has. And not just different rights. Human rights go beyond animal rights, in that there are ways of treating an animal that are permissible if the animal is non-human but not permissible if the animal is human. So-called *species-ism* is built into the idea of human rights; those who reject species-ism reject human rights. It follows that if human rights are grounded in the worth that one has *qua* human being, that worth has to go beyond the worth that any non-human animal has.

It is commonly assumed that all human rights are universal; but that seems to me not correct. For some human rights, there are circumstances such that those in one or another of those circumstances do not have the right even though they are human. The right to police protection is an example. For anyone who has a right to police protection, the status sufficient for having the right is that of being a human being; it's not required that one be some particular kind of human being. But in many societies of the past there was no police force. Accordingly, those whose circumstance was that of living in such a society did not have a right to police protection; they were not wronged on account of not being protected by police. By contrast, the right not to be tortured for the pleasure of the torturer is a human right that is universal. Not only is having the status of being human sufficient for possessing the right; in any circumstance in which a human being ever finds himself, he has the right.

The distinction employed in the last several paragraphs, between one's *status* and one's *circumstance,* is such that sometimes it's not clear whether a description is a description of one's status — that is to say, of what one is like — or of one's circumstance. It would be desirable if I could offer a precise definition of the two concepts. I cannot. Nonetheless, we need the distinction. If we said that a human right is a right one possesses just by virtue of being human, it would turn out that there

were very few human rights, only those that are universal. The right to
police protection would not be a human right. Being a human being is
not sufficient for having the right; one also has to be in a particular sort
of circumstance.

The various UN declarations on human rights all declare or assume
that human rights are grounded in the dignity of the rights-holders;
likewise, most theoretical attempts at grounding human rights attempt
to ground them in the dignity of the rights-holders.[4] Since it is my view
that rights in general are grounded in the worth of the rights-holder, I
agree that a dignity-grounding is what we must look for.

Those who favor a dignity-grounding of human rights all assume, so
far as I know, that *qua* human we are all equal in dignity. Human beings
vary greatly in the worth they have on account of native endowments,
achievements, relations in which they stand, and so forth. But it's assumed that there is something about our being human that gives us
equal dignity — a dignity greater than that of any animal and one we
cannot lose, short of ceasing to be human. My discussion of natural human rights in *Justice: Rights and Wrongs* was thus predicated on the conviction that all human beings are uniquely precious, not just those who
are capable of fully functioning as persons but also infants who are not
yet capable of so functioning, Alzheimer's patients who are no longer
capable, and the mentally impaired who are never capable.

Because of the equal, ineradicable, and animal-transcending dignity
each human being has *qua* human being, none may be carved up for
stew, none may be shot and tossed into a dumpster for waste manage-
ment to haul away, none may be deposited on a mountain side to die,
none may be tortured for the vengeance or the pleasure of the torturer.
To do any of these things to any human being would be to demean
them, to treat them with under-respect, to treat them in a way that does
not befit their worth. Human rights are what respect requires for the
equal, ineradicable, and animal-transcending dignity that we each have
qua human being.

The big challenge facing the theorist who believes that there are human rights and that they are grounded in our equal, ineradicable, and
animal-transcending dignity, is to identify that feature or relationship of
human beings on which that dignity supervenes. To identify successfully
that feature or relationship would be to *ground* human rights. And there
must be such a feature or relationship. Worth, dignity, excellence, does
not settle on things willy-nilly; always there's something about the thing
that gives it worth, something that accounts for its worth, something on

4. An important exception is Alan Gewirth. In the fifteenth chapter of *Justice: Rights
and Wrongs*, I lay out Gewirth's theory and explain why, in my view, it is unsuccessful.

which its worth supervenes. If the piano sonata that you composed is a fine sonata, then there's something about your composition that makes it fine. We may find it difficult if not impossible to put into words what that is; but it makes no sense to say that it's a fine sonata but that there's nothing about it that makes it fine.

Almost all secular attempts at accounting for the dignity that grounds human rights do so by appealing to certain capacities that human beings possess; and almost all of those, in turn, follow Kant in appealing to the capacity for rational agency. Ronald Dworkin stands out from the crowd in suggesting that the dignity in question supervenes not on possession of certain capacities but on the way in which we human beings are "created." Human beings, says Dworkin, are masterpieces of natural- and self-creation; our equal, ineradicable, and animal-transcending dignity supervenes on that.

Why Capacity Accounts of Human Dignity Do Not Work

In *Justice: Rights and Wrongs,* I argued that the attempt to account for the dignity that grounds human rights by reference to the capacity for rational agency cannot be successful. Let me here cite two reasons for that conclusion.

First, the capacity for rational agency comes in degrees, so the worth a human being has on account of possessing the capacity also comes in degrees. But that violates the equal-worth proviso. Add to this that human beings also do a better or worse job of exercising whatever particular capacity for rational agency they possess; and if human beings have worth *qua* rational agents, then, of those who have the same capacity, presumably those who exercise it better have more worth.

Corresponding to the capacity for rational agency is the property of *possessing that capacity to some degree or other and of exercising one's particular capacity with some competence or other;* and that property does not come in degrees. Either one has it or one does not; one cannot have it to some degree or other. So someone might suggest that the equal, ineradicable, and animal-transcending dignity that we all have just *qua* human supervenes on possessing that property.

But notice that the reason for thinking that dignity supervenes on possessing that property is the prior conviction that dignity supervenes on possessing and exercising the capacity. And as we have just noted, both the extent of the capacity for rational agency that one possesses, and the competence with which one exercises the extent of one's capacity, come in degrees. So the equal dignity that supervenes on possessing the capacity to some degree or other and exercising it with some competence or other is inextricably linked to the differential dignity that supervenes on the particular extent of the capacity one possesses and one's competence in exercising it. It is, in fact, just the minimum of the differential dignity that we each have by virtue of our particular possession and exercise of the capacity. The very thing that gives some bit of dignity to each human being gives a highly differentiated dignity. If that's the best we can do, we'll have to ask ourselves, "What then?" But rather than spending time answering that question, let's take note of a second, more menacing, problem.

Some of the higher animals appear to be capable of rational agency; so the dignity that supervenes on possession of the capacity is not animal-transcending. To cope with this fact, we could "beef up" the capacity for rational agency until we felt sure that no non-human animal has the capacity. We could say that the relevant capacity is the capacity for rational *moral* agency, or that it is the capacity to form, revise, and enact a life-plan. I assume that no non-human animal has those capacities. Or we could take a slightly different tack and say that the relevant capacity is the capacity to function as a person; functioning as a person includes possessing the capacity for rational agency but more as well. Presumably no non-human animal is capable of functioning as a person.

But the more we beef up the capacity to assure ourselves that no non-human animal possesses the capacity, the greater will be the number of human beings who also do not possess the capacity. It was already true of the non-beefed-up capacity for rational agency that some human beings do not possess the capacity. Infants do not yet have the capacity; adults suffering from dementia no longer have the capacity; those human beings who are severely impaired mentally from birth never have the capacity.

In *Justice: Rights and Wrongs* I explored the possibility of getting those human beings who lack the capacity for rational agency into the "circle of dignity" by thinning out the relevant relation between a human being and the capacity. Though infants do not possess the capacity for rational agency, many of them stand in the relation to that capacity of *going to possess* it, Alzheimer's patients stand in the relation to that capacity of *once having possessed it,* and those who are severely impaired mentally from birth stand in the relation to that capacity of *being member of a species whose adult properly formed members possess it.* Indeed, every human being stands in relation to the capacity in that last relationship. But at this point we have to ask ourselves two questions. Does standing in that relation to the capacity give one sufficient dignity to ground one's human rights? And do not those well-formed primates who are in fact capable of rational agency have more dignity?

I should make clear that I too am of the view that the capacity for rational or moral agency gives those who possess the capacity great worth — differential worth, since the capacity comes in degrees. So too the capacity for forming, enacting, and revising a life-plan gives great worth to those who possess it, as does the capacity for functioning as a person. My point is that there are some human beings who lack these capacities.

So far as I can see, every attempt to account for some equal, ineradicable, and animal-transcending dignity that we possess *qua* human beings by appealing to a capacity of some sort will confront exactly the same problems as those confronted by the attempt to account for that dignity by reference to the capacity for rational agency. And as to Dworkin's non-capacity account: severely impaired human beings are not masterpieces of natural- and self-creation.

Does Human Nature or the *Imago Dei* Ground Human Rights?

So what to do? Some will continue to believe that there are natural human rights but will give up on the attempt to discover what grounds them; why bang one's head against the wall? Others will conclude that it was a mistake to believe that there are natural human rights. They may continue to hold that there are natural rights of other sorts — the rights of persons, for example. Or they may scrap the whole idea of natural rights. But suppose that we are not yet ready to give up in despair on the attempt to articulate a dignity-grounding of human rights. Which direction of search looks most promising?

Well, standing in some relation to someone or something sometimes gives us worth. So we might try to find some being, or type of being, and some relation, such that every human being stands in that relation to that being or a being of that type, and such that standing in that relation to the being bestows on one the worth we are looking for. It will, of course, have to be a relation such that standing in the relation to the being in question does not presuppose any capacities on one's part,

I think that easily the most plausible candidate for the being in question is God. Those who believe that there is no God will of course not find God a plausible candidate. But even they can ask, in hypothetical mode, whether theism provides a way of grounding human rights. The main question to consider is what might be the worth-bestowing relation.

A suggestion often made by theologians is that human rights are grounded in the dignity we all have on account of bearing the *imago dei*. To decide whether this suggestion is correct, we have to know what constitutes the *imago dei*. The history of Christian (and Jewish) thought contains a quite astounding diversity of understandings of the *imago*. To the best of my knowledge, however, all of them are of one or the other of two sorts.

Some writers understand the *imago dei* to consist of resembling God with respect to the possession and exercise of certain capacities; others understand it to consist of resembling or representing God with respect to the exercise of a certain role in creation — the role of "having dominion," for example. All the roles proposed require exercising certain capacities. So the main point made above concerning secular attempts to ground dignity in capacities applies here as well: whatever capacities one might single out, some human beings do not have those capacities. Some do not yet have them, some no longer have them, some never have them. But if a given human being does not possess those capacities, then of course she does not resemble God with respect to possessing them, nor does she resemble or represent God with respect to the role in creation that the capacities enable. If the *imago dei* is understood in either of the traditional ways, there are human beings who lack the *imago dei*.

Though I know of no theologian who explicitly takes note of this implication of his position, few if any would find it acceptable. There is a long theological tradition which holds that the image of God in us has been impaired by sin; but few theologians would accept that some human beings lack the image entirely. So is there some way of understanding the *imago dei* that does not have this implication?

In *Justice: Rights and Wrongs* I proposed a nature-resemblance account of the *imago dei*, in place of the standard capacity-resemblance and role-resemblance accounts. No matter how seriously impaired a human being may be, she nonetheless possesses human nature. And in possessing such a nature, she resembles God. Human nature is like the divine nature in that mature, properly functioning specimens of human nature possess God-like capacities and play a God-like role in creation;

Every human being bears the *imago dei*, thus understood. So the question to be considered is whether our bearing the image so understood bestows on us an equal, ineradicable, and animal-transcending dignity. Does the dignity we are looking for supervene on standing to God in the relation of bearing the image of God, image being understood along nature-resemblance lines?

We can treat the question in two stages. Is the fact that one possesses human nature sufficient, by itself, to impart to one the relevant dignity? If not, does the relevant dignity supervene on resembling God with respect to possessing such a nature? If the right answer to the former of these two questions is "Yes," then those secularists who agree that human beings have a nature thereby have a way of grounding natural human rights. In place of the standard capacity accounts of human dignity, theirs will be a human nature account.

In *Justice: Rights and Wrongs,* I suggested that a way to think about the first of these two questions is to regard our nature as our design-plan and then to consider what we would say about other cases of well-formed and malformed exemplifications of a design-plan. I offered the following case. Suppose that my neighbors to the east and to the west both own examples of the same model of automobile; both own Jaguars, let us say. The example that my neighbor to the east owns runs like a top, and I admire it enormously. The example that my neighbor to the west owns has been in a serious crash. It has been, as they say, "totaled." The repair shops all tell my neighbor that repair is impossible. Sell it for scrap, they say.

Would I advise my neighbor to the west to reject this advice and hold onto his automobile? Would I tell him that the repair shops, in giving their advice, were ignoring the fact that his automobile is an example of a truly noble model, and that his own Jaguar is, on that account, to be admired and prized? Would I advise him to build an addition to his garage, hire a wrecker to deposit his ruined Jaguar gently in the garage, and keep it protected with a dust cover?

I would not give him that advice. The conclusion I drew from the analogy in *Justice: Rights and Wrongs* is that possessing human nature cannot, all by itself, ground human rights.

There may be some readers who would give different advice. Even though the Jaguar of my neighbor to the west is a total wreck, they would advise him to keep it and treasure it on the ground that the model itself, the design-plan, is truly noble. If there are such readers, I invite them to take the next step of comparing my neighbor's wrecked example of that truly admirable model with an operating example of a somewhat less admirable model — a well-running Toyota, let us say. Is not the latter automobile more admirable than the former? Be it granted that *the model* of which the former is an example is more admirable than *the model* of which the latter is an example. But we are talking now not about the models but about the automobiles. I judge that the latter automobile is more admirable than the former.

The application is obvious. It may be that a severely impaired human being has some worth just on account of possessing human nature. But does not a well-functioning chimpanzee or porpoise have more worth? What we need for our purposes is an animal-transcending worth.

What then about *resembling* God with respect to the nature one possesses? Does the fact that one resembles God in possessing a nature such that those in whom it is properly functioning possess God-like capacities — does the fact of that resemblance impart to a human being the requisite dignity even if she herself is so severely malformed that she does not have those capacities? Not so far as I can see. If possessing human nature does not itself impart to one the requisite dignity, I fail to see how resembling God with respect to possessing such a nature does so.

A Theistic Account of Human Dignity

Several times now I have made the point that if it is by virtue of our standing in some relation to God that we all have the equal, ineradicable, and animal-transcending dignity that grounds human rights, it will have to be a relation such that standing in the relation in no way presupposes capacities on one's part. If one adopts what I called a *nature-resemblance* account of the *imago dei,* then standing to God in the relation of bearing the image of God satisfies that criterion; it does not presuppose any capacities on one's part. But though the relation satisfies that criterion, it nonetheless proved not capable of doing the work required. We have to look for a different relation.

In *Justice: Rights and Wrongs,* I suggested that the relation to God of being loved by God does the work required. Initially, the suggestion does not look promising. Love as attraction will not do the work required since, rather than bestowing worth, such love acknowledges the worth already there. Love as benevolence or benefaction fares no better. Such love may well bring about the enhancement of the worth of its object. But what we are looking for is not a form of love that *causes* or *brings about* enhancement of worth but one that *as such* bestows worth on its object. It's the *being loved* that gives one the worth, not what the love causes. The fact that the Alzheimer's patient is a recipient of love-bestowing worth has to be compatible with the fact that she remains an Alzheimer's patient.

So what about love as attachment? Well, here it's important that we be clear on the difference between love that *bestows* worth on the beloved and love that gives to certain ways of treating the beloved what I shall call *transitive moral significance.* A passage from John Calvin's commentary on Genesis is useful for making the point. Calvin is commenting on Genesis 9:6, "Whoever sheds the blood of a human, by a human shall that person's blood be shed, for in his own image God made humankind." This is Calvin's comment:

> Men are indeed unworthy of God's care, if respect be had only to themselves; but since they bear the image of God engraven on them, he deems himself violated in their person. Thus, although they have nothing of their own by which they obtain the favour of God, he looks upon his own gifts in them, and is thereby excited to love and to care for them. This doctrine, however, is to be carefully observed, that no one can be injurious to his brother without wounding God himself. Were this doctrine deeply fixed in our minds, we should be much more reluctant than we are to inflict injuries.

Calvin is here ascribing transitive moral significance to the act of injuring a human being: by injuring the human being, one wrongs ("wounds," "violates") God. On first reading of the passage, it appears to be Calvin's view that injuring a human being has this transitive moral significance because he or she bears the image of God: "since they bear the image of God engraven on them, [God] deems himself violated in their person." But on closer reading it appears that that was not his thought. God, says Calvin, is "excited to love and to care" for human beings by discerning in them his gift to them of his image. Discerning the image evokes the love; but it is because God loves human beings that injuring them has the transitive moral significance that Calvin ascribes to it: "no one can be injurious to his brother without wounding God himself." Let's add what seems to be implied: God's love for human beings is God's attachment to them, the attachment being evoked by God's "discerning" that they image God; God's care for human beings is then evoked by God's attachment to them.

On account of God's attachment to human beings, one wrongs God by injuring a human being. This transitive moral significance of injuries done to one's fellow human beings is awesome indeed, as Calvin suggests, and constitutes an important element in the complete picture. But the fact that injuring a human being has this transitive moral significance does not imply that the human being *herself* has a worth that she would not have had absent God's attachment to her. It does not imply that I wrong *her* by injuring her. Wronging God by injuring her is not to be identified with wronging *her* by injuring her. If I wantonly destroy a piece of furniture you made of which you are proud and to which you are attached, I wrong you; but I do not wrong the piece of furniture. If God's love of human beings is to account for the worth that grounds human rights, that love has to impart to *them* a worth that otherwise they would not have; giving transitive moral significance to injuring them is not enough.

So once again, what sort of love might do the work required? Well, imagine a monarch. He's a good monarch, loved by all his subjects; he bestows on all of them the great good of a just political order that serves the common good. But he's rather lonely. So in addition to being a benefactor to all his subjects, he decides to choose a few of his subjects as people that he would like to be friends with. This, for the ones chosen, is an honor. "I am honored that you would choose me for a friend," they say. No doubt over the course of time various goods in their lives will ensue from being friends with the monarch. But just to be chosen as one with whom the king would like to be a friend is an honor. Those chosen will cite that fact under "Honors" in their *curricula vitae*. Those not chosen will be envious.

And now for the crucial point. To be honored is to have worth bestowed on one. Admittedly this is somewhat mysterious. But the indicator of the fact that this is what happens is that to be honored is to acquire new ways of being demeaned, new ways of being wronged, a new ground for respect; and that's possible only if there has been some alteration in one's worth. The most obvious way in which one can now be demeaned is, of course, by having the honor itself belittled. One who has not been chosen by the monarch for friendship sarcastically remarks to someone who has been chosen, "Big deal!" The latter has a right to be angry; this is a snub. Depending on the situation, the snub may also amount to snubbing the one who gave the honor; but in any case, it amounts to snubbing the one honored. Honoring bestows worth.

Sometimes an honor is bestowed as a way of recognizing worth, sometimes not. The monarch's choice of a few subjects as those he would like to be friends with is not his way of declaring that these are the most estimable of his subjects. The monarch must, of course, spot some potential for friendship in those he chooses; and in some cases there will be obstacles to the realization of the potential that the monarch, in cooperation with his subject, has to work at overcoming. But that's different from selecting them for friendship because they are the most estimable in the realm and as a way of declaring that they are.

The application of the analogy will be obvious. Suppose that one is chosen by God as someone with whom God wants to be friends.[5] That is to be honored by God. And to be honored by God is to have worth bestowed upon one. Add now that every human being has the honor of being chosen by God as someone with whom God wants to be friends. Then every human being has the worth that being so honored bestows on one.

A question to raise is whether, on this view of things, it is purely whimsical and arbitrary on God's part to choose human beings as the creatures with whom God wants to be friends. Might God just as well have chosen, say, crocodiles? No. I remarked that though the monarch does not look for the most estimable people in the realm when settling on those he would like to be friends with, he does look for those in whom he sees potential for friendship. Crocodiles lack the potential for being friends with God. It's incompatible with crocodile nature. To be a friend with God one has to have the nature of a person. Crocodiles at their best cannot be persons. Of all the animals, it's only human animals that can function as persons.

The very same consideration that makes it understandable why God did not choose crocodiles for friendship makes it understandable why

5. "The will for fellowship [is God's] very being." Karl Barth, *Church Dogmatics*, Vol. 2, Part 2, 26.

God chose human beings. Since it's in our nature to be persons, we have the potential for friendship with God. Of course there are blockages to the realization of that potential that have to be overcome by God and by us. The moral breach between us of our having wronged God will have to be repaired; and those who cannot presently function as persons will have to be healed, in this life or the life to come, of that deep malformation.

Earlier I said that, so far as I could see, possessing human nature does not, by itself, provide us with a worth sufficient for grounding human rights, and that resembling God with respect to possessing such a nature does not add the requisite worth. It now turns out, however, that human nature and the *imago dei* are not irrelevant to a full account of human dignity. They make it understandable that God would choose human beings for friendship and not the non-human animals. Given our nature, we have the potential for friendship; given their nature, they do not.

Notice that the answer I have given to the question whether God's desire for friendship with human beings and not with other animals is whimsical and arbitrary is not an explanation of God's desire for friendship with human beings. Our possessing human nature provides the potential for friendship between God and us. It's a necessary condition for friendship. But it's not an explanation. The explanation for God's wanting to be friends with us is presumably much like the explanation for why we want to be friends with some fellow human being. We seek to become friends with someone not because we think he merits it, not because his worth requires it, but because we anticipate that our friendship will be a significant good in the lives of both of us. So too for God's desire to be friends with us.

Those who are not theists will of course not accept this theistic account of human worth. But there are also a good many theists who, for one reason or another, will not accept it. So it's worth asking, in conclusion, whether one finds, in any of the theistic traditions, the theme that God honors each human being by choosing him or her as someone with whom God wants to be friends, or whether this idea amounts to an *ad hoc* innovation on my part motivated by trying to secure a dignity-grounding for human rights.

This theme — of God as honoring us by choosing us as creatures God wants to be friends with and then taking steps to overcome the obstacles to friendship — this theme is in fact pervasive in the Christian tradition. Let me quote a recent sounding of the theme. It occurs in a passage from Marilyn Adams's book, *Horrendous Evils and the Goodness of God.* Nowhere in her book does Adams have human rights in mind; so I cannot be accused of "cherry picking." In the final judgment, says Adams, "God will be seen to have honored the patriarchs by making them His friends, Israel through election and the giving of the Law, making them a nation by His going out and coming in with them, through all of their trials. According to the Christian point of view, the Maker of all things has honored the human race by becoming a member of it, honored all who suffer horrendous evils by identifying with them through His passion and death. Still more amazing, God will be seen to have honored even the perpetrators of horrors by identifying with their condition, becoming ritually cursed through His death on a tree, taking His stand with the cursed to cancel the power of curse forever!"[6]

6. Marilyn McCord Adams, *Horrendous Evils and the Goodness of God* (Ithaca: Cornell University Press, 1999), 127.

PART THREE

Just and Unjust Love

Chapter Fifteen

WHAT IS FORGIVENESS?

IN THE PREFACE I REMARKED that a persistent theme in discussions about the relation between love and justice is the theme of conflict: love often is, or appears to be, unjust; justice often is, or appears to be, unloving. It's time to take up that theme and analyze some examples of real or apparent conflict. A consequence of our previous discussion is that the examples now look somewhat different from the way they looked before. Examples that were previously seen as cases of real or apparent conflict between benevolence-love and justice are now also to be seen as cases of real or apparent malformation of care.

Warfare is thick with examples of real or apparent conflict between benevolence-love and justice. We ought to protect these people here against assault and menace; not to do so would be irresponsible. But how can we do so without wronging those people over there? I will not be analyzing examples of this type, important though they are, mainly because doing so with adequate depth would require a book of its own. Instead I will analyze examples of three other types of real or apparent tension that have received attention in the literature on love and justice. Forgiveness of a wrongdoer is sometimes said to violate justice, along with such near relatives of forgiveness as pardon, amnesty, and the like. Gratuitous benefits are sometimes distributed in a way that violates justice. And love is sometimes unjust in its paternalism. I will take these up in the order of mention.

HANNAH ARENDT ON THE DISCOVERY OF FORGIVENESS

In a well-known passage in her book *The Human Condition,* Hannah Arendt remarked that "the discoverer of the role of forgiveness in the realm of human affairs was Jesus of Nazareth."[1] She goes on to say that "the fact that [Jesus] made this discovery in a religious context and articulated it in religious language is no reason to take it any less seriously in a strictly secular sense" (215).

Forgiveness, she says, is "the necessary corrective for the inevitable

1. (Garden City, NY: Doubleday Anchor Books, 1959), 214-15.

damages resulting from action" (215). It constitutes "redemption from the predicament of irreversibility — of being unable to undo what one has done." The remedy for unpredictability, by contrast, "is contained in the faculty to make and keep promises. The two faculties [of forgiving and of promising] belong together in so far as one of them, forgiving, serves to undo the deeds of the past, whose 'sins' hang like the sword of Damocles over every new generation, and the other, binding oneself through promises, serves to set up in the ocean of uncertainty, which is the future by definition, islands of security without which not even continuity, let alone durability of any kind, would be possible in the relationships between men" (212-13).

I think Arendt was correct when she said that Jesus was the discoverer of the role of forgiveness in human affairs; her account of his "discovery" seems to me not quite on target, however. Arendt's claim that Jesus was the discoverer of the role of forgiveness in human affairs presupposes that the ancient pagan ethical writers did not recognize the importance of forgiveness. In the next chapter I will defend that claim, and ask whether the failure of the ancient pagan writers to praise and urge forgiveness was merely accidental. But Arendt's claim also presupposes that the writers of the Hebrew Bible were no different from the ancient pagan ethical writers on this score.

Over and over the writers of the Hebrew Bible declare that God's love for God's wayward human creatures is manifested in God's forgiveness of sinners. As we saw in previous chapters, the modern day agapists extrapolated from this declaration to claim that divine forgiveness is not just one among other manifestations of divine love but exemplary of God's love in general and paradigmatic for ours. Seldom, however, do the writers of the Hebrew Bible attribute forgiveness to human beings;[2] and never (to the best of my knowledge) do they enjoin someone to forgive his fellows. The emphatic insistence by Jesus that we human beings are to forgive each other was thus indeed new.

Luke reports Jesus as saying on one occasion, "If another disciple sins, you must rebuke the offender, and if there is repentance, you must forgive. And if the same person sins against you seven times a day, and turns back to you seven times and says, 'I repent,' you must forgive" (Luke 17:3-4). One imagines the disciples talking with each other about this injunction and finding it hard to swallow; must one really forgive someone *seven* times? To check out whether Jesus really meant to say that one is to forgive a repetitively repentant wrongdoer, Peter asks Jesus, in Matthew's narrative, "Lord, if my brother sins against me, how of-

---

2. Two examples: Esau apparently forgives Jacob in Genesis 33, and Joseph apparently forgives his brothers in Genesis 45.

ten should I forgive? As many as seven times?" Jesus offers a hyperbolic reply, "Not seven times but, I tell you, seventy-seven times" (Matthew 18:21-22). Jesus then goes on to tell the parable of the servant whose master forgave his huge debt but who himself refused to forgive the small debt of one of his own debtors. The master, upon hearing of the behavior of his servant, had him punished severely. Jesus explained, as the point of the parable, that if we do not, out of mercy, forgive those who wrong us, our heavenly Father will not forgive us.

So Arendt was correct in her claim that Jesus' teaching and practice constituted a decisively new event in the history of forgiveness. But it was not certain "experiences in the small and closely knit community of his followers" that led Jesus to his "discovery" (215). Jesus was led to his "discovery" by his conviction that God's forgiveness of us, and our forgiveness of each other, are intertwined: we are to be like God in forgiving those who wrong us, and we are to pray that God will forgive our wronging of God as we forgive those who wrong us.

Forgiveness Thought to Violate Justice

Forgiveness has long appeared to many a violation of justice. So if forgiveness is motivated by love, then forgiveness is the site of conflict, real or apparent, between justice and love. Consider how Anselm stated his problem with forgiveness. Addressing God in the *Proslogion*[3] he asks:

> How do you spare the wicked if You are all-just and supremely just? For how does the all-just and supremely just One do something that is unjust? Or what kind of justice is it to give everlasting life to him who merits eternal death? How then, O good God, good to the good and to the wicked, how do You save the wicked if this is not just and You do not do anything which is not just? Or, since your goodness is beyond comprehension, is this hidden in the inaccessible light in which You dwell? (*Proslogion*, 9)

Anselm assumes that forgiveness requires foregoing punishment. But justice requires that the wrongdoer be punished. The ancient formula for justice was "rendering to each what is due him or her." What's due the wrongdoer is punishment. Hence to forgive him is to violate justice.

Anselm's solution, if one can call it that, was remarkably unhelpful.

---

3. I am using the translation by M. J. Charlesworth (Notre Dame: University of Notre Dame Press, 1979).

After a number of tentative probes he settled on the following proposal. In speaking of God as just, we must distinguish between God's being just relative to us and God's being just relative to Godself. God is just relative to us when God renders to us what is due us; God is just relative to Godself when God does what befits God's nature as the supreme good. In sparing the wicked "You are just," says Anselm to God, "not because you give us our due, but because You do what befits You as the supreme good" (*Proslogion,* 10). "In sparing the wicked You are just in relation to Yourself and not in relation to us" (10).

Anselm's argument, that relative to himself God is just not only when punishing the wrongdoer but also when forgiving him, goes as follows. Whatever God does that accords with God's will befits God's goodness, since God's will is itself good. Accordingly, "that alone is just which You will, and that is not just which You do not will" (11). Now God wills to save some and not others. Accordingly, the salvation of the former and the damnation of the latter are both just in relation to God. "It is just in relation to You, O just and benevolent God, both when You punish and when You pardon." Indeed, "it [would not be] just for those to be saved whom You will to punish, and it [would not be] just for those to be damned whom You will to pardon" (11). Thus the relation of God's mercy to God's justice is that "Your mercy is derived from Your justice, since it is just that You are so good that You are good even in forgiving" (11).

I submit that this is not Anselm at his best. Distinguish, he says, between God's being just relative to us and God's being just relative to Godself. Understand the former as rendering to us what is due us, and understand both as grounded in God's acting in accord with God's good will. Observe, next, that it is in accord with the will of God that some wrongdoers be forgiven. Conclude that whereas God is not just relative to them, on account of the fact that God does not render to them what is due them, God is nonetheless just relative to Godself, since God's forgiveness of some wrongdoers is as much in accord with God's good will as God's punishment of others.

This helps not at all in resolving the initial perplexity. What perplexed Anselm was that, in forgiving wrongdoers, God appears to be doing what justice forbids. No, says Anselm; though God is unjust *relative to the wrongdoer* when forgiving him, God is not unjust *relative to Godself.* Even if we grant that relative justice is a coherent concept, which I doubt, Anselm does no more than replace his original perplexity with its near relative. Using the conceptuality Anselm proposes, we face the following question: if God is unjust relative to wrongdoers when God forgives them, how can it be good for God to forgive them? How is God's goodness compatible with God's treating persons in a way that is unjust relative to them? To declare that God's treating them in this way is not unjust relative to God does not explain how it can be good of God to treat them in a way that is unjust relative to them. We remain as perplexed as ever.

To this may be added that the solution has no application whatsoever to human forgiveness. If forgiveness requires foregoing punishment, and if foregoing punishment of the wrongdoer is an infraction of justice, how are we to explain the fact that Jesus commands us to forgive each other?

WHAT IS FORGIVENESS?

It would be a happy state of affairs if there were consensus on the nature of forgiveness; we could then proceed immediately to consider the charge that forgiveness is a violation of justice. But there is no such consensus. Even a cursory review of the twentieth-century philosophical and theological literature on forgiveness turns up fundamental disagreements.[4] "Forgiveness is primarily a matter of how I *feel* about you (not how I treat you)," says Jeffrie Murphy; "thus I may forgive you in my heart of hearts or even after you are dead."[5] On the contrary, says Richard Swinburne. For you to forgive me is to undertake "that in future you will not treat me as the originator of an act by which I wronged you." "Feelings need not be involved."[6] Forgiveness is the overcoming of feelings of resentment and indignation, says Murphy, this time citing Bishop Butler. Jean Hampton insists on a distinction. Though forgiveness is the overcoming of hatred for the wrongdoer, it is not the overcoming of feelings of resentment and indignation over what was done to one.[7]

Given these and other such disagreements, there is no option but to devote the remainder of this chapter to arriving at an understanding of the nature of forgiveness. Only then can we address the question whether forgiveness violates justice.[8] Much more could be said about

4. For an excellent review of this literature, see the essay by Nigel Biggar, "Forgiveness in the Twentieth Century: A Review of the Literature, 1901-2001," in Alistair McFadyen and Marcel Sarot, *Forgiveness and Truth* (Edinburgh and New York: T&T Clark, 2001). Also useful is Anthony Bash, *Forgiveness and Christian Ethics* (Cambridge: Cambridge University Press, 2007).

5. "Forgiveness and Resentment," in Murphy and Hampton, *Forgiveness and Mercy,* 21.

6. *Responsibility and Atonement* (Oxford: Oxford University Press, 1989), 85, and 87 n. 8.

7. See the essays in Murphy and Hampton, *Forgiveness and Mercy.*

8. I have discussed forgiveness on three previous occasions: "Does Forgiveness Undermine Justice?" in *God and the Ethics of Belief,* ed. Andrew Dole and Andrew Chignell (Cambridge: Cambridge University Press, 2005), 219-47; "The Place of Forgiveness in the Actions of the State," in *The Politics of Past Evil,* ed. Daniel Philpott (Notre Dame: University of Notre Dame Press, 2006), 87-111; and "Jesus and Forgiveness," in *Jesus and Philosophy:*

forgiveness than I will be saying here; I will say only enough for us to be able to consider whether forgiveness violates justice.

Begin with the fact that forgiveness cannot be dispensed hither and yon indiscriminately. As I argued in Chapter Four, forgiveness presupposes that someone has been wronged, deprived of something to which she had a right; it presupposes that an injustice has occurred. It furthermore presupposes that the one doing the forgiving *recognize* that someone has been wronged, *recognize* that an injustice has occurred.

Most writers on the matter take for granted that only the one wronged can do the forgiving. I have no stake in whether this is true; but it seems to me that it is not. We say such things as "I think I have finally forgiven my uncle for the way he took advantage of my father" and "I find it very difficult to forgive the officials of the university for the shabby way they treated our field hockey team."

Someone might suggest that such remarks indicate not that the thesis should be discarded but that we should employ a richer and more expansive understanding of how a person can be wronged. One can be wronged not only by how one is treated personally but by the treatment accorded those with whom one identifies. I identify with my father; that's why I was wronged by how my uncle treated him and why I am in a position to forgive my uncle. I identify with our field hockey team; that's why I was wronged by how the university officials treated the team and why I am in a position to refrain from forgiving those officials.

Perhaps this is correct; I'm not sure. But if it is, it assumes a very expansive understanding of identification. After being incensed at a priest I know because of a story I read in the newspaper about his abuse of a young boy, I may eventually come to forgive the priest. But suppose I did not know the boy and do not know the man he has become. Do I nonetheless identify with him, and is it because of that identification that I too was wronged by the priest? If we do say that I identify with the boy and was thus myself wronged, I fear that we are using the word "identify" in such a way that it is true by definition that if I forgive someone, then either I was wronged directly or wronged indirectly on account of being identified with the one who was directly wronged.

Let me present my account of forgiveness in two stages. First I will describe the context required if forgiveness is to occur. Then I will say what forgiveness does within such a context. To avoid irrelevant controversy, I will confine myself to speaking of the direct victim as doing the forgiving.

New Essays, ed. Paul Moser (Cambridge: Cambridge University Press, 2008). Though I continue to agree with much of what I said in those essays, I now think that some of what I said there about forgiveness was either mistaken or deficient. A few passages in this chapter have been taken over from those essays.

The prerequisite context has five essential components. It is my impression that, with one exception, the claim that these are conditions for the occurrence of forgiveness is non-controversial; we will get to the exception shortly. I can forgive Hubert for the wrong he did me only when (1) Hubert did wrong me; (2) I rightly believe that he was blamable for doing so;[9] (3) I continue to remember the deed and who did it, and continue to condemn it; (4) I feel resentment or some similar negative emotion at the deed done; and (5) I feel anger or some similar negative emotion at Hubert for having done it. Only when these conditions are met is it possible for me to forgive Hubert for the wrong he did me.

I have several times cited the first of these as a prerequisite of forgiveness. Let me briefly explain why the others are as well. I can forgive Hubert for wronging me only if I rightly believe that he is blamable for doing so. If I believe that he is not blamable — he acted under duress, out of non-culpable ignorance, out of ineradicable weakness of will, or whatever — I excuse him; I do not blame him.[10] Though forgiving resembles excusing in important respects, it is nonetheless not only distinct from excusing but forestalled thereby.

Second, if I am to forgive Hubert for the wrong he did me, I must continue to remember the deed done, I must continue to remember that it was Hubert who did it, and I must continue to condemn the deed. Forgetting what was done to me, or forgetting that Hubert did it, whether because I actively put the memory out of mind or because it just gradually fades away, resembles forgiveness. But forgiving is not forgetting; forgetting forestalls forgiveness. If one has forgotten, one cannot forgive. Forgiving is not to be identified with letting bygones be bygones — no matter whether one lets the bygones be bygones because one no longer holds the agent culpable, because one no longer actively remembers the deed done or who did it, or because one no longer condemns it as wrong.

Third, it is possible to believe that one has been wronged by someone without experiencing any negative affect toward either deed or doer. One might dismiss act and agent as beneath one's attention. "I can't be bothered with insults from scum like this." Such affectless dismissal is not forgiveness; it forestalls forgiveness. It does not treat the deed and its doer with the moral seriousness that forgiveness requires.

So what is it to forgive Hubert for the wrong he did to me? The most philosophically sophisticated and detailed account of forgiveness presently available is that by Charles L. Griswold in *Forgiveness: A Philosophi-*

---

9. In my *Justice: Rights and Wrongs,* I argue that one can wrong someone without being blamable for doing so.

10. Most English translations of the New Testament have Jesus on the cross praying concerning his executioners, "Father, forgive them; for they do not know what they are doing" (Luke 23:34). I think what Jesus is asking God to do is excuse them.

cal Exploration.[11] Griswold's account presupposes his insistence that the only negative emotion relevant to forgiveness is toward the wrongdoer; he calls it resentment. Thus, he implicitly denies the fourth on my list of prerequisites of forgiveness, the presence of a feeling of resentment or some similar negative emotion toward the deed done. Griswold then analyzes forgiveness as including the following four components: forswearing revenge, moderating resentment, committing oneself to let go of any lingering resentment, and communicating to the offender that forgiveness is granted.

Two additional factors that Griswold cites as components of forgiveness seem to me better viewed as prerequisites than components, namely, the wrongdoer's re-framing of herself and the victim, and the victim's re-framing of herself and the wrongdoer. Let me quote Griswold on what he has in mind by these re-framings:

> In order to qualify for forgiveness, the offender would have to show that she has sympathetically entered into the situation of her victim, and understands the victim's narrative from that point of view. The offender would also have to offer a narrative accounting for how she came to do wrong, how that wrong-doing does not express the totality of her person, and how she expects to become worthy of approbation. The offender who presents a request for forgiveness presents a narrative of guilt, regret, and remorse, explains how she came to do the injury, describes the moral sentiments that ensued, and convincingly depicts a change of ways that will unfold over time.
>
> For her part, the victim must re-frame both her view of the offender and her view of herself. . . . Re-framing your perspective on the offender, and eventually yourself, means that your resentful "stories" . . . must be revised. Furthermore, you must re-frame your view of yourself, in part insofar as your self-definition is affected by your oppositional relation to enemies or oppressors. (183-84)

I judge that seldom does anything so elaborate as these re-framings take place; if such re-framings were a prerequisite (or component) of forgiveness, forgiveness would seldom occur. For my immediate purposes, however, this point is not important. What's important to note is that, since Griswold holds that it is only toward the wrongdoer that one feels negative affect, not toward the deed done, forgiveness on his account includes committing oneself to let go of *all* negative affect evoked by the wrongdoing, and forgiveness is full and complete only when all negative affect has in fact disappeared.

11. (Cambridge: Cambridge University Press, 2007).

My problem with this analysis is the following. Griswold insists, as do I, that forgiving is not forgetting. To the contrary: forgiveness *requires* remembering what was done to one and who did it, and *requires* continuing to condemn it. Now if one takes what was done to one with moral seriousness, then I doubt that one can remember and continue to condemn it without feeling at least some negative affect toward it. The only way to get rid entirely of this negative affect would be to forget what was done to one or no longer condemn it. But to say it yet again, forgiving requires remembering and continuing to condemn.

But suppose that I am mistaken about this; suppose that one can remember and condemn what was done to one while feeling no negative affect toward it. Surely forgiveness does not require *committing* oneself to getting rid of negative affect toward the deed done, and surely full and complete forgiveness is *compatible* with continuing to feel resentful of what was done to one. Forgiveness, so I suggest, requires letting go of one's negative feelings toward the *wrongdoer;* it does not require letting go of one's negative feelings toward the deed done.

A satisfactory account of forgiveness requires distinguishing, as Griswold explicitly declines to do, between one's negative affect toward the wrong done and one's negative affect toward the wrongdoer. One can fully forgive the wrongdoer while continuing to resent what he did. A satisfactory theory of forgiveness must explain how this delicate balancing act can be brought off, and it must explain why it is (or is not) sometimes good to bring it off.

I think Griswold is correct in suggesting that the clue to how this balancing act is to be brought off lies in a certain alteration in how the victim views the wrongdoer. But Griswold does not succeed in getting a clear fix on what this alteration in perspective consists of — this *re-framing*, as he calls it.[12] I suggest that forgiveness is the enacted resolution of the victim no longer to hold against the wrongdoer what he did to one — or to use biblical language, no longer to count the sin against him.[13] Mere resolution is not enough; forgiveness requires that one *enact* the resolution, act on it. If one resolves not to hold the deed against the wrongdoer but, for whatever reason, never acts on one's resolution — one finds it too difficult, one shortly falls into a permanent coma, whatever — then, though one is willing to forgive, one does not actually forgive.

An explanatory qualification is in order. One's resolution not to hold

12. Here is what Griswold says in one place about the "re-framing" that forgiveness requires by the victim of the wrongdoer: "it must involve something like distinguishing that 'part' of the self responsible for the injury from the 'whole person'"(57). I find this too vague to be helpful.

13. Cf. 2 Corinthians 5:19: "In Christ God was reconciling the world to himself, not counting their trespasses against them."

the deed against the wrongdoer may be partial, in that it consists of resolving not to hold the deed against him in some ways but not all. So too
one's enactment may be partial, in that one succeeds in enacting one's
resolution in some ways but not all. And the *scope* of one's resolution
may expand over time, as may the scope of one's enactment. For our
subsequent discussion it will be important to keep these points in mind,
that forgiveness is often partial in the two ways mentioned, and often
takes the form of a process rather than a full and complete resolution
enacted on the spot.

What is it no longer to hold against someone what he did to one, no
longer to count it against him? He did it after all, one remembers that
he did, and one continues to condemn it. Arendt spoke of redemption
from the predicament of being unable to undo what was done. Strictly
speaking, there is no redemption from that predicament; there is no
undoing of the wrong done, no undoing of guilt.

Some writers suggest, implicitly or explicitly, that not to hold against
someone the wrong he did one is to treat the deed as not having been
done.[14] That seems to me not quite correct; not even when one excuses
someone for what he did does one do that. To forgive is not to treat the
act as not having been done but to enact the resolution *not to hold the act*
against *the wrongdoer.*

And what is it for me not to hold against Hubert what he did to me?
It is for me to engage him as I would if I regarded that deed as not belonging to his moral history. It does in fact belong to his moral history
and I know that it does; I remember it, I condemn it, and I regard
Hubert as blamable. But I now act on the resolution to engage him as I
would if I believed that it was only part of his personal history, not part
of his moral history.

By the *moral history* of a person I mean that ensemble of things he did
that contribute to determining his moral condition, things he did that
contribute to determining in which respects and to what degree he is a
morally good person and in which respects and to what degree he is
morally bad. The point of introducing the idea of a person's moral history is that we need not, and do not, regard everything a person does as
part of his moral history. If Hubert wronged me, but it turns out that
he's not blamable because he acted out of non-culpable ignorance,
then, rather than thinking worse of him for what he did to me, I excuse
him. To excuse him is to view the deed as not part of his moral history. It
is part of his personal history; he did it. But it's not part of his *moral* history; it does not put a blot on his moral condition.

One can imagine a society whose members did not accept excuses.

---

14. We will find Swinburne saying this in a passage to be quoted shortly.

They would count everything a person did that wronged someone as contributing, negatively, to his moral character. If the deed wronged someone and Hubert did it, then it belongs to Hubert's moral history; it places a blot on his moral character. No excuses allowed. Our society is not such a society.[15]

Though forgiving the wrongdoer is not only different from excusing him but precluded thereby, forgiving resembles excusing in that one enacts the resolution to engage the person as one would if the deed done were only a wrong-inflicting component of his personal history, not a negative component of his moral history. While not excusing him, one nonetheless enacts the resolution to engage him as one would if one did excuse him — with the exception, of course, that one believes, about him, that he is in fact not to be excused for what he did.[16] Full and complete forgiveness comes as close as possible to engaging him as one would if one excused him while nonetheless *not* excusing him. If one excuses him, one declines to hold the act against him for the reason that one believes that it does not belong to his moral history; if one forgives him, one resolves not to hold the act against him even though one believes that it does belong to his moral history.

Is holding the deed against the wrongdoer a kind of pretence on one's part? If I no longer hold against Hubert the wrong he did me, am I *pretending* that it does not belong to his moral history? I think not. Suppose the officials in some department of justice decide not to press charges against someone even though they believe that he committed an infraction of the law. Though the state will then not hold the infraction against the person, neither the state nor its officials acting in their capacity will henceforth *pretend* that he did not violate the law. Or suppose that some head of state decides to pardon someone who has been judged guilty of some infraction; neither the state nor its head henceforth pretends that he had not been judged guilty.

FORGIVENESS EVOKED BY REPENTANCE

If forgiving Hubert is what I have suggested it is, why would I do such a thing? We in our society do not find it problematic that I do not hold against Hubert the wrong he did me when I think he's not blamable. But if I believe he is blamable, why would I nonetheless engage him as I

15. I am told that if someone who is an Eastern Orthodox priest kills someone, he is no longer eligible to serve as priest even if the killing was accidental and he has no moral culpability.

16. I assume that believing, about him, that he is not to be excused, counts as a way of engaging him.

would if I excused him? I remember what was done to me and continue to condemn and resent it; I remember that it was Hubert who did it and continue to condemn and feel angry at him for having done it. In such a situation, why would I enact the resolution not to hold the deed against him in my engagement with him? Why would I forgive him?

If the case is of the usual sort, what leads me to forgive Hubert is that I have come to believe that he has altered his relation to what he did in a morally significant way. He remains blamable for having done it; it's a stain on his moral character. He cannot change that. But I believe that he has now morally distanced himself from what he did to me by joining me in condemning it. With unmistakable sincerity he has told me that he is sorry for what he did. If the wrong done is the sort of thing for which compensation can be given, he has offered compensation. Hubert's overall moral condition is now significantly different from what it was before his repentance. He is a morally different person from the one who wronged me, better in an important respect. That's why I resolve no longer to hold the deed against him.

If the wrong done was not serious, and if the victim is of a forgiving disposition, forgiveness in response to the recognition that the wrong-doer is penitent may emerge almost effortlessly. As I pointed out earlier, however, forgiveness often requires effort, and many find that the effort is beyond them. Many are the victims who cannot bring themselves to forgive, even when they concede that the wrongdoer is penitent. There's a side of themselves that wants to forgive; but they find it impossible to resolve to do so. Or they resolve to do so but find it impossible to carry out the resolution. Forgiveness is often partial, maybe usually, and is often slow and difficult.

CAN ONE FORGIVE AN UNREPENTANT WRONGDOER?

Can I forgive Hubert if I believe that he is not contrite? Believing that he continues to stand behind what he did, can I nonetheless form and enact the resolution not to hold it against him? Suppose I believe that Jesus commands us to forgive the one who has wronged us whether or not he is penitent.[17] Can I, out of what I believe to be my Christian duty,

17. Jesus is nowhere in the New Testament reported as issuing any such command. Whereas he enjoins us to love our enemies and seek to do them good, he nowhere enjoins us to forgive them. Cf. what *The Kairos Document,* issued in South Africa in 1986, says on the matter: "The Biblical teaching on reconciliation and forgiveness makes it quite clear that nobody can be forgiven and reconciled with God unless she or he repents of their sins. Nor are *we* expected to forgive the unrepentant sinner. When he or she repents we must be willing to forgive seventy times seven times but before that we are expected to

form and act on the resolution not to hold against him what he did to me even though I believe that he is impenitent?

I doubt it. I can be *willing* to forgive him — when he repents. I can have a forgiving disposition toward him. But it appears to me that no longer to hold against someone the wrong he did one while believing that he himself continues to stand behind the deed, requires not treating the deed or its doer with the moral seriousness required for forgiveness; it is to downplay rather than forgive. "I suppose he did wrong me; but it's not worth making anything of it."[18]

But suppose I am mistaken about this. Suppose it is possible fully and completely to forgive the person who has wronged one while knowing full well that he continues to stand firmly behind what he did. Then I would say, first, that such an action is unacceptably arbitrary. We are to suppose that one continues to hold against some people the wrong they did one; one is not a moral wimp who waves aside all wrongs done to one. So why is one not holding this wrong against this wrongdoer, when one holds other wrongs against other wrongdoers? What is the morally relevant difference?

Second, and more important: in the absence of repentance, to enact the resolution not to hold the deed against the wrongdoer is to insult him and to demean oneself, thereby wronging both alike. Consider the situation. Hubert agrees with me that what he did should be counted as belonging to his moral history; but he insists, over my objection, that what he did was not wrong. Now I say to him, "You agree that you are responsible for what you did to me, but you don't see anything wrong in it. I disagree. What you did to me was wrong. But I have resolved not to hold it against you. I forgive you. I have resolved henceforth to treat you as I would if I excused you." I submit that this is both to demean myself and to insult Hubert by refusing to treat him and what he did with full moral seriousness. "Keep your forgiveness," he snaps; "I did nothing wrong." Far better to join with Hubert in counting the deed as part of his moral history and then go on to insist, against his protests, that it was wrong.

Richard Swinburne makes the point well. Unless the wrongdoing is trivial, it is wrong for the victim "in the absence of some atonement, at

---

preach repentance to those who sin against us or against anyone. Reconciliation, forgiveness and negotiations will become our Christian duty in South Africa only when the apartheid regime shows signs of genuine repentance" (§3.1).

18. An implication of this position is that one cannot forgive the wrongdoer who is dead if one believes he was never penitent, nor the wrongdoer who has sunk into dementia. In such cases, one lives with the regret that forgiveness never became possible. There is no escape in this life from this feature of our human condition. We have to cope with it, not pretend that we have it in our power to undo it.

least in the form of apology, to treat the [act] as not having been done."[19] If I have murdered your wife and you decide to overlook my offence and interact with me as if it had never happened, your attitude "trivializes human life, your love for your wife, and the importance of right action. And it involves your failing to treat me seriously, to take seriously my attitude towards you expressed in my action. Thereby it trivializes human relationships, for it supposes that good human relations can exist when we do not take each other seriously" (86).

The therapeutic tradition has caused a good deal of confusion on this point by denominating as forgiveness a process or activity quite different from that which philosophical and theological writers have in mind by "forgiveness." I have highlighted the moral and social dimension of forgiveness: forgiveness, in the normal case, is a response by the victim to indications of repentance on the part of the wrongdoer. The pair, repentance and forgiveness, is a moral social engagement. By contrast, what the therapeutic literature has in mind by "forgiveness" is an a-social and a-moral process that is entirely internal to the victim. The therapist offers to help the victim overcome her negative feelings toward the deed and its doer without in any way engaging the wrongdoer. If the victim finally arrives at the point where those negative feelings are gone, she is said to have forgiven.[20]

Though getting over one's negative feelings toward the wrongdoer is a component of forgiveness, getting over them in this way is not forgiveness. As Anthony Bash puts it in his discussion of forgiveness therapy, "relief, inner peace and transformed and reordered relationships, can come about other than through forgiveness. Forgetting, excusing, collusion, denial and condoning may also produce the same effects. Forgiveness is not only about feeling better: it is about addressing the moral issues that caused the unforgiveness. The fact of the morally wrong acts and the ensuing guilt that arises from having done them need to have been addressed if the term 'forgiveness' is to be a moral — rather than simply a relational, existential — term" (173).

19. *Responsibility and Atonement* (Oxford: Oxford University Press, 1989), 85-86. A few pages back I argued that not holding the deed against the wrongdoer is not to be equated with treating the deed as not having been done.

20. Anthony Bash discusses forgiveness therapy in the third chapter of *Forgiveness and Christian Ethics*. Jeffrie Murphy discusses it in the seventh chapter of his *Getting Even* (Oxford: Oxford University Press, 2003). Bash describes the therapy as follows: "The result of a 'forgiveness intervention' is typically a diminution of unforgiving feelings toward the wrongdoer. This usually comes about through a psychological reordering of a victim's feelings and thoughts towards the wrongdoer. Forgiveness, so it is thought, is the means to better psychological health and so to the benefits that better psychological health brings" (37). It is an "*intrapersonal* phenomenon" (42). The "intervention does not involve dialogue and engagement with the wrongdoer" (41).

Forgiveness therapy is a way of getting to the point where bygones have become bygones; it is closely related to, though not quite identical with, getting to that same point by forgetting what was done to one. When forgiveness proves impossible, letting bygones be bygones, or getting them to become bygones, is the best one can do; sometimes this second best may be indispensable for getting on with one's life.[21] But the moral question I raised is always on the horizon. Is one taking the deed and its doer with sufficient moral seriousness if one consigns the episode to a mere bygone? And if not, is one then not demeaning oneself and insulting the wrongdoer?

It is often said that to condition forgiveness on the wrongdoer's repentance is to allow the wrongdoer to continue to have control over one. And so it is, in a way. Finding it impossible to forgive, one may try to escape the wrongdoer's psychological control by getting to the point where the deed is for one a mere bygone. But letting the deed become, or getting it to become, a mere bygone, though it extricates one from the wrongdoer's psychological control, does not extricate one from the fact that one has been wronged and that the wrongdoer continues to stand behind what he did. The unrepentant wrongdoer continues to have that sort of moral control over his victim. The victim may put the deed out of mind; but that does not alter the moral fact that she has been wronged by someone who has no regrets.

THE FOCUSED NATURE OF FORGIVENESS

One last point about forgiveness. In her insightful and provocative discussion of forgiveness and related phenomena, Jean Hampton argues that, strictly speaking, overcoming one's anger at the wrongdoer is preparation for forgiveness rather than a component thereof; and she contends that not holding the deed against the wrongdoer is a possibility opened up by forgiveness, perhaps something the forgiver hopes for, but not part of forgiveness itself. Forgiveness itself, she says, is a "change of heart" of the following sort:

> The forgiver who previously saw the wrongdoer as someone bad or rotten or morally indecent to some degree has a change of heart when he "washes away" or disregards the wrongdoer's immoral ac-

---

21. Abraham Lincoln, as portrayed in Doris Kearns's *Team of Rivals: The Political Genius of Abraham Lincoln* (New York: Simon & Schuster, 2005), was almost supernaturally capable of not letting his anger at how he was treated by certain members of his cabinet, especially Stanton, influence his interactions with them.

tions or character traits in his ultimate moral judgment of her, and comes to see her as still *decent, not* rotten as a person, and someone with whom he may be able to renew a friendship.

Hampton goes on to say that "when one has a change of heart towards one's wrongdoer, one 'reapproves' of her, so that one is able to consider renewing an association with her. The change of heart is the new understanding of the wrongdoer as a person one can be 'for' rather than 'against'" (83). This is of course closely similar to what, earlier in this chapter, we found Griswold saying.

I am dubious. Forgiveness, and the repentance that is the counterpart of forgiveness in the normal case, seem to me typically much more focused than they appear to be to Hampton.[22] I think one forgives the wrongdoer *for* his act of wrongdoing, and that to forgive him for his act of wrongdoing is to enact the resolution no longer to hold *that deed* against him, this resolution including the resolution to overcome one's anger at him *for the thing he did.* Thus I can forgive a wrongdoer for what he did to me and still regard him as a rotten person overall; conversely, my forgiving him for what he did to me neither presupposes that previously I regarded him "as someone bad or rotten or morally indecent" (82), nor does it imply that I now see him in a different and better light. I may have thought, and may continue to think, that he's a fine person and that what he did to me was quite out of character.[23]

An implication of this focused understanding of forgiveness (and repentance) is that I may forgive Hubert for what he did to me — act on the resolution no longer to hold it against him — and still want nothing to do with him. Forgiveness is often granted in the hope, and sometimes

22. In *Getting Even*, Murphy offers an explanation of repentance that is diffused in the same way that Hampton's explanation of forgiveness is: "Repentance is the remorseful acceptance of responsibility for one's wrongful and harmful actions, the repudiation of the aspects of one's character that generated the actions, the resolve to do one's best to extirpate those aspects of one's character, and the resolve to atone or make amends for the harm that one has done" (41). Griswold also understands repentance and forgiveness as less focused than I think they are. About repentance he says, for example, that "the offender must commit to becoming the sort of person who does not inflict injury, and that commitment must be shown through deeds as well as words" (50). And about forgiveness he says that he agrees with Hampton that forgiveness requires "a change in the injured person's belief that the wrong-doer is simply a 'bad person' with whom one ought not consort. . . . Without that, we should hardly be willing to credit her with forgiveness" (54).

23. I think it is probably because Hampton understands forgiveness as a less focused phenomenon than I take it to be that she speaks of hatred of the wrongdoer whereas I am inclined to speak of anger at the wrongdoer. Anger at someone is always anger at them *for* something they said or did. Hatred may be similarly focused, but it need not be. Hampton usually speaks simply of hatred of the wrongdoer, not of hatred of the wrongdoer *for* some specific act of wronging.

the expectation, of reconciliation. But one can accept someone's apology for the wrong he did one, and forgive him for that wrong, while nonetheless holding out little if any hope for reconciliation. Or perhaps the more precise thing to say is that reconciliation will sometimes have to be confined to reconciliation over this one deed. A focused understanding of repentance and forgiveness requires, as its complement, a focused understanding of reconciliation.

Chapter Sixteen

HOW THE RECOGNITION OF FORGIVENESS CAME ABOUT AND WHAT'S ITS POINT?

OUR GOAL IN THIS PART of our discussion, Chapters Fifteen through Seventeen, is to determine whether forgiveness is a violation of justice. But before we address that issue, we should take up a question posed in the preceding chapter but left unanswered. Hannah Arendt claimed that Jesus was the one who discovered the importance of forgiveness. This claim implies that the ancient pagan ethicists did not recognize its importance. Was she right about that? And if she was right about that, why did they not recognize its importance? Was it an oversight on their part, or does it tell us something important about their way of thinking about ethical issues?

Addressing that last question will lead naturally to a question that our discussion of the nature of forgiveness ineluctably raises: what's the point of that moral social engagement which consists of repentance by the wrongdoer and forgiveness by the one wronged? In case one's anger proves an impediment to getting on with life, deal with that; if necessary, enlist the help of a therapist to get bygones become bygones. But why forgive?

FORGIVENESS IN THE ANCIENT PAGAN WRITERS

This is not the place for a comprehensive survey of what the writers of pagan antiquity had to say about forgiveness, nor am I competent to offer such a survey.[1] Let me instead look at two representative figures, Aristotle and Seneca — Aristotle as representative of the Peripatetic school of ancient eudaimonism, Seneca as representative of the Stoic school.

In Book 4, section 5, of the *Nicomachean Ethics,* Aristotle discusses the

---

1. Charles L. Griswold offers a brief survey in the opening nineteen pages of his *Forgiveness: A Philosophical Exploration.*

ethics of anger. Following his usual strategy of explaining a virtue by locating it at the midpoint between extremes, he declares that "good temper is a mean with respect to anger" (1125b 27).[2] "Good temper," he says, is his own term for the virtue in question. In ordinary speech "the middle state [is] unnamed," as are the extreme states — though "the excess might be called a sort of irascibility" (1125b 28-30).

Aristotle then goes on to say that the good-tempered man is "the man who is angry at the right things and with the right people, and further, as he ought, when he ought, and as long as he ought" (1125b 31-32).

> For the good-tempered man tends to be unperturbed and not to be led by passion, but to be angry in the right manner, at the things, and for the length of time, that reason dictates; but he is thought to err rather in the direction of deficiency; for the good-tempered man is not revengeful, but rather tends to forgive.
>
> The deficiency, whether it is a sort of inirascibility or whatever it is, is blamed. For those who are not angry at the things they should be are thought to be fools, and so are those who are not angry in the right way, at the right time, or with the right persons; for such a man is thought not to feel things nor to be pained by them, and, since he does not get angry, he is thought unlikely to defend himself; and to endure being insulted and to put up with insults to one's friends is slavish. (1125b 33–1126a 8)

Anger at the person who has harmed one is a good thing, provided it be of the right duration, intensity, etc.; not to feel anger would be "slavish." Aristotle offers no hint of conditions under which it would be good to work toward overcoming one's anger at the person who harmed one. He says that the good-tempered man "tends to forgive." But by the tendency to forgive he does not mean the tendency not to hold the injury against the repentant wrongdoer; he means simply the tendency not to get angry. And he describes this tendency in the good-tempered man as something to be "blamed." Good-tempered people have a bad tendency to get less angry than they should.[3] In short, there is in Aristotle no recognition of forgiveness as we have understood it, and hence, of course, no praise of forgiveness.

The likeliest place to find an affirmation of "the role of forgiveness in the realm of human affairs" by a writer of pagan antiquity would be in

---

2. I am using the translation by W. D. Ross, ed. J. O. Urmson, in *The Complete Works of Aristotle,* ed. Jonathan Barnes (Princeton: Princeton University Press, 1984).

3. Aristotle speaks in a rather similar way about our tendency to forgive in *Nicomachean Ethics,* 7.6; 1149b 4-6.

Seneca's *On Mercy (de Clementia)*.[4] *De Clementia* was addressed by Seneca to the young Nero. Book I, which is most of what has been preserved, consists of a multifaceted argument, with many examples, for the conclusion that clemency in punishment by a ruler yields a number of desirable results. In the fragment of Book II that we have, Seneca tells us what clemency is.

Clemency is mildness in the imposition of the punishment due a person. When a range of punishment is specified in a legal or quasi-legal system for misdeeds of a certain sort, clemency consists of choosing the more lenient. "The following definition will meet with objections," says Seneca, but "it comes very close to the truth. We might speak of mercy [clemency] as 'moderation that remits something of a deserved and due punishment'. The cry will go up that no virtue ever gives any one less than his due. But everyone realizes that mercy is something which 'stops short of what could deservedly be imposed'."[5] Seneca offers the following examples to elucidate his analysis:

> In one case, [the clement person] may simply administer a verbal admonition without any punishment, seeing the man to be at an age still capable of correction. In another, where the man is patently labouring under an invidious accusation, he will order him to go scot-free, since he may have been misled or under the influence of alcohol. Enemies he will release unharmed, sometimes even commended, if they had an honourable reason — loyalty, a treaty, their freedom — to drive them to war. All these are works of mercy [clemency]. (2.7; 164)

Clemency thus exhibits what Seneca calls "freedom of decision." "It judges not by legal formulae, but by what is equitable and good. It can acquit or set the damages as high as it wishes. All these things it does with the idea not of doing something less than what is just but that what it decides should be the justest possible." In short, clemency is what the Greeks called *epiekeia*, usually translated as "equity" and explained by Aristotle as follows:[6]

> The equitable is just, but not the legally just but a correction of legal justice. The reason is that all law is universal but about some things it is not possible to make a universal statement which will be correct.

4. I am using the translation by John M. Cooper and J. F. Procopé in *Seneca: Moral and Political Essays* (Cambridge: Cambridge University Press, 1995).

5. Seneca, *On Mercy*, 2.3, in *Seneca: Moral and Political Essays*, 160.

6. Martha Nussbaum has a very interesting discussion of equity, *epikeia*, in her essay "Equity and Mercy," in *Philosophy and Public Affairs* 22.2 (1993): 83-125.

In those cases, then, in which it is necessary to speak universally, but not possible to do so correctly, the law takes the usual case. . . . When the law speaks universally, then, and a case arises on it which is not covered by the universal statement, then it is right . . . to correct the omission. . . . Hence the equitable is just. . . . And this is the nature of the equitable, a correction of law where it is defective owing to its universality. . . .

It is also clear from this what sort of person the equitable person is. For a person who chooses and does such things, and who is not zealous for strict judgment in the direction of the worse, but is inclined to mitigation, even though he can invoke the law on his side — such a person is equitable and this trait of character is equity, being a kind of justice and not a distinct trait of character. (*Nicomachean Ethics* 1137b34-1138a3)[7]

There are two differences, both minor, between Aristotle's understanding of equity and Seneca's. Aristotle describes equity as attending to the full particulars of the case and then *correcting* the application of the relevant law so as to achieve justice in this case; Seneca describes clemency as attending to the full particulars of the case and then, so as to achieve justice in this case, choosing the milder from the range of punishments that the law specifies. And whereas Senecan clemency always takes the form of relative mildness in punishment, Aristotelian equity might in principle impose a more severe punishment than the law specifies.[8]

Seneca is at pains to emphasize that clemency is neither forgiveness nor pardon. "Forgiveness . . . is failing to punish what in your judgment should be punished, while pardon is the remission of a penalty that is due" (2.7; 164). "The wise man does nothing that he ought not to do and omits nothing that he ought to do. So he will not excuse a punishment which he ought to exact" (164). He may "do the same as he would if he forgave [him, but he does it] without forgiving, since to forgive is to confess that one has left undone something which ought to have been done" (164).

Seneca is likewise emphatic in saying that clemency is based not on pity but on moral reasoning concerning the most just punishment. Pity is a vice, not a virtue, something that all good men avoid. "The fault of a petty mind succumbing to the sight of evils that affect others . . . is a fea-

7. The translation of the last paragraph of this passage is from Nussbaum, in "Equity and Mercy," 92.

8. Nussbaum, in "Equity and Mercy," offers some interesting suggestions, however, as to why Aristotelian equity will usually prove to be milder than legal justice.

ture very familiar in the worst kind of person. There are women, senile or silly, so affected by the tears of the nastiest criminals that, if they could, they would break open the prison. Pity looks at the plight, not at the cause of it. Mercy [clemency] joins in with reason" (2.7; 161).

In short, in praising clemency as he does, Seneca is not praising forgiveness. It's one thing to choose the more lenient punishment from the range permitted by the law because it best fits the particulars of the case; it's quite another thing no longer to hold against someone the wrong he did one. In practicing Senecan clemency, one holds the wrong against the wrongdoer.

GRISWOLD'S EXPLANATION OF WHY THE ANCIENTS DID NOT RECOGNIZE AND PRAISE FORGIVENESS

In *Forgiveness,* Charles L. Griswold argues that it was what he calls the "perfectionism" of the ancient ethicists that prevented them from clearly distinguishing forgiveness from other rather similar phenomena and from praising it. What he means by describing ancient ethics as "perfectionist" is that it focused attention on how the fully wise and virtuous person — the perfected person — would act.

Plato and the Stoics held that such a person — the Stoics called him a "sage" — is invulnerable in the sense that he realizes that the only true goods in his life are the goods of virtuous action, these being goods whose possession lies entirely within his own control. The sage is like everyone else in his susceptibility to being deprived of what the Stoics called "preferables"; but the presence or absence in one's life of one and another preferable does not determine whether one acts virtuously, and hence does not determine how good one's life is. "In the classical perfectionist outlooks," says Griswold, "forgiveness is not a virtue because the perfected soul is by definition almost, or entirely, immune from receiving injury, or from doing injury" (15).[9] The word "injury" is ambiguous here. The Stoic sage is vulnerable to impairments in the preferables in his life; he is not vulnerable to impairments in his happiness, his *eudaimonia,* impairments in how well he lives his life.

The view of the Peripatetics concerning the invulnerability of the fully wise and virtuous person was close to that of the Stoics; they arrived at their conclusions by a somewhat different path, however. Contrary to the Stoics, they held that it is almost impossible for someone reared among people who are living their lives badly to become fully virtuous;

---

9. This sentence occurs in the course of Griswold's discussion of Nietzsche, whom he interprets as rejecting forgiveness for the same reason as the ancients.

becoming virtuous is, in that way, not entirely up to oneself. They agreed with the Stoics, however, that the person who has become fully wise and virtuous is not vulnerable to impairments in his happiness. What is the case, they thought, is that the virtuous person who lives in straitened circumstances finds that she is thereby deprived of opportunity for the full display of her virtue.

Forgiveness, says Griswold, has no place within such perfectionist outlooks as these. Forgiveness is

> appropriate to an outlook that emphasizes the notion of a common and irremediably finite and fallible human nature, and thus highlights the virtues that improve as well as reconcile but do not aim to "perfect." . . . Forgiveness is a virtue against the background of a narrative about human nature and its aspirations that accepts imperfection as our lot (in a religious view, our lot absent divine grace, and in a secular view, our lot unalterably). Our interdependence as social and sympathizing creatures; our embodiment and our affective character; our vulnerability to each other; our mortality; our standing to demand respectful treatment from one another, as befits creatures of equal dignity, and our obligations to one another; the pervasiveness of suffering — most often unmerited where it is intentionally inflicted — and of pain, violence, and injustice: these are part and parcel of that imperfection. . . . Forgiveness is responsive to the demands of a world so understood, and in a way that helps to enable its possessor to live a good life. (14-15)

Forgiveness is indeed a response to the demands of a world that is imperfect in the way Griswold describes. But the near single-minded concentration of the ancient ethicists on what the fully wise and virtuous person would do did not lead them to deny or overlook the fact that most of us are imperfect creatures living in an imperfect world. They would have been mystified by Griswold's references to equal dignity, and they would have meant something different by the term "obligations" than what he means; but they would have affirmed that our condition is as he describes it. The perfectionist ethic of the ancients was as much a way of coping with imperfection as is our practice of repentance and forgiveness. The right question then is this: why did they choose their way of coping? Why did they not choose the way of repentance and forgiveness?

The perfectionism of the ancient writers seems to me to have been accidental. The Stoics could not have given up their conviction that it is possible here in this world to become a perfected sage without revising a good deal of the rest of their thought; but without revising anything they could have given advice to the person who is not yet a sage as to how to live in the interim — in addition to advising him to work at becoming a sage. In fact they did give a bit of such advice. Nonetheless, they did not recommend forgiveness. And as for the Peripatetics, they did talk about the plight of the person who lives among bad people or in straitened circumstances; bad people inhibit one's becoming virtuous, straitened circumstances constrict the scope of virtuous action. But they too did not recommend forgiveness.

In short, even if the ancient writers had been less perfectionist in their focus than they were, even if they had focused less on the person who is fully wise and virtuous and had taken time to give advice to those of us who are still wayfarers on the road to wisdom and virtue, they would still not have recommended forgiveness. What accounts for their failure to do so has to be something other than their perfectionism, something deeper in their thought than the happenstance of their focus on the person who is fully perfected in wisdom and virtue. That deeper factor is indicated by the terms "dignity" and "obligations" that Griswold used when describing our condition.

Griswold remarks that "the idea of the inherent dignity of persons" was missing from ancient pagan ethical thought (9). He appears to believe that it was missing because of the "aristocratic" assumptions of ancient ethics; the ancients did not believe in *equal* dignity. He is right about that. But the more fundamental point is that they did not believe in the *inherent* dignity of human beings, be it equal or not. Or if some did, this conviction did not enter systematically into their understanding of the structure of practical reason.

When the ancient eudaimonists reflected on the structure of practical reason, they thought exclusively in terms of life-goods, more specifically, in terms of wellbeing. Only incidentally did they take note of the worth of human beings and of the actions that respect for such worth requires of us. Thus they did not develop an account of rights. On my view of rights, as consisting of what respect for the worth of persons and human beings requires, they could not have developed a theory of rights given their failure to acknowledge systematically the worth of persons. They took note of being harmed, that is, of impairment in wellbeing; they took no note of being wronged, of being treated with under-respect. One can be harmed without being wronged and one can be wronged without being harmed. Forgiveness presupposes that someone has been wronged.

In short, the practices of forgiveness and repentance are necessarily missing where there is no recognition of the inter-connected phenomena of the worth of human beings, of rights, of being wronged, of duties, of guilt. It was because the ancient eudaimonists did not, in any systematic way, recognize these phenomena, that forgiveness and repentance were not only not praised by them but not recognized.[10] Hannah Arendt was right in her assumption. The discovery of forgiveness was not possible within the framework of the ancient ethicists.

The fact that Jesus discovered forgiveness "in a religious context and articulated it in religious language is no reason," said Hannah Arendt, "to take it any less seriously in a strictly secular sense" (214-15). True. But what we have seen is that one cannot just insert forgiveness into any ethical orientation whatsoever. There are frameworks of thought within which forgiveness can find no home. Forgiveness entered the world along with the recognition of divine and human worth, of being wronged, of rights, of duty, of guilt. It cannot occur where those are not recognized.[11]

IMAGINING A COUSIN OF FORGIVENESS

It would have been possible for the ancient writers to recognize something in the region of forgiveness, a cousin, if you will. When speaking about the perfectionist focus of ancient ethical thought, we have to be

10. It was for the same reason that they did not and could not understand virtue as *moral* virtue. Thomas Reid makes the point in a remarkably perceptive passage; I know of no other philosopher who has. After distinguishing between doing something because one judges that it is on the whole good for one, and doing something because one recognizes that it is one's duty, Reid says this: "If there be no virtue without the belief that what we do is right, it follows that a moral faculty, that is, a power of discerning moral goodness and turpitude in human conduct, is essential to every being capable of virtue or vice. A person who has no more conception of moral goodness and baseness, of right and wrong, than a blind man has of colours, can have no regard to it in his conduct, and therefore can neither be virtuous nor vicious" (*Essays on the Active Powers* [1788; repr. Cambridge, MA: MIT Press, 1969], 5.4; 398). This is true, Reid adds, when we speak "of virtue in the strict and proper sense, as it signifies that quality in a man which is the object of moral approbation." But we "sometimes use the word *virtue* in such a latitude, as to signify any agreeable or useful quality, as when we speak of the virtues of plants" (398). It is in this sense that the ancient eudaimonists used the word. For them, a virtue is a habit whereby one engages in a "prudent prosecution of [one's] interest" (399), that is, in a prudent prosecution of what is good on the whole for one.

11. It is rather often said that the most important and disruptive addition of Christianity to the thought of the ancient pagan ethicists was that of the corrupt will. Aristotle had the idea of a weak will; no one, so it is said, had the idea of a corrupt will. I do not dispute that this was indeed an important and disruptive addition. But more disruptive yet was the introduction of the idea of moral guilt as opposed to ethical error — of the upright person as opposed to the wise person. It would be possible to work out a version of eudaimonism that incorporates the idea of a corrupt will; it is not possible to work out a version of eudaimonism that incorporates the ideas of duty and guilt, the ideas of rights and wrongs.

clear on just what sort of perfection the ancient writers had in mind. What they had in mind was not the morally perfect human being — the one who always does what he ought to do, the one who never wrongs anybody. They had in mind the fully wise and virtuous human being, the one who always does what he should do, the one who makes no mistakes in his judgments about goods and evils in his life and in the lives of others, neither about natural goods and evils nor about the goods and evils of action.[12]

The natural and appropriate emotional response to the recognition that one did not act as one should have acted because of an error in judgment on one's part concerning the worth of some life-good or life-evil is *regret;* one regrets what one did. In case one's error has the effect of harming someone else, it's appropriate that one express one's regret to the person harmed. Expressing regret for harming someone is something like expressing contrition for wronging someone; but obviously it's not the same.

Now suppose you have harmed but not wronged me and that, sometime later, you come to me and say that you now regret what you did. You are wiser after the fact; you realize that you made a mistake. You should not have done what you did. That constitutes a distancing from the deed not unlike the distancing of the person who repents of the wrong he did me.

What would be an appropriate response on my part to your expression of regret? Would it be appropriate for me to do something like not hold the deed against you? Literally not holding the deed against you is not in the picture, since not to hold it against you is to engage you as I would if I viewed the deed as not part of your moral history when in fact it is and I know it is. In the case we are considering it is not part of your moral history, not something you ought not to have done. It's no more than something you should not have done. We might call what's in view in this case your *sagacity-history,* and correspondingly, your *sagacious* character.

In my engagement with you I can treat this deed as not part of your sagacity-history. I know you did it; but in my engagement with you I can

12. The reader should be reminded of how, throughout my discussion, I have been using the words "should" and "ought." When I say that a person *should* do something, I mean that that would be the best thing for them to do. When I say that they *ought* to do something, I mean that it is their obligation to do that. Something may be the best thing for one to do without its being obligatory. For example, selling my present automobile and buying a new one may be the best thing for me to do; it will usually not be obligatory. Failure to do what one should do may be no more than unwise; failure to do what one ought to do makes one guilty, blameworthy. If one ought not do something, then one should not do it; the converse does hold.

treat it as not reflecting on your practical wisdom. What makes this appropriate is that you yourself declare that it was a mistake on your part; you no longer stand behind it. Though not the same as forgiveness, this is, structurally speaking, a cousin to forgiveness. To the best of my knowledge we have no name for this stance.

So once again, if you express regret for what you did to me, would it be appropriate for me to respond with this nameless cousin of forgiveness? Would it be appropriate for me, in my engagement with you, to treat you as if there had not been this failure of practical wisdom on your part? I think it would be appropriate.

The ancient writers, without discarding their eudaimonistic framework, might have taken note of, and recommended, this nameless cousin of forgiveness. But they did not. Why not? My best guess is that they assumed that practicing this nameless cousin of forgiveness would (or might) require foregoing punishment of the person who did what he should not have done; and they all assumed that foregoing punishment would be a violation of justice. If this speculation is correct, then we have to conclude that what accounts for the absence of any systematic recognition of repentance and forgiveness by the ancient ethicists was not only their failure to recognize inherent rights and obligations but also their commitment to (at least) the negative side of the reciprocity code. Consider Aristotle's account of "corrective" justice in Book 5 of the *Nicomachean Ethics*. In a transaction in which one party "is in the wrong and the other is being wronged, and . . . one inflicted injury and the other has received it," injustice has the character of an "inequality." So "the judge tries to equalize it; for in the case . . . in which one has received and the other has inflicted a wound, or one has slain and the other been slain, the suffering and the action have been unequally distributed; but the judge tries to equalize things by means of the penalty, taking away from the gain of the assailant" (1132a 4-10). Corrective justice consists of the equalizing of gains and losses; it consists of redressing the imbalance created by the injury. To forego such equalizing would be a violation of justice.

WHY FORGIVE?

Why forgive? What's the point of no longer holding against Hubert the wrong he did me? What's the point of engaging him as I would if I believed that his act was not part of his moral history, not a blot on his moral character? Why not either forget the wrong he did me or continue to hold it against him, even if he is contrite? Why walk the tightrope of remembering and resenting the wrong he did me while no longer holding it against him and hence no longer being angry at him for having done it?

Because forgiveness is *due* the penitent wrongdoer, says Griswold in one place. "Forgiveness is commendable because it is what the offender is due. . . . Forgiveness recognizes . . . that a wrong-doer who has taken all the necessary steps to rejoin the moral community would be disrespected in turn if forgiveness were withheld" (69).

I find this claim implausible, that repentance places on the victim the *obligation* to forgive, that not to forgive would be to *wrong* the wrongdoer, making the wrongdoer now the victim and the victim now the wrongdoer. Repentance is not, in this way, an obligation-generating act; my repentance does not put me in the position of having a morally legitimate claim on your forgiveness. Imagine the following domestic situation. The husband has wronged his wife. He now expresses genuine contrition. Then he adds, "And if you don't forgive me, you will be guilty of wronging me." This seems to me so far from expressing the moral truth of the situation as instead to be morally grotesque.[13]

The situation seems to me rather that the wrongdoer *offers* the victim his repentance in the *hope* that the victim will regard him in a new moral light, treat him as having a new moral identity. The victim should then respond to this offer, or try to respond, by offering forgiveness in return. But the "should" here is not the should of moral obligation but the "should" of this being the best thing to do. It's an act of supererogatory grace on the part of the victim to forgive. If the victim finds it impossible to forgive, her appropriate response is not feeling guilty but regretful. In the texts that first recognized and commended forgiveness, the Hebrew and Christian scriptures, forgiveness of the penitent sinner is consistently presented not as a duty but as an act of gratuitous love. The repentance of the sinner does not obligate God to forgive.

Forgiveness, says Arendt, "serves to undo the deeds of the past." She does not mean this literally, of course, since she also says that forgiveness is "the remedy for the irreversibility of human action," "the possible redemption from the predicament of irreversibility — of being unable to undo what one has done." Given that human action is irreversible, nothing can undo the wrong one did or the wrong one suffered; nothing can undo one's guilt or one's having been wronged. But

---

13. Not only does Griswold say what I quoted him above as saying. He also says that the moral value of forgiveness "lies in part in a change of heart on the victim's part, the letting go of resentment, and seeing the offender in a new light." And then he adds that "because the sentiments are not wholly at the command of the will, the forswearing of resentment cannot be obligatory" (68). These sentences seem to me to strike a very different note from those quoted above, a correct note, let me add.

Arendt is right; forgiveness is a remedy for misdeeds of the past. Our question is: what does this remedy do? What is the good that forgiveness brings about, or aims to bring about?

Let me quote Jean Hampton's answer:

> [Forgiveness] makes possible the benefits that come from a renewed relationship. And it also liberates each of them from the effects of the immoral action itself. The forgiver is no longer trapped in the position of the victim defending herself, and the wrongdoer is no longer in the position of the sinner, stained by sin and indebted to his victim. But perhaps the greatest good forgiveness can bring is the liberation of the wrongdoer from the effects of the victim's moral hatred. If the wrongdoer fears that the victim is right to see him as cloaked in evil, or as infected with moral rot, these fears can engender moral hatred of himself.[14]

John Burnaby, in *Christian Words and Christian Meanings*, makes a similar but slightly different point: "We shall be to one another what we were before, save for one important difference. I know now that you are a person who can forgive, . . . and that to keep me as a friend, or to avoid becoming my enemy, is more important to you than to maintain your own rights. And you know that I am a person who is not too proud to acknowledge his fault, and that your goodwill is worth more to me than the maintenance of my own cause. Forgiveness does not only forestall or remove enmity; it strengthens love."[15]

Contra Hampton, I think the emotion we are dealing with here is usually not *hatred* but *anger*. When I am inexcusably wronged, I am angry at the wrongdoer for what he did to me; usually I don't *hate* him. Given that correction, both Hampton's and Burnaby's comments seem to me wonderfully perceptive. Repentance and forgiveness bear the potential of liberating both victim and malefactor from the on-going morally destructive effects of the wrongdoing and of giving to each a new insight into the moral character of the other; thereby they open up the possibility of a renewed relationship. Punishment of the wrongdoer achieves neither of these; it neither liberates the parties from the moral pit in which they find themselves nor does it enable reconciliation. Nor does forgetfulness or any other form of "bygoning" by the victim achieve these goods; they too do not liberate victim and malefactor from that

14. Jean Hampton, "Forgiveness, Resentment, and Hatred," in *Forgiveness and Mercy*, p. 86.

15. John Burnaby, *Christian Words and Christian Meanings* (New York: Harper & Brothers, 1955), 87. I owe this reference to Vincent Brümmer.

moral pit nor do they open up the possibility of a renewed relationship based on reconciliation.

But given what I have called the *focused* nature of forgiveness and of the repentance that evokes it, one may tender forgiveness without expecting these benefits and without in fact bringing them about. The person who apologizes for some act of wronging me and whom I forgive for this act may remain unrepentant of all the other ways in which he has wronged me; he may be a scoundrel of whom I expect that he will wrong me again in the future. In such a case, forgiveness does not bring about the goods Hampton and Burnaby cite, nor does the forgiver expect that it will.

So suppose I judge that my forgiveness of the wrongdoer for the wrong he did me will not actualize these goods, in particular, that it will not make reconciliation possible except narrowly over this one act. Though the wrongdoer's repentance for this deed makes possible my forgiveness of him for this deed, there remain all the other ways in which he wronged me of which he has not repented and all the wrongings that I fear or expect he will perpetrate on me in the future. Is there then any reason to go ahead and forgive him for this one deed? If forgiving him for this one deed has no chance of bringing about the goods that Hampton and Burnaby mention, why forgive? Why does Jesus enjoin that one forgive the repentant wrongdoer seventy-seven times if one fully expects that he will wrong one a seventy-eighth time?

The answer to this question will not be found by looking yet farther afield for beneficial effects of forgiveness on the flourishing of victim or wrongdoer. If forgiveness is a good even in such cases, that's because it is an intrinsic good in the life of the wrongdoer that it's appropriate for the victim to choose as an end in itself; to do so is an act on her part of caring about the wrongdoer.

To forgive you for the wrong you did me upon discerning that you are penitent is to free you from the burden of this part of your past being a determinant of how I engage you henceforth. Such liberation from the past is an intrinsic good in your life; witness the fact that the repentant wrongdoer hopes for forgiveness. It's a good in your life that I no longer hold against you what you did to me; it's a good in your life that I am no longer angry with you on that account. My holding it against you would be an evil in your life; your flourishing would be impaired. The fully flourishing life does not contain such modes of treatment. That's why love forgives even when causal effects enhancing one's wellbeing or that of the wrongdoer are not to be expected.

Forgiveness as a mode of caring about the other is hard to bring off. It does not come naturally. What comes naturally is nursing one's anger and lusting for revenge.

Chapter Seventeen

DOES FORGIVENESS VIOLATE JUSTICE?

ANSELM'S PROBLEM WITH FORGIVENESS

We are ready for the question: does forgiveness violate justice? Or to put the question more precisely: does *full and complete* forgiveness violate justice? The person who wronged me has made clear that he repents of what he did; in response, I no longer hold it against him and no longer harbor negative feelings toward him because of what he did. What's the problem with that?

The problem, said Anselm, is the relation of punishment to forgiveness, on the one hand, and of punishment to justice, on the other. Forgiveness requires sparing the wrongdoer from punishment. So prominent is this aspect of forgiveness in his mind that in *Proslogion,* 9 and 11, he scarcely mentions forgiveness; he speaks instead of *sparing* and *saving* from punishment. But sparing the wrongdoer from punishment for his misdeed is a violation of justice. "What is more just than that the good should receive good things and the bad receive bad things" (*Proslogion,* 10)? It follows that to forgive the wrongdoer is to violate justice. To the best of my knowledge, everybody who thinks that forgiveness is a violation of justice agrees with Anselm's identification of the problem.

Why does Anselm hold that justice requires punishment of the wrongdoer? Anselm's question, "what is more just than that the good should receive good things and the bad receive bad things," gives the clue. Anselm embraced the reciprocity code and understood punishment as retribution. Punishment redresses the injury done to the victim by imposing an equivalent injury on the wrongdoer; as such, punishment implements the negative side of the reciprocity code.

DOESN'T JESUS' TEACHING IMPLY
THAT PUNISHMENT IS NOT REQUIRED?

To deal with the questions before us, whether forgiveness requires foregoing punishment of the wrongdoer and whether foregoing punishment is a violation of justice, it will be necessary to present what I regard as the best account of punishment presently available. Before we get to that, however, let me say that I find it confounding that Anselm, with no hesitation, embraced the reciprocity code and the retributive rationale for punishment that goes along with it.

Anselm knew Scripture well and took it as authoritative. He would have known that Jesus enjoined rejection of the reciprocity code. He would have known that Jesus taught that we are not to repay evil with evil but always to seek the good of self and neighbor, even of those who are one's enemies. He would have known that the writers of the epistolary literature in the New Testament taught the same thing. We are to reject the retributive rationale for punishment, not only of the repentant wrongdoer but also of the *unrepentant* — though nowhere does Jesus or any New Testament writer say that we are to *forgive* the unrepentant wrongdoer. Only if punishment brings about life-goods is punishment to be imposed.

In assuming that justice requires retributive punishment of wrong-doing, Anselm was in line with the majority opinion in the Christian tradition; it's that majority opinion that I find confounding. A common assumption in Christian theology has been that "God's justice must be satisfied." This assumption has led, among other things, to theories of the atonement according to which Christ, in allowing himself to be crucified, suffered on our behalf, thereby satisfying the requirements of retributive justice. It is we who are punished, not Christ; but it is Christ who undergoes the hard treatment that God assigned as our punishment, not we ourselves. Our status now is said to be that we are forgiven.

That Christ's suffering was in some way *for us* is undeniably a component of New Testament teaching. But if God forgives us for our wrong-doing, then the idea that our punishment took the form of Christ suffering on our behalf cannot be the right account of Christ's suffering *for us*. If you have been convicted of wrongdoing and been sentenced, and I now serve the sentence on your behalf — pay the fine, substitute myself for you in prison, whatever — then the situation is not that you have been forgiven and that punishment of you for your wrongdoing has been foregone. The situation is rather that the hard treatment I submit to *counts as* your punishment. By way of *my* subjection to hard treatment, *you* are punished.[1] It's not forgiveness that is taking place but vicarious punishment.

1. On the theory of the atonement sketched out in the text above, it is we who are punished, not Christ; the imposition of hard treatment on Christ counts as punishment of us for our wrongdoing. Christ is innocent; there is nothing to punish him for. On a somewhat different theory of the atonement, Christ takes our sins onto himself, so that whereas we were once guilty, we now no longer are. Christ is now guilty. The suffering Christ undergoes is then punishment of him for his wrongdoing. But this account resembles the

Why have so many Christian theologians and ethicists thought that justice requires retributive punishment of the wrongdoer when Jesus clearly teaches that we are not to return evil for evil — that we are to stop thinking in terms of paying back, getting even, evening things up, redressing injury with injury, harm with harm, evil with evil? Why has the declaration that God does not punish the repentant sinner but forgives him, and the injunction that we are to do likewise, not jolted Christian theologians and ethicists into concluding that justice does not require punishment? Why has it instead led them into calling vicarious punishment of the wrongdoer, *forgiveness* of the wrongdoer?

I don't know. Possibly because Jesus' teaching on this matter is less clear than I take it to be. More likely, I think, because the reciprocity code, and the idea of punishment as retribution that goes along with it, have had such a tight grip on human thought and imagination that not even Jesus' rejection of the code and his injunction to forgive rather than punish have been sufficient to loosen that grip, not even on those who take his words as authoritative. All about us people talk about getting even, giving malefactors what they have coming to them; it's hard to resist thinking the same way. My own tangential contact with the American criminal justice system convinces me that its fundamental rationale in the mind of the public is retribution, this overlaid with the rationales of deterrence and social protection.

THE REPROBATIVE THEORY OF PUNISHMENT

But what is punishment? Different writers answer that question differently. So just as we have to offer our own understanding of forgiveness, so too we will have to offer our own understanding of punishment.

In a seminal article titled "The Expressive Function of Punishment," Joel Feinberg articulated a rationale for punishment that I find attractive.[2] He offers his rationale as an alternative to the traditional retributive rationale. So before we look at Feinberg's rationale, let us remind ourselves of the structure of the retributive rationale.

The idea of retribution is the idea of redressing the injury done to

---

other in that we are not forgiven. We have no guilt; Christ is the guilty one. There is nothing to forgive us for.

In my discussion of Pauline justification in Chapter Twenty, I will argue that this is not what Paul is teaching in Romans, and that, in any case, it is ontologically impossible. If I wronged you at a certain time, then ever after it remains the case that I wronged you at that time and that I am guilty of having done so.

2. See Joel Feinberg, *Doing and Deserving* (Princeton: Princeton University Press, 1970), 95-118.

the victim by the imposition of an equivalent injury on the wrongdoer.[3] The point of doing this, say those who favor the retributive rationale for punishment, is that thereby an imbalance created by the wrongdoing is rectified. The theory does not claim that this rectification of imbalance is an intrinsic good in the life of either victim or wrongdoer, nor does it claim that it proves always to be an instrumental good in the life of one or the other; rather it claims that the moral order is thereby vindicated. Many retributive theorists assume or claim that this vindication of the moral order is (prima facie) obligatory; a few hold the weaker view that it is something we *should* do, *ceteris paribus*.

The idea of punishment as rectifying an imbalance goes back into antiquity. In her essay "The Retributive Idea"[4] Jean Hampton presents an interesting contemporary articulation of the idea. Those who wrong others, she says, "objectively demean them. They incorrectly believe, or else fail to realize, that others' value rules out the treatment their actions have accorded the others, and they incorrectly believe or implicitly assume that their own value is high enough to make this treatment possible. So, implicit in their wrongdoings is a message about their value relative to that of their victims" (124). Punishment, by subjecting the wrongdoer to hard treatment, sends a counter-message to the effect that the message of relative worth implicit in the wrongdoer's action was mistaken. Punishment is thus the assertion of

> moral truth in the face of its denial. If I have value equal to that of my assailant, then that must be made manifest after I have been victimized. By victimizing me, the wrongdoer has declared himself elevated with respect to me, acting as a superior who is permitted to use me for his purposes. A false moral claim has been made. Moral reality has been denied. The retributivist demands that the false claim be corrected. The lord must be humbled to show that he isn't the lord of the victim. If I cause the wrongdoer to suffer in propor-

3. Some writers use the term "retributive theory" more broadly, to apply to any theory of punishment which holds that the person being punished must *deserve* the hard treatment of the punishment on account of his guilt. Though I find it not at all clear what's being claimed here with the term "deserve," I suppose it would be correct to say that Feinberg's account of punishment requires that the person being punished *deserve* his hard treatment. The current Merriam-Webster's Collegiate Dictionary gives, as the first meaning for "retribution," *to pay back*. This, of course, is what the Latin *re-tribuere* meant. For this reason, I think it best to call a theory of punishment a "retributive" theory only if it sees *redressing the injury done to the victim by the imposition of an equivalent injury on the wrongdoer* as the rationale for punishment.

4. The essay is the fourth chapter of *Forgiveness and Mercy*, which she co-authored with Jeffrie Murphy. Murphy contributed the first, third, and fifth chapters, Hampton the second and fourth.

tion to my suffering at his hands, his elevation over me is denied, and moral reality is reaffirmed. I master the purported master, showing that he is my peer. (125)

In short, "retributive punishment is the defeat of the wrongdoer at the hands of the victim (either directly or indirectly through an agent of the victim's, e.g., the state) that symbolizes the correct relative value of wrongdoer and victim. It is a symbol that is conceptually required to reaffirm a victim's equal worth in the face of a challenge to it. . . . [Its] *telos* is not so much to produce good as it is to establish goodness" (125-26). Punishment strikes "a blow for morality." It "plants the flag of morality" (130).[5]

Feinberg begins the presentation of his alternative rationale for punishment by exploring the difference between punishments and penalties — examples of a penalty being a parking ticket, a library fine, an offside penalty in soccer, and disqualification from some competition for failing to answer all the questions in the application form. Both penalties and punishments belong to the type, "infliction of hard treatment by an authority on a person for his prior failing in some respect (usually an infraction of a rule or command)." The question is, what differentiates punishments from penalties within this type?

Feinberg's answer is that punishment has a symbolic significance that the infliction of a penalty does not have. Specifically, "punishment is a conventional device for the expression of attitudes of resentment and indignation, and of judgments of disapproval and reprobation, on the part either of the punishment authority himself or of those 'in whose name' the punishment is inflicted. Punishment, in short, has a *symbolic significance*" (98).

Let me unpack this a bit. By "reprobation" Feinberg means "the stern judgment of disapproval" (101) — that is, *moral* disapproval. Hard treatment for something a person did, on the one hand, and moral reprobation and resentment of it, on the other, often occur separately. The fine imposed when one returns a library book late can be rather hard treatment; but its imposition does not have the symbolic significance of conveying a judgment of moral disapproval on deed or doer or of express-

5. Hampton's account is an insightful analysis of most if not all cases of wrongdoing in which the malefactor treats the victim as he does in order to secure some personal advantage. But many cases of wrongdoing are not of this sort. People sometimes wrong others for good and noble reasons; the wrongdoer seeks to achieve some great good for his fellows and finds it necessary to deceive some people, exile others, kill yet others, and so forth. In such cases, there is no attempt on the part of the wrongdoer to elevate his own worth relative to that of the victim; rather, the great good that he is pursuing blinds him to the fact that the worth of those who are his victims rules out this way of treating them.

ing resentment or indignation — though a moralistic librarian may accompany the fine with such a judgment. It has no particular symbolic significance whatsoever; it's just a device for encouraging people to return borrowed books promptly. Conversely, though a verbal denunciation is a reprobative judgment and expresses the emotion of resentment or indignation, it is not the imposition of hard treatment.

Unique to punishment, on Feinberg's view, is that hard treatment has gotten connected with a judgment of moral disapproval of deed and doer and with feelings of indignation, resentment, and anger. To use the language of speech-act theory: the act of subjecting the wrongdoer to hard treatment *counts as* the illocutionary act of condemning him and his deed. One performs the illocutionary act of condemning him and what he did *by* performing the act of subjecting him to hard treatment. In turn, by performing the illocutionary act of condemning him and his deed, one expresses feelings of indignation and resentment for what he did and anger at him for doing it. To quote Feinberg, "To say that the very physical treatment itself expresses condemnation is to say simply that certain forms of hard treatment have become the conventional symbols of public reprobation. This is neither more nor less paradoxical than to say that certain words have become conventional vehicles in our language for the expression of certain attitudes, or that champagne is the alcoholic beverage traditionally used in celebration of great events, or that black is the color of mourning" (100).[6]

It should be noted that the focus of punishment, on this account, is entirely on the wrongdoer and his deed: the imposition of hard treatment on him counts as condemning *him for his deed,* and it is a way of expressing resentment of *the deed done* and anger at *him* for doing it.[7]

Feinberg notes that most of the benefits regularly claimed for certain kinds of punishment — rehabilitation of the wrongdoer, deterrence of similar wrongdoing by others, protection of the public from the wrongdoer — are only loosely connected with its nature as a judgment of condemnation and an expression of negative feelings toward deed and doer. Punishment does not always achieve those life-goods; and often there are other ways of achieving those goods than punishment. However, there is one social benefit of punishment that is intimately con-

6. Aristotle did not think of hard treatment imposed on a wrongdoer as a mode of condemnation; he thought of it as a way of correcting an inequality.

7. I hold that institutions, such as the state, can perform illocutionary acts, but that they cannot have feelings of resentment and anger and hence cannot express such feelings. Thus whereas both aspects of Feinberg's theory, the illocutionary act aspect and the expression of feelings aspect, hold for punishment performed by persons, only the first aspect holds for punishment performed by institutions. I will not clutter the text above with explicit recognition of this qualification.

nected to its nature, namely "symbolic nonacquiescence," as Feinberg calls it (102).

Punishment conveys to those who have ears to hear that society does not condone what was done. Referring to paramour killings, which were allowed in Texas until rather recently, Feinberg argues that the demand that such killings be punished, whatever else it may be, is "the demand that . . . the state *go on record* against paramour killings and the law *testify to the recognition* that such killings are wrongful." He observes that "punishment no doubt would also help deter killers," and "this too is a desideratum." But deterrence "is not to be identified with reprobation, for deterrence might be achieved by a dozen other techniques from simple penalties and forfeitures to exhortation and propaganda. By contrast, "effective public denunciation and, through it, symbolic nonacquiescence in the crime seem virtually to require punishment" (103).

Above I spoke of the *retributive* rationale for punishment. What shall we call the rationale for punishment that Feinberg has articulated, and what shall we call punishment imposed for that reason? Feinberg calls his theory of punishment the *expressive* theory; he gives no name to the punishment itself whose rationale is spelled out in the theory. It would be odd to call it "expressive punishment." I propose highlighting the illocutionary-act aspect of punishment on his account by calling the rationale for punishment that he articulates, the *reprobative rationale,* and calling punishment imposed for that reason, *reprobative punishment* or *punishment as reprobation.*

When reprobative punishment is exercised properly, it's an intrinsic good in the life of punisher and wrongdoer, and an important instrumental good for society in general, perhaps also for the wrongdoer. Of course the hard treatment which is a component of reprobative punishment is, as such, a diminution of the wrongdoer's wellbeing. But the entire package is a good in his life — not an evil imposed to redress an evil. Recall that Moses cited reproving one's neighbor as an example of loving the neighbor (Leviticus 19:17).

Feinberg introduced his discussion by distinguishing two genera of the type, *infliction of hard treatment by an authority on a person for some prior failing on his part,* one having penalties as its members, the other having punishments as its members. At various points in his discussion he assumes that there is also a third genus of the type. The members of this third genus have no common name so far as I know. Mentioning some of its most prominent members will give the idea, however: hard treatment imposed on a wrongdoer for the purpose of rehabilitating him, hard treatment imposed on a wrongdoer for the purpose of deterring others from doing the sort of thing he did, and the hard treatment of incarceration, house arrest, or exile imposed on a wrongdoer for the purpose of protecting society from further acts of wrongdoing on his part.

Hard treatment imposed for these reasons is often called "punishment." I think Feinberg is right to hold that, strictly speaking, they are not that. Punishment is backward-looking; one punishes someone for what he did. Both the retributive and reprobative rationales for punishment incorporate this backward-looking feature. But hard treatment imposed for the purpose of rehabilitation, deterrence, or protection, lacks this backward-looking feature. It is focused exclusively on bringing about some future good.

A final point before we move on. When one has Feinberg's account of punishment in mind and then reads Paul's description of governmental authority in Romans 13, what leaps out at once is Paul's declaration that government is God's servant "to execute wrath (*orgē*, anger) on the wrongdoer." Paul cites deterrence as a beneficial effect of governmental punishment. But executing anger on the wrongdoer is what governmental punishment is as such — or what it *should be* as such. Punishment, when done with proper intent, is a way of expressing anger at the wrongdoer and reproving him for what he did. Nowhere does Paul say that it is the task of government to repay, to get even, to even things up, to pay back evil with evil, to redress injury with injury. Nowhere does he suggest that retributive punishment is a legitimate function of government. At the end of the preceding chapter he said that if there is to be vengeance, evil repaid by evil, it's up to God to do it. The God-given task of government is reprobative punishment, not retributive punishment.

DOES FORGIVENESS REQUIRE FOREGOING PUNISHMENT?

We are now prepared to address Anselm's two assumptions. Begin with this: does forgiving the wrongdoer require that one forego punishing him for what he did and require declining to support the imposition of punishment on him by others? Many who have written about forgiveness have claimed that it does not require this. Here our distinction between partial forgiveness and full and complete forgiveness becomes indispensable. Though partial forgiveness is compatible with punishing the wrongdoer or supporting the imposition of punishment, full and complete forgiveness is not.

Let's assume that the punishment in question would be just. Forgiveness consists of engaging someone as one would if one regarded what he did as part of his personal history but not part of his moral history; it consists of engaging him as one would if one excused what he did — with the exception that one continues to believe, about him, that he is in fact blamable for what he did. But punishment, be it retributive or reprobative, is *for* the wrong done; to impose it or support its imposition is to engage the person *as a wrongdoer*. If one engaged him as one would if one excused him, one would oppose the imposition of punishment; a person is not justly punished if his act of wronging is to be excused. Partial forgiveness is compatible with imposing and supporting the imposition of punishment; while supporting the imposition of punishment one might, in various other ways, engage the wrongdoer as one would if one excused him. But full and complete forgiveness is incompatible.

The person who has been wronged is thus faced with a choice. He can impose or support the imposition of punishment, but then his forgiveness will necessarily be partial at best; or he can commit himself to full and complete forgiveness, but then he will have to oppose the imposition of punishment. The question to be considered, then, is whether to choose the latter of these is somehow to violate justice. Anselm and many others have held that it is. If they are right about that, then one ought not choose that option. And if one ought not choose that option, one ought not offer the wrongdoer full and complete forgiveness. We'll address this question shortly.

Does Forgiveness Require Foregoing Hard Treatment Aimed at Rehabilitation, Protection, or Deterrence?

What about rehabilitation, protection, and deterrence? Does full and complete forgiveness require that one oppose the imposition of hard treatment on offenders for those reasons? Well, recall that I may believe that the person who wronged me is genuinely repentant of what he did to me and may forgive him for that while nonetheless believing that he is likely to do the same sort of thing again, to me or others. Thus, even though I fully and completely forgive him for this act, I may believe that he should be rehabilitated and that society should be protected until he is. If I also believe that the best way to bring about these goods is to impose, or support the imposition of, certain forms of hard treatment on him, then I will be in favor of that.

The situation for deterrence is different. We are to suppose that there is a law or rule in effect, and that sanctions have been attached to the violation of this law or rule. Let us assume that the law or rule is just, that the sanctions are just, and that the sanctions are justly imposed. The imposition of the sanctions on someone is hard treatment; it's the threat of this imposition that functions as deterrence.

Now if the sanctions are justly imposed, they will be imposed only on those who did in fact break the rule or law; nobody will be "framed."

And they will be imposed only on those who are blamable for breaking the rule or law — that is, not excusable. Thus to impose or support the imposition of sanctions on the wrongdoer is perforce not to engage him as one would if one excused him. Full and complete forgiveness is incompatible with imposing or supporting the just imposition of hard treatment on a wrongdoer for the purpose of deterrence.

Here too, then, the person who has been wronged is faced with a choice: if he imposes or supports the imposition of deterrence-sanctions, his forgiveness will have to be at most partial; if he commits himself to full and complete forgiveness, he will have to oppose the imposition of deterrence-sanctions. The question to be considered is whether to choose the latter of these is somehow to violate justice. If it is, he ought not choose that option. And if he ought not choose that option, he ought not offer the wrongdoer full and complete forgiveness. Only partial forgiveness of a certain sort would be acceptable.

DOES FOREGOING REPROBATIVE PUNISHMENT VIOLATE JUSTICE?

What we have seen, so far, is that full and complete forgiveness requires foregoing reprobative punishment and requires foregoing the imposition of deterrence-sanctions, when such imposition would be just. The question that remains is whether such foregoings would violate or undermine justice.

Start with punishment. If one believes in retributive punishment and holds that, whenever possible, it *ought* to be imposed on each and every wrongdoer for each and every act of wrongdoing — a preposterous position in my view; life would be a horror — then one will of course hold that to forego punishment is to violate justice. But suppose that one rejects the retributive rationale and instead embraces Feinberg's reprobative rationale. Is it the case, on this rationale, that to forego punishment is perforce to violate justice?

What reason might one have for thinking that it is? Well, consider the following famous (or infamous) passage in Kant's *Metaphysical Elements of Justice:*

> Even if a civil society were to dissolve itself by common agreement of all its members (for example if the people inhabiting an island decided to separate and disperse themselves around the world), the last murderer remaining in prison must first be executed, so that everyone will duly receive what his actions are worth and so that the bloodguilt thereof will not be fixed on the people because they failed to insist on carrying out the punishment; for if they fail to do

so, they may be regarded as accomplices in this public violation of legal justice.[8]

Kant gives no indication that he means what he says here to apply only to unrepentant murderers; one has to assume he means it to apply both to the repentant and the unrepentant. At the very end of the passage he speaks of *legal* justice as violated by the release of murderers; from the passage as a whole it's clear that he regards this violation of legal justice as also a violation of moral justice.

Kant claims that failure to punish wrongdoers is a double violation of justice. First, what is due a wrongdoer is that he receive a punishment befitting the gravity of his wrongdoing — in Kant's words, that he "duly receive what his actions are worth." To fail to impose on him the punishment due him is to violate justice; justice requires rendering to a person what is due him or her. Whether this is true is, of course, the very question that we are presently considering. So let's move on to Kant's second reason. To fail to punish the wrongdoer is to become an accomplice in his wrongdoing; bloodguilt for the deed is now on our hands as well as his. "Accomplice" is of course used metaphorically. What Kant means, no doubt, is that to forego punishing a wrongdoer is to condone his wrongdoing. It is one's condoning of his wrongdoing that makes one complicit in it.

Is it true that foregoing punishment of the wrongdoer constitutes condoning what he did — along with sending a message of condonation and perhaps becoming an accomplice in his wrongdoing? The point is directly relevant to Feinberg's reprobative rationale for punishment: to punish is to condemn what is done and to send a message of non-condonation. Rather than considering the claims in general, let's focus on those cases in which foregoing or urging the foregoing of punishment is motivated by forgiveness. Does foregoing or urging the foregoing of reprobative punishment of the wrongdoer because one has fully and completely forgiven him constitute condoning his wrongdoing and sending a message to that effect?

Hampton quotes the same passage from Kant that I have been referring to and comments: "I agree with Kant that we would be accomplices in the crime if we failed to punish its perpetrator, because we would be condoning the evidence it gave us of the relative worth of victim and offender, or to put it another way, because we would be acquiescing in the message it sent about the victim's inferiority. Kant takes it as fundamental that to be committed to morality is to be committed to asserting and

8. Immanuel Kant, *The Metaphysical Elements of Justice*, trans. John Ladd (Indianapolis: Bobbs-Merrill, 1965), 102.

defending it no matter what the consequences. Hence it is morally required that we send an annulling message after a crime so that the victim's value receives its proper defense" (131).

Hampton explicitly concedes that mercy may sometimes be appropriate, understanding mercy as "the suspension or mitigation of a punishment that would otherwise be deserved as retribution, . . . granted
out of pity and compassion for the wrongdoer" (158). Her thought is
that the obligation "to annul the wrongdoer's immoral message" (159)
may sometimes conflict with other and weightier obligations, "in particular, to the wrongdoer as a human being" (158). But her heart is not in
this concession. The discussion is brief; and it closes not with an affirmation of the value of mercy but with a warning against it; mercy "risks undermining both the deterrent message and the expression of the value
the wrongdoer has transgressed" (159).

Note the structure of the argument now before us. Feinberg's
reprobative rationale for punishment holds that if I punish someone,
then I condemn what he did and send a message of non-condonation.
Kant and Hampton hold that if I forego punishment, then I condone
what was done and send a message to that effect. The Kant-Hampton
conditional is a denial of the antecedent (and the consequent) of
Feinberg's conditional. The Feinberg conditional does not imply the
Kant-Hampton conditional; to suppose that it does would be to commit
the fallacy of denying the antecedent. But the two conditionals are compatible. So we have to consider the Kant-Hampton conditional on its
merits.

I find it implausible to suppose that not explicitly condemning or
urging the condemnation of some wrong is perforce to condone it and
send a message to that effect. Issuing condemnations of everything that
one does not condone would take up far too much of one's time and
sour all one's relationships. Whether or not, in a given case, not explicitly condemning or urging the condemnation of some wrong constitutes condoning it and sending a message to that effect depends entirely on context.

Add to this the point that though reprobative punishment of someone for what he did is a way of condemning deed and doer, punishment
is not the only means available for issuing a condemnation. So why hold
that not doing it this way perforce counts as condoning it? If a person in
authority makes clear by his speech that he firmly condemns some deed
and firmly blames the person who did it, but then goes on to declare
that, because the offender has repented, out of mercy he will forego
punishing him, why would that constitute condoning the deed and
sending a message of condonation? It's true that mutely declining to
punish an offender is readily interpreted as condoning what he did. But

declaring that the person before one is guilty, and then announcing that, because he has repented, one will for the sake of some good forego punishment — surely foregoing punishment in that context is not reasonably interpreted as condoning what he did and sending a message of condonation.

So far, then, we have uncovered no reason to conclude that foregoing reprobative punishment of a wrongdoer is, as such, condoning what he did and sending a message to that effect. But what about the following consideration? Feinberg observes that on the expressive theory of punishment, the proportioning of severity of punishment to severity of crime that is traditionally demanded of corrective justice can be understood along the following lines. Take as a given that condemnation is the sort of speech act that comes in degrees of emphasis, and add the thesis that, in general, the worse the crime, the more emphatic should be the condemnation. The way this general principle gets implemented, when condemnation takes the form of punishment, is that the worse the crime, the harder the treatment imposed on the criminal.

Now suppose that an authority, after issuing an emphatic verbal condemnation of what the person before him has done, announces that because the offender has repented, out of mercy for the offender or his family, or for the sake of social peace, he will forego applying the specified punishment. Let our previous point be conceded, that this entire package does not constitute condoning what the person did, nor does it send a message of condonation. Nonetheless, this total package would seem too weak a condemnation compared to that pronounced on someone else who committed the same crime and is sentenced, say, to twenty years in prison. So does not the whole package send the message that this person's wronging is less odious than that of the other person? If so, that would violate justice, would it not, since the crime was in fact of the same magnitude? If there is a system in place for expressing judgments as to the relative severity of crimes — worse crime, harder treatment — then to break with the system and give some crime a less harsh treatment than the system specifies, or no hard treatment at all, would be to send a wrong message, would it not? Talk as loudly as one will, one's actions carry the message that it was not such a bad crime after all.

I don't see it. Suppose that the criminal code has a variety of words to indicate the relative severity of crimes — as in fact our criminal code does: "first-degree murder," "second-degree murder," "manslaughter," etc. Suppose that the jury convicts the person in the dock of second-degree murder, that the judge gives a speech about the heinousness of such a crime, and sentences him in accord with the criminal code, but that the executive then steps in and, because the offender has repented, he, out of mercy for his plight and that of his family, reduces his sentence. Would any reasonable person interpret this whole package as carrying the message that it was not such a bad crime after all? Would not any reasonable person conclude that the jury and judge had determined that he had committed a terrible crime for which severe punishment was appropriate, but that the executive had decided, out of mercy and because the offender had repented, to reduce the punishment?

In short, I see no reason to conclude that foregoing reprobative punishment is perforce a violation of justice. Of course, if the executive pardons the wrongdoer because he is white, male, wealthy, socially prominent, or of a certain religion or nationality, that would send a wrong message about morality. But on the face of it, pardoning a repentant wrongdoer out of mercy is significantly different from pardoning on the basis of such factors.

Does Foregoing Deterrence-Sanctions Violate Justice?

We saw that full and complete forgiveness of a wrongdoer not only implies that one will decline to impose or support the imposition of reprobative punishment on him; it also implies that one will decline to impose or support the imposition of deterrence-sanctions on him. That raises the question whether this would in some way violate justice. If so, then it would be wrong to extend full and complete forgiveness.

Let's confine our reflections to those cases in which the rule or law to which sanctions are attached is just, in which the sanctions themselves are just, and in which the sanctions are justly imposed. As we noted earlier, a condition of the sanctions being justly imposed on someone is that he have violated the law and be culpable for doing so. Let's add that justice requires the existence of a system to deter the actions that this system seeks to deter.

The system seeks to deter all violations of the rule or law for which the agent is culpable — not just those violations for which the agent remains subsequently impenitent, but *all* violations. I doubt that a repentance-exception attached to the rule or law even makes sense (such-and-such is forbidden unless one repents afterwards), but if it does, such an exception would conflict with the aim of deterring all actions of such-and-such a sort, not just those for which the agent remains impenitent. It would equally conflict with the aim of the system if a repentance-exception were attached to the sanctions rather than to the laws — i.e., if it were specified that the sanctions are to be imposed only on those who culpably violate the law and do not subsequently repent.

What remains to consider is selective *application* of the sanctions. Suppose that Hubert has violated the law in wronging me as he did, but that he is now repentant and that, in response to his repentance, I offer him full and complete forgiveness. I will then decline to impose or support the imposition on him of the deterrence-sanctions attached to the law. Does that refusal violate justice in some way?

Well, consider the following. Suppose that I combine my advocacy of exempting Hubert from the application of the sanctions with resistance to extending the same exemption to other repentant violators. That would be unfair to those others, unjust; why only Hubert and his wronging of me?[9] So suppose that, to avoid this injustice, I mount a campaign in favor of the general principle that all repentant violators be exempted from the imposition of the sanctions. Were this principle accepted, that would undermine the system. And surely it is wrong to advocate a principle that, if accepted, would undermine the system. The fact, if it is a fact, that one expects to be a voice crying in the wilderness would not make it right.

My conclusion is that when there is a just deterrence-system in place and when justice requires the existence of such a system, then one would violate justice if one refrained from applying the sanctions to someone who has violated the law because one fully and completely forgives him.[10] One's forgiveness has to be partial.

My argument raises a theological quandary. Hebrew and Christian scriptures pervasively present God as issuing laws to human beings and attaching sanctions to those laws, and never do they suggest that those laws and sanctions have a repentance-exception attached. God is also presented as offering full and complete forgiveness to the penitent wrongdoer; this is a manifestation of God's love that we can count on. But my argument implies that if this is a principle we can count on, the deterrence-function of the sanctions is undermined.

My response to this quandary is that God's justice system — if we may call it that — should not be thought of along deterrence lines but along reprobative lines. God's punishment of human beings for their wrongdoing is a condemnation of what was done and an expression of God's

9. As my argument in the next chapter will make clear, it's not the mere arbitrariness of wanting to extend an exemption only to Hubert that makes what I do unfair and unjust; it's the favoritism that's the problem.

10. My argument explicitly presupposes that the deterrence-system is a just system. As to whether the American system of criminal justice is a just deterrence-system, the following remarks of Jeffrie Murphy are very much to the point: "I cannot help thinking . . . that many of the unspeakably brutish conditions that we tolerate in our jails and prisons flow not from stated legitimate desires for justice and crime control but rather from a vindictiveness so out of control that it actually becomes a kind of malice. If we are tempted so to demonize those who have wronged us and start viewing them as monsters, we would be wise to recall Nietzsche's famous warning: 'Take care that when you do battle with monsters that you do not become a monster'" (*Getting Even*, 34).

anger. Full and complete forgiveness, as we saw earlier, requires foregoing reprobative punishment. But what we also saw is that such foregoing
does not, as such, violate or undermine justice.

Chapter Eighteen

JUST AND UNJUST GENEROSITY

JUSTICE IN THE PARABLE OF THE LABORERS IN THE VINEYARD

Sometimes one's bestowal of a good on someone other than oneself, or one's distribution of some good among a number of persons, is morally required of one; it's one's duty. But sometimes it is not out of duty but out of generosity that one bestows or distributes some good; it's an act of gratuitous generosity. Yet gratuitous generosity sometimes perpetrates injustice. Though one would wrong no one if one did not bestow or distribute the good, in bestowing or distributing the good as one does, one wrongs someone. The question to be considered in this chapter is, what makes gratuitous generosity sometimes unjust?

The justice of God's generosity was the theme of several of Jesus' parables, for example, that of the laborers in the vineyard, already discussed in an earlier chapter. Recall how the parable goes. The owner of a vineyard hired some day laborers early in the morning, saying that he would pay them the going daily wage. He hired others at nine o'clock, telling them he would pay them whatever was just *(dikaios)*. He hired an additional group around noon, another around three o'clock, and a final group around five o'clock. When the working day was over, he instructed his manager to pay the workers, beginning with those hired last and ending with those hired first.

Those hired last were given an amount equal to the going daily wage. Those hired first took note, and expected considerably more. But everybody was paid the same. So they grumbled. They had worked long hours through the heat of the day whereas the five o'clockers had worked only one hour when the heat was moderating. It wasn't fair to give equal pay for unequal work. It was an in-your-face injustice.

Nygren, as we saw, interpreted the landowner as saying that surely he was permitted to be generous to the latecomers even if that meant treating the early workers unjustly. I called attention to the fact that what the landowner actually said was quite different — not that he was permitted to dispense his generosity as he wished even though, in so doing, he was treating the early workers unjustly, but that he was not treating the early workers unjustly. "Friend," he said to one of the grumblers, "I am doing you no injustice *(adikos);* did you not agree with me for the usual daily

207

wage? Take what belongs to you and go; I choose to give to this last the same as I give to you. Am I not allowed to do what I choose with what belongs to me? Or are you envious because I am generous?" When discussing the parable earlier, I dropped the discussion at this point; I did not express my own view about the landowner's reply.

The landowner obviously expresses Jesus' point of view. Some who hear or read the parable will agree with the landowner on that account; they accept what Jesus says because Jesus said it. I think most others will believe that the grumblers have a case. The landowner was not obligated to be charitable to anyone; his obligation was to pay the workers what was due them for the work they had done. But if he was going to go beyond his obligations and be generous, then he was obligated to be just in his generosity. The policy that he settled on was patently unjust: a big dollop of charity to those who worked only one hour and none to those who worked all day. The response of the landowner to the grumblers ignores this point. Yes, of course he's permitted to be generous; nobody said he wasn't. But he's not permitted to be so patently unjust in how he dispenses his generosity.

It's not hard to imagine a scenario in which the charge of injustice is somewhat mitigated. Suppose the landowner was aware of the fact that these workers all had families dependent on them and that the going daily wage was barely enough to support a family. That's what led him to act as he did; he cared about these workers and their families. This interpretation fits the point about the kingdom of God that Jesus was using the parable to make. It's important to everyone that they have a place in the kingdom. That's why God treats the late-coming Gentiles the same as the Jews who have labored long and hard in the vineyards of Torah.

The early workers have an obvious response. If all along it was the landowner's intention to give everybody an amount equal to the going daily wage, whether they had earned it or not, why didn't he announce this to everybody at the beginning? Then everybody could freely have decided how much work he wanted to put in.

Of course the landowner was no fool; he knew that if he openly presented this option to all the day laborers at the beginning of the day, he would not have enough workers to get the work done. So he manipulated the situation so as both to get the work done and to be seen as generous. The result of his curious combination of generosity with pay for work done was that he wronged the early workers; he perpetrated injustice.

Let's come back to the parable after exploring what it is, in general, that makes generosity sometimes unjust.

THE ARISTOTELIAN PARADIGM AND WHY IT HAS TO BE REJECTED

Our concern here is solely with those cases in which the distribution of some good to one or more parties is not required by justice but is an act of pure generosity — cases in which none of the recipients would have been treated unjustly had no distribution been made. Refusal to make the distribution might reflect poorly on the character of the person who declines the opportunity to be generous; but it would not constitute wronging anybody.

Anyone acquainted with the Western philosophical tradition will at this point think immediately of Aristotle's formula for justice in distributions. Aristotle held that justice in distributions always takes the form of equality of some sort, and injustice, the form of inequality of some sort. I judge that the statement of Aristotle's idea that Joel Feinberg gives in one of his articles is more illuminating of what Aristotle had in mind than are Aristotle's own formulations. When divisible goods are being distributed, says Feinberg, "the Aristotelian paradigm [is that] justice requires that relevantly similar cases be treated similarly and relevantly dissimilar cases be treated dissimilarly in direct proportion to the relevant differences between them."[1] Injustice in such cases consists in "arbitrary and invidious discrimination of one kind or another: a departure from the requisite form of equal treatment without good reason" (299).

Is the Aristotelian paradigm, as formulated by Feinberg, correct? Does it give us what we are looking for? Does it pinpoint what it is that makes generosity sometimes unjust?

Let's be clear what we are asking here. In my account of justice I affirmed the traditional principle that treating someone as justice requires consists of rendering to that person what is due him or her. The question before us now is not whether the Aristotelian principle is an alternative account of justice that ought to be taken seriously, nor is it whether the Aristotelian principle is an account of justice that proves, on analysis, to be the same as the traditional one. The question is whether the Aristotelian principle explains why it is that, in some generous distributions, one or more persons are not receiving what is due them — why it is that one or more persons are wronged.

A couple of preliminary comments. There's a difference in how the Aristotelian principle is formulated in the two sentences that I quoted from Feinberg. The idea expressed in the first sentence is that justice in distributions consists of treating relevantly similar cases similarly and relevantly dissimilar cases dissimilarly. The idea expressed in the second

---

1. "Noncomparative Justice," in *The Philosophical Review* 83.3 (1974): 297-338, here 310.

sentence is that justice in distributions requires that similar cases be treated similarly unless one has a good reason for doing otherwise — or as Feinberg puts it in other places, unless one has a *morally relevant* reason for doing otherwise. The first sentence speaks of relevant similarities and dissimilarities. The second speaks of morally relevant reasons. According to the first formulation, dissimilarity in one's assignment of goods has to be justified by pointing to some relevant dissimilarity among the potential recipients; otherwise the assignment is unjust. According to the second formulation, dissimilarity in one's assignment of goods among potential recipients has to be justified by some morally relevant reason; otherwise the assignment is unjust.

The difference is only skin deep. The idea behind both formulations is the following. Suppose one has some good that one wishes to distribute and that there are a number of persons for whom it would be a good. Then justice requires that one distribute it equally or proportionately among those persons unless one has some morally relevant reason for excluding some or giving some less; and a morally relevant reason will always consist of some morally relevant difference between the included and the excluded. What makes a distribution unjust is that it is a departure from equality or proper proportionality that cannot point to a morally relevant difference. Either there is no reason; the distribution is arbitrary. Or the reason is not a morally relevant reason; for example, one withholds the benefit from those people there because they have a skin color one doesn't like.

Reflection on a few cases makes clear that if the Aristotelian principle is to have any plausibility whatsoever, one has to be exceedingly lax and generous in what one is willing to count as morally relevant similarities and dissimilarities. Often the relevant similarities and dissimilarities will not be in the persons as such but in one or another relational property that they possess or lack.

For example: come Christmas, I give gifts to those to whom I am especially attached — family and friends. The children on my block are not much different from my own children; nonetheless, I don't give them gifts. And my neighbor is not much different from my friend; but I don't give him a gift either. We all agree that there is nothing unjust in this sort of partiality. So if the Aristotelian principle is to hold for such cases, we have to regard the possession and lack of the relational property of *being someone to whom I am attached* as constituting a morally relevant similarity and dissimilarity. This is just one of many examples of the point.

The example can be used to make another preliminary point. When selecting Christmas gifts for my children, my attention is focused entirely on doing my best to insure that they will more or less equally prize the gifts I give them; the thought that I am giving presents only to my children and not to the children on my block never crosses my mind. But in applying the Aristotelian principle, one has to attend not only to relevant similarities and dissimilarities within the distribution class on which one is focused but also to relevant similarities and dissimilarities between those within that class and those outside. It is especially when one attends to the latter similarities and dissimilarities that one comes to realize how lax and generous the idea of a morally relevant reason has to be if the Aristotelian principle is to come out true. Of course, if the good that one is distributing is non-divisible, then the distinction between these two sets of similarities and dissimilarities disappears; in such cases, there are no similarities and dissimilarities among the members of the distribution class, since the class has only one member.

Enough by way of preliminaries. Does the Aristotelian principle explain what makes the just exercises of generosity just and the unjust exercises unjust? Well, suppose that I am seated at my desk, getting ready to write out checks for my end-of-the-year charitable contributions. Over the course of the year I have sorted out the appeals for funds that came my way, filing those from organizations that seemed to me to serve a worthy cause and to be needy of funds, and tossing the others into the wastebasket. Now I open my file and find that I have collected appeals from thirty organizations, to none of which I feel any particular attachment.

As I am wondering how to proceed, the Aristotelian paradigm comes to mind. I conclude that what it tells me to do is rank these organizations in terms of some combination of worthiness and need, and then proportion my contributions accordingly. But as I am reflecting further on whether to employ this understanding of the principle as my guide, it occurs to me that I have been almost entirely passive up to this point. I have made no attempt to search out needy and worthy organizations. I have simply taken the appeals that arrived in the mail and sorted them into two categories. But surely there are many needy and worthy organizations that happen not to have had me on their mailing list. Is that a morally relevant reason for treating them differently from those that did have me on their list? I'm not sure; I find that I don't have a very good grip on this concept of a morally relevant reason. But it doesn't seem like a morally relevant reason. It's hard to see why one would think it was, other than that one wants to keep the Aristotelian paradigm from coming out false for this case.

I dismiss these unsettling thoughts and return to asking myself whether I should follow the Aristotelian paradigm for the organizations whose appeals I have kept. Should I rank them in terms of some combination of worthiness and need and then proportion my contributions accordingly? For no particular reason I decide that this year I don't want to spread my charity thin in the way that this would require. I will select just a few, four or five perhaps, and concentrate my charity on them.

Now I have to select those few. I carefully re-read the brochures in my file, this time looking for anything I can seize on as a morally relevant reason for tipping my decision one way or another. After several hours of this, I find myself paralyzed; I cannot choose. So in desperation I assign numbers to the various organizations and make my choice by rolling dice. Or perhaps I hit on graphic design as the deciding factor and give my money to the five organizations whose brochures strike me as the most attractive. Or perhaps I notice that a few of these organizations list the members of their board of directors; I find this apparent openness appealing and decide to give my money to them. Or I notice that four of them have their home offices in my state; that tips me toward them. Or I recall that I visited Africa in the course of the year and was very moved by what I experienced there, so I decide to give all my money this year to organizations that work in Africa. It's easy to go on in this vein and imagine other such ways of making my decision.

So far as I can see, none of these ways of making my decision constitutes treating any organization unjustly. If those I pass over become aware that I have passed them over, they will regret my doing so; but they cannot claim to have been wronged. Yet the Aristotelian principle has surely not been satisfied. In no case did I have a morally relevant reason for choosing as I did; in no case was my departure from equal treatment based on morally relevant similarities and dissimilarities among the organizations. In each case my choice was more or less whimsical and arbitrary. How is the location of an organization's home office relevant? How is the aesthetic quality of its brochure relevant?

Or if one declares that the fact that an organization came up with a winning number on a roll of the dice is a morally relevant reason for including it within my benefactions, then surely the idea of a morally relevant reason is no longer doing any work; it's not explaining anything. One's only reason for calling such a fact "morally relevant" is that one wants to prevent the Aristotelian paradigm from implying that the form my generosity took in this case was unjust.

Feinberg suggests that we are offended by arbitrary discriminations and find them unjust because they are "offensive to reason." "The principle that relevantly similar cases should be treated in similar ways, put in just that general way, is a principle of reason, in much the same way as Aristotle's principles of identity, contradiction, and excluded middle are 'laws of thought.' It is *absurd* to treat relevantly similar cases in dissimilar ways" (319). We are, of course, offended by many arbitrary discriminations and we do find many of them unjust. But as for myself, the examples of arbitrary discrimination that I have given seem to me not at all offensive or unjust; they do not violate some principle of justice. And they represent just the tip of the iceberg.

Suppose someone offers to fund a scholarship at his alma mater and insists that the criteria for eligibility include the requirement that the candidate have been born in the same small Minnesota village that the donor came from. The university authorities will try to talk him out of such a quirky stipulation; but in doing so, they cannot claim that it would be unjust. Or suppose that some millionaire decides to dispense some of his wealth by tossing $100 bills out of his Manhattan hotel room; is anybody wronged by this erratic behavior? Or suppose the Gates Foundation decides to concentrate its AIDS endeavors on Africa because the first person suffering from AIDS that Bill Gates met was born in Africa. Hardly a morally relevant reason; but is anybody wronged?

And then there are all the cases of arbitrary random assignment of indivisible goods. Suppose I decide to bequeath my automobile to one of my children. After trying and failing to find some "rational" way of deciding to whom to give it, I resort to chance. I have my children pull straws, throw dice, or whatever. Those who lose in the draw will naturally be regretful; but they cannot claim to have been wronged.

The Aristotelian formula is patently mistaken. Its grip on Western thought is not because of its truth but in spite of its falsehood.

Explaining the Injustice of Unjust Distributions

My conclusion thus far is negative. The Aristotelian paradigm was offered as an explanation of why certain exercises of generosity are just and others unjust. The paradigm says that what makes a selective exercise of generosity just is the presence of a morally relevant reason for including these persons but excluding those from one's benefaction, even though those would also benefit from the benefaction. And it says that what makes a selective exercise of generosity unjust is the absence of a morally relevant reason for including these persons but excluding those, when those would also benefit. We have found cases of just generosity whose justice the paradigm does not illuminate, since the paradigm implies that those cases are unjust. It would be desirable if we could go beyond this negative conclusion and gain some insight into why some benefactions are just and some unjust. And let's keep in mind that it's possible that though the Aristotelian paradigm does not explain all cases, it does explain some.

Let's approach the matter from the side of injustice. Let's look at some examples of unjust generosity in the hope of discerning what makes them unjust.

Suppose that I have promised to bequeath the art prints that I own to my children; and suppose, further, that after considerable discussion we have agreed on a distribution that makes all the children equally happy. Then in the course of a party that I throw for my neighbors one evening one of the neighbors admires one of my prints and I, pleased by his admiration, impulsively say "Here, it's yours." Flush with good feeling and a bit too much wine, I then grandly announce that everybody is free to select one of my prints as theirs to take home. When everybody is gone, I have none left. Only next morning do I remember, to my horror, that I had promised them to my children.

My generosity is clearly a violation of justice. But being flush with good feelings for these people on this occasion seems a morally relevant difference between them and everybody else. Had I not made the promise to my children, my generosity to my neighbors would not have been unjust; and a defender of the Aristotelian paradigm would have pointed to my good feelings for these people as the relevant similarity among them and the relevant dissimilarity from everybody else. So having a morally relevant reason for making one's distribution as one did proves not to be sufficient for justice. What made my distribution unjust was not that I lacked a morally relevant reason for making the distribution as I did; what made it unjust was that, in being generous to the neighbors, I broke a promise to my children. My breaking of my promise is what made my generosity unjust, not my departure from equal treatment of everybody who might benefit from my paintings without a morally relevant reason for my departure.

And consider once again an example that we used in a previous chapter. Sam is a bachelor who likes to offer candy every now and then to children on the block. None of the children on the block has a right to receive candy from Sam; giving out candy is gratuitous generosity on his part. And since Sam has not promised the candy to anyone, he is not wronging any promisee by giving candy to the children on the block. Let us also agree that he is not wronging the children in the next block by giving candy only to those who live on his block — though for the Aristotelian it's a nice question why living on this block rather than that block counts as a morally relevant principle of discrimination.

But Sam has taken a strong dislike to one of the children on the block, Roger. Why he dislikes Roger is not entirely clear to him. He has no reason to think that Roger has a bad character; Roger has always treated him politely, and Sam has never seen Roger being mean to other children. But there's something about the look on Roger's face that turns Sam off; perhaps he dislikes that look because of some episode buried deep in his memory. In any case, whenever Sam distributes candy, he sees to it that Roger gets none.

Sam's charity is patently unjust; in making his distribution as he does, he wrongs Roger. Why? Why is his exclusion of Roger from his benefactions unjust whereas his exclusion of the children on the neighboring block is not unjust? Suppose Sam had tossed all the candy up into the air and that, in the ensuing scramble, everybody managed to get some except Roger. Add that Roger is as agile as any of the other children. This outcome would be unfortunate; one hopes that some of the children would take pity on Roger and give him some of their candy. But it would not be unjust. Sam's exclusion of Roger from his generosity was unjust because his exclusion of Roger was motivated by inexcusable ill-will. No such ill-will motivated his exclusion of the children in the neighboring block from his largesse, and no such ill-will would account for Roger winding up with no candy had Sam tossed it all up into the air.

Consider, next, a case Feinberg presents that is more or less of the opposite sort. Imagine a father who is making out bequests to his two sons, A and B. "Let us suppose," says Feinberg, "that A and B are roughly of the same age, size, health, appearance, abilities, beliefs, and ideals, that each has the same basic financial needs and that the bequests more than fulfill them in each case." And now suppose "that the father leaves everything else after those basic needs have been met — say, one million unsuspected dollars — to A simply because he likes A better" (315). Feinberg thinks that this would be a case of injustice. I agree; son B is wronged by such treatment.[2]

Why? If B's needs are adequately met by the bequest from his father, why is he wronged? Isn't the father permitted to dispose of that extra million dollars as he wishes? Suppose he had donated all of it to some charitable organization. Then surely B would not have been wronged. So why is he wronged if the father gives the million dollars to B's brother?

It's the father's favoritism that is the culprit. The bestowal of the million dollars on son A is an act of favoritism on the father's part; B is wronged by that favoritism. Parents sometimes like one of their children more than another, perhaps they usually do. I dare say that ideally they would like all their children equally. The fact that often they don't is not as such, however, a blot on their moral character. But when a parent's liking of one child more than another takes the form of favoritism in the distribution of goods, then the disfavored child is wronged. An important normative component in the role of parent in our society — it may be different in other societies — is that parents are to do their

2. Feinberg takes the example from A. D. Woozley, who thinks it would not be a case of injustice.

best to be even-handed in promoting the good and respecting the worth of their children. Favoritism is a violation of this role-obligation.

One way of interpreting Jesus' parable of the prodigal son is that the elder son is accusing the father of favoritism for his scoundrel brother;[3] though the elder son does not actually say that the father's favoring of the younger son is an injustice to him, it's not implausible to suppose that that is the idea. As the elder son is coming in from the fields, he hears the noise of a party in the family home. He inquires from someone what's going on and learns that a party is being thrown to celebrate the return of his dissolute younger brother. The elder brother is very angry and refuses to join the party. The father goes out and pleads with him to join the festivities. The elder son responds, "Listen! For all these years I have been working like a slave for you, and I have never disobeyed your commands; yet you have never given me even a young goat so that I might celebrate with my friends. But when this son of yours came back, who has devoured your property with prostitutes, you killed the fatted calf for him!" (Luke 15:29-30).

The father does not concede the charge of favoritism but then go on to contend that no injustice was done. He contests the charge; the elder son is misinterpreting the situation. It's not favoritism that led him to throw the party. Remember, "all that is mine is yours. But we have to celebrate and rejoice because this brother of yours was dead and has come to life, he was lost and has been found" (15:31-32).[4]

Finally, consider the following example.[5] A small manufacturing company is holding its annual Christmas party. Since the company has been unusually profitable this year, the owner has decided to share some of the wealth and give out bonuses; he's never done that before. So at a certain point in the festivities he stops the music, says that he has a surprise announcement, and declares that he will now hand out bonuses. He explains that for some time he contemplated proportioning the size of a person's bonus to her position in the company, the quality of her work, and so forth; but eventually he decided that that was getting too complicated. Give them all a five thousand dollar bonus, he decided. So he calls the workers forward one by one, in alphabetical order. But he fails to call out Joseph's name, Joseph being the only person of color who works for the firm. Some of the workers notice the omission and call it to the attention of the owner. The owner blandly replies,

---

3. Earlier I suggested that the parable can also be interpreted as an appeal by the elder son to the reciprocity code.

4. There's a fascinating and pointed contrast between the elder son referring to the one who returned as "this son of yours" and the father referring to him as "this brother of yours."

5. My example is an adaptation of an example of Scott Dolff.

"You're right; I did skip Joseph. There's no bonus for Joseph." Where-upon he sits down.

Joseph rightly feels hurt and angry. I would say that he has been wronged; the way in which the owner dispensed his generosity was un-just. But why? Neither Joseph nor anyone else had a bonus coming; no-body would have been wronged had the owner not given any bonuses. So why is Joseph wronged by not receiving a bonus? The answer is that Joseph has been snubbed, demeaned, treated as if he were of less worth than the other workers; there's no other way to read the situation. The owner might have chosen some random procedure for distributing bo-nuses to only some of the people in the firm; those who did not win a bonus in the raffle would be regretful, but they could not claim they had been wronged. It was the owner's demeaning of Joseph in how he distributed his generosity that made his distribution unjust.

Let's pull things together. Feinberg states the Aristotelian paradigm as declaring that injustice, in the sorts of cases we are considering, con-sists of "departure from the requisite form of equal treatment without good reason" (299). It's the absence of a morally relevant reason for dif-ferentiating between the included and the excluded that accounts for the injustice of unjust exercises of generosity. Extrapolating from the cases we have considered, I suggest that it is seldom the absence as such of a morally relevant reason that accounts for the injustice of an unjust distribution. The implicit assumption, that the default option in the ex-ercise of generosity is that everybody who can benefit is to be treated equally, is false. Even if we expand the notion of a morally relevant rea-son so far that it no longer has any explanatory content, benefactors do not need morally relevant reasons for distributing their benefactions as they do. Without violating justice, they can employ quirky reasons or re-sort to chance procedures.

There is no one thing that explains the injustice of unjust generosity. Sometimes what makes a distribution unjust is that distributing the lar-gesse to these people breaks a prior obligation to distribute it to other people. Sometimes what makes a distribution unjust is that a nefarious reason is guiding the distribution. Sometimes what makes a distribution unjust is that it amounts to treating one person as of less worth than oth-ers when they are in fact of equal worth. No doubt if we continued look-ing at examples we would find yet other sources of injustice in generosity.

GENEROSITY DOES NOT IN GENERAL GENERATE NEW RIGHTS

An implication of the Aristotelian paradigm as it applies to generosity is that, where the good is divisible and nobody has a prior right to a share in the benefactor's generosity, generosity generates in certain people a right to a share in the good. Once the benefactor begins his distribution, then he finds that he has generated, in those who are relevantly similar to the initial recipients, the right to a share that is equal or proportionate to the share the initial recipients received. If any receive, then all who are relevantly similar have a right to receive.

But if the conclusion that I drew just above is correct, this implication is mistaken. It's not true in general that generosity generates new rights and that it is the violation of those generated rights that accounts for injustice in generosity. Roger had a prior right not to be treated with culpable ill-will; it was the violation of that prior right that accounted for the fact that he was wronged. Son *B* had a prior right not to be the victim of his father's favoritism; it was the violation of that prior right that accounted for the fact that *B* was wronged. Joseph had a prior right not to be treated as of less worth than his fellows on account of his being a person of color; it was the violation of that prior right that accounted for the fact that he was wronged by the owner's omission of him in the distribution of bonuses. Generosity, to be just, must attend to the rights that we already have.

IS MERCY DIFFERENT?

None of my examples has been an example of generosity in the form of mercy. Mercy comes in two forms. One form is mitigation of the severity of punishment; the other is alleviation of the plight of the unfortunate. Does mercy in either of these two forms require different conclusions from those I have drawn?

I think not. Start with mercy of the former sort, mitigation-mercy. Examples of this sort that come immediately to mind are pardons issued by governmental officials — in the United States, by the president of the country and by the governors of the states. We, the citizens of the United States, expect that the president, with the assistance of the justice department, will be reasonably systematic in selecting the most worthy candidates for pardon. If the president departs from that expectation by tossing coins or allowing his choice to be determined by favoritism or prejudice of one kind and another, we are disturbed and regard the process as unfair and unjust. But suppose that in some kingdom there is the longstanding practice of the king employing a random procedure for selecting ten prisoners for release each New Year's Eve. So far as I can see, no one is wronged by such a procedure; justice is not violated.[6]

---

6. Something not all that different from this practice seems to have been in force in

Mercy in the form of alleviating the plight of the unfortunate is no different. Let it be noted that mercy in the form of alleviation of hardship is not always an exercise of gratuitous generosity; sometimes it is obligatory. The Samaritan in Jesus' parable of the good Samaritan was, I would say, obligated to come to the aid of the wounded man, as were the priest and the Levite — though it was compassion rather than recognition of duty that led the Samaritan to act as he did. And I have a so-called *imperfect* duty to show mercy to some of the unfortunates who accost me with their pleas for aid as I walk about Manhattan. But not all such mercy is obligatory; some goes above and beyond the call of duty. A good deal of volunteer work is like that — volunteering to help out at the local soup kitchen, volunteering to help out in a nearby retirement home, and so forth. Does volunteering to help out on one occasion imply that if one fails to help out on all relevantly similar situations, one is acting unjustly? Of course not.

BACK TO THE PARABLE OF THE WORKERS IN THE VINEYARD

Let's return to the parable from which we began. Did the owner of the vineyard wrong anyone by the highly unusual way in which he combined generosity with paying workers a just wage for the work they did? Everybody but the five o'clock workers disliked the owner's combination of generosity with just pay; the early workers disliked it intensely. But was anyone wronged?

I fail to see that anyone was. The landowner did not act out of ill-will toward anyone, nor did he act out of favoritism. Did he then perhaps break an implicit agreement between himself and the early workers? Had he led them to believe that the only principle on which he would act was equal pay for equal work and unequal pay for unequal work? Certainly not. He was entirely open with the early workers about the basis on which he would pay them: the going daily wage for those who worked the full day, a just wage for those who arrived a bit later. He said nothing as to how he would pay later workers. He kept his word. Did his actions perhaps demean the early workers, treat them as of less worth than those who came at five o'clock? Not so far as I can see.

The owner did not cite a morally relevant reason for the unusual way in which he dispensed his largesse. In fact he didn't cite any reason at all; he just declared that he was permitted to be generous. As we have

---

Palestine at the time of Jesus. The practice is described as follows in Matthew 27:15: "Now at the festival the governor was accustomed to release a prisoner for the crowd, anyone whom they wanted."

seen, selective generosity may be just even in the absence of any morally relevant reason for one's selection. The early workers strongly preferred that the landowner pay each worker what he had earned and then, if he wished to be generous, give everybody an equal-sized gift. Better yet would have been proportioning the size of the gift to the length and onerousness of the work. But the fact that they strongly preferred these arrangements does not establish that the landowner wronged them in not choosing one of them.[7]

7. David Reidy called my attention to the fact that my discussion in this chapter is very relevant to the extensive discussions about justice and luck that have been taking place in recent years. A good introduction to the discussion can be found in the article by Kasper Lippert-Rasmussen, "Justice and Bad Luck," in the online Stanford Encyclopedia of Philosophy: http://plato.stanford.edu/entries/justice-bad-luck/.

Chapter Nineteen

JUST AND UNJUST PATERNALISM

IN THE PRECEDING CHAPTER we discussed cases in which the generous bestowal of a good on one person or group of persons wrongs another. But sometimes generosity wrongs the very person on whom the good is bestowed — or those very persons. Our project in this chapter is to discuss what is probably the most common form of this sort of unjust well-doing, namely, *paternalism*. The bearing of agapism on political life will come to the fore more than it has hitherto.

COLES ON THE TERRORS WROUGHT BY LOVE

"It is difficult to write of generosity today," says Romand Coles in a chapter titled "Questioning *Caritas*," "without conjuring up images of the terror wrought by a religion that at once placed the movement of *caritas* and *agape*, giving and love, at the foundation of being and swept across the Americas during the Conquest with a holocaust of 'generosity'."[1] Coles goes on to offer a diagnosis of what it was that led Christians and others to spread terror in the name of love.

> Dominant modes of imagining and understanding generosity in Western history — I have in mind here particularly many of those rooted in various forms of either Christianity or modern rational subjectivity — have been constituted on the idea of a self-identical ground from which is given all being, truth, moral value, and beauty. Perhaps this self-origination is sometimes understood better as an internally differentiated dynamic flow, a giving always moving beyond itself, and in this sense less stable than a self-identity. Yet even as in some sense dynamic, *even in its movement*, the fount of giving is self-identical insofar as this flow does not receive — and even precludes reception of — alterity. . . . The profoundest goals, meanings, and textures of the generous act do not emerge from a receptive encounter with the other. . . . Such an orientation is destined to

---

1. In Romand Coles, *Rethinking Generosity: Critical Theory and the Politics of Caritas* (Ithaca: Cornell University Press, 1997), 1.

manifest itself repeatedly, as it has already for centuries, in ugly encounters: violent conflicts within the church and at its boundaries. Insofar as generosity does not understand itself to be deeply rooted in a receptive encounter with others, it will proliferate a blindness, theft, and imperialism despite its best efforts. (2-3)[2]

The passage is not entirely consistent. The diagnosis suggested by the words "a self-identical ground from which is given all being" is that Christians have thought of generosity, divine and human, as an outpouring of new loci of goodness, the motive and form of the outpouring lying entirely within the agent because there is as yet no other to be encountered, no "alterity" to whom one can be receptive.

I find this diagnosis implausible. Once new loci of goodness have been created, distinct from the agent, then, if those loci are living things, the possibility opens up of generosity in the form of promoting the flourishing of those loci. In Chapter Fourteen I proposed calling the production of good, *benefaction*. Benefaction comes in several forms, not only in the form of creation but also in the form of seeking the flourishing of those loci of goodness already there. How could any Christian overlook the fact that God's benefaction as creator is followed by God's providential benefaction, seeking the flourishing of the beings created? In Mark, Jesus is recorded as saying, "The Son of Man came not to be served but to serve" (10:45). And how could any Christian overlook the fact that we are enjoined to do likewise — to promote the flourishing of those loci of goodness already there, our neighbors?

The other, and more plausible, interpretation of Coles's diagnosis of what it was that led Christians to spread terror in the name of love is that, though Christians realized full well that generosity, divine and human, takes the form not only of creation but also of love for what is already there, their love for the other did not emerge from "a receptive encounter with the other." Though they recognized that they were confronted with "alterity," "the profoundest goals, meanings, and textures of the generous act [did] not emerge from a receptive encounter with the other." In short, their love for the other took the form of terror because it was paternalistic.

No doubt Coles is right about this; the generosity that spread terror was highly paternalistic. Paternalism does not always spread terror, however, nor is it always even wrong. I submit that the root cause of the ter-

2. Coles adds the following: "This malignancy at the heart of the loving gift rears its head in *City of God,* when Augustine writes that to love my neighbor as myself is to try to give him or her what I myself most need and want, namely the will to love God. Hence the generosity engendered by the Augustinian Christian narrative is one whose overarching aim is given entirely from within itself" (3).

ror spread by generosity in the conquest of the Americas was not that it
was paternalistic generosity rather than generosity that emerged from a
receptive encounter with the other. The root cause of the terror was
that it was a generosity of benevolence rather than a generosity of care.
It paid no attention to what justice required. It did not view the Indians
as bearers of an ineradicable dignity; it saw them as members of an out-
group, the out-group of savages who had to be brought into Christian
civilization. It did not ask whether it was wronging them.

We must not tar all the Europeans with the same brush. The generosity of some took the form of resisting rather than spreading terror. And
terror was by no means always spread in the name of generosity. One
does not have to read much of the history of the conquest of the Americas by the Europeans to see that it was at least as often greed and vengeance that caused the terror as misguided love. Coles would surely
agree. But injustice wreaked by paternalistic love was his concern in
"Questioning *Caritas*," as it is mine in this present chapter.

WHAT IS PATERNALISM?

"Paternalism" is a term that is protean in its meanings, used differently
by different writers. It would serve no purpose to canvas those differences here. Let me instead explain how I will be using the term.[3]

Paternalism comes in two main forms. One form, call it *paternalism A*,
consists of bestowing on someone, without any decision on his part, that
which one regards as enhancing his good, thus regardless of his views
on the matter, if any. The bestowal may or may not be coercive. I treat
an overweight acquaintance of mine paternalistically if, in defiance of
his own view as to the benefits of exercise, I give him the gift of a year's
membership in a health club because I think exercise would be good
for him. No coercion there. By contrast, the paternalism of the European colonists toward the native Americans was coercive. They did not
describe the habits and accomplishments of European civilization to
the native Americans and then ask whether they wished to receive them.
They forced these on them.[4]

3. There is a fine discussion of paternalism, coercion, and related phenomena in the
first two chapters of Joel Feinberg's *Social Philosophy* (Englewood Cliffs, NJ: Prentice-Hall,
1973).

4. In a chilling passage in *On Liberty*, J. S. Mill says that coercively paternalistic treatment of "barbarians" raises no problems. "We may leave out of consideration those back-
ward states of society in which the race itself may be considered as in its nonage. The early
difficulties in the way of spontaneous progress are so great, that there is seldom any
choice of means for overcoming them; and a ruler full of the spirit of improvement is war-

Paternalism of the other form, call it *paternalism B,* consists of putting pressure on someone to *decide to act* in a way that one regards as good or right, or to *decide to refrain from acting* in a way that one regards as bad or wrong, when one believes that the person himself is not inclined so to act or refrain from acting. It may be a particular action that one pressures him to perform or refrain from performing, or it may be actions of a certain type. In the latter case, one may expect or hope that, as a consequence of the pressure, the recipient will develop a habit of so acting or refraining. The habit may be a moral or spiritual virtue. Thus one may expect or hope that, as a consequence of one's pressure, he will become a better person.

The pressure may take the form either of carrots or sticks — either of benefits or burdens — attached to the action or inaction in question. The attachment of burdens constitutes coercion. Or the pressure may take the form of hectoring. Offering someone reasons for acting or not acting a certain way does not, as such, constitute pressure. But if one's offering of reasons is so persistent as to become hectoring, then the offering of reasons has become a form of pressure.

Nobody holds that all cases of paternalistic treatment of others are wrong. Sometimes we find ourselves in the position of being responsible for a person's good when she herself is incapable of making a decision on the matter at hand. She is an infant, or severely impaired mentally, or psychologically disturbed, or recovering from surgery, or in a coma, or mentally confused, or fallen into dementia. Nobody sees anything wrong in paternalism in such cases; on the contrary, paternalism may be obligatory. It will, of course, be paternalism of form A, since human beings of the sorts mentioned are not capable of making decisions.

Though children who are not suffering from impairments of the sorts mentioned are capable of making decisions, on many issues they are not capable of making reflective decisions concerning their present and future good; they have not yet attained "the age of reason." Their flourishing requires that responsible adults make certain decisions for them and, when necessary, pressure them into conforming. Many forms of paternalistic treatment of children are not only permissible but obligatory.

Let's have a term for those whose powers are sufficient for making a reflective decision concerning their good; let's call them *deliberative*

---

ranted in the use of any expedients that will attain an end, perhaps otherwise unattainable. Despotism is a legitimate mode of government in dealing with barbarians, provided the end be their improvement, and the means justified by actually effecting that end. Liberty, as a principle, has no application to any state of things anterior to the time when mankind have become capable of being improved by free and equal discussion. Until then, there is nothing for them but implicit obedience to an Akbar or a Charlemagne, if they are so fortunate as to find one" (96-97).

adults.[5] Just as the paternalistic treatment of those who are not deliberative adults is often justified, so too is the paternalistic treatment of deliberative adults who voluntarily place themselves under such treatment.
An obvious example is deliberative adults who, finding themselves af-
flicted with destructive desires that they cannot control on their own,
place themselves under the paternalistic care of a person or institution
because they have a second-order desire to restrain or eliminate those
destructive desires. Since the person *wants* to be treated paternalistically
with respect to those destructive, first-order, desires, nobody regards it
as wrong to treat him thus. The particular way in which the caretaker
treats him may wrong him; but treating him paternalistically does not as
such wrong him.

Our social engagements are filled with many other, less obvious, examples of voluntary submission to paternalistic treatment. When I pre-
pare to teach a lecture course in philosophy I compose a syllabus of topics that I think would be good for the students to engage and a set of
writings that I think would be good for them to read. I do not — not
usually, anyway — consult them as to what they think would be good for
them to discuss and read; I make that decision for them. I treat them paternalistically. But in signing up for the course, they have voluntarily
submitted to my paternalism. This is but one of many examples of the
point. We all regularly find ourselves in situations where we say, "Don't
ask me. Tell me. I trust your judgment."

WHY SOME ARE RELUCTANT TO APPROVE ANY PATERNALISTIC TREATMENT OF DELIBERATIVE ADULTS

There is deep reluctance, in some popular brands of liberal political
theory, to concede the permissibility of paternalistic treatment of deliberative adults who do not voluntarily submit to the treatment. Or to
make the same point from the opposite angle: there is a strong inclination in those brands of liberal political theory to insist that deliberative
adults ought always to be treated as autonomous.[6]

---

5. A person may be capable of making a reflective decision concerning some of her
goods and not others. Thus the concept we really need is that of a deliberative agent concerning the matter at hand. But I think that no confusion will ensue if we employ the non-
relative concept to discuss the issues. It should also be noted that at least some teenagers
satisfy the concept of rational adult.

6. The term "autonomous" is even more protean in its meanings than "paternalism."
Robert P. George, in *Making Men Moral: Civil Liberties and Public Morality* (Oxford: Oxford
University Press, 1993), 147ff., unravels some of these different meanings. I will be using
"treating X as autonomous" as the antonym of "treating X paternalistically."

I think it unlikely, however, that anyone does in fact believe that the paternalistic treatment of deliberative adults who do not voluntarily submit to such treatment is always and as such wrong; I think it likely that everyone, if pressed, would concede that exceptions of one sort and another have to be allowed.[7] It will prove illuminating, nonetheless, to consider the principle in its unqualified form before we consider it as most commonly qualified.[8]

What do those who are inclined to reject all paternalistic treatment of non-consenting deliberative adults see as wrong with such treatment? What makes it unacceptable in principle? Different writers answer this question somewhat differently; but the core idea is almost always the same. If I treat some non-consenting deliberative adult paternalistically, I am not paying him due respect as a rational moral agent.

Why is that? Why am I not paying him due respect as a rational moral agent? It seems right to describe paternalism A as not paying the recipient due respect as a rational moral agent; the agent bestows what he regards as the good without the recipient making any decision whatsoever as to whether or not to receive it. But in paternalism B, the subject, or recipient, must decide what to do. The difference that paternalism of this sort makes is that, in making his decision, the subject of the paternalism must now take into consideration the benefits or burdens that the paternalist has attached to the course of action or inaction in question.

Over and over in his writings John Rawls uses a phrase borrowed from Kant, "free and equal rational being." I suggest that the term "equal" is the clue to the answer to our question. It cannot be said that in attaching benefits or burdens to some course of action or inaction that you are considering, and then leaving it up to you to decide, I am not treating you as a rational moral agent. What can be said, however, is that I am not treating you as my *equal qua* rational moral agent. That's the idea. Deliberative adults have a right not to be treated as inferior *qua* rational moral agents. To treat a fellow deliberative adult as one's inferior *qua* rational moral agent is to treat him with under-respect,

7. In his essay "Foundations of Liberal Equality," *Tanner Lectures on Human Values*, vol. 11 (Salt Lake City: University of Utah Press, 1989), Ronald Dworkin comes very close to affirming the principle without qualification. After distinguishing various forms of paternalism, he says that the only form that is sometimes permissible is "endorsed paternalism," which seeks to coerce a person into behavior he does not presently value but which eventually results in or contributes to his "conversion" to believing it valuable (78). Only if such paternalism is short term is it permissible, and only if it does not significantly constrict his choices in case the "conversion" never occurs.

8. Feinberg calls the principle in its unqualified form "anarchistic," and devotes several pages in his *Social Philosophy* to considering it. He states the principle thus: "Society and the state should grant to every citizen 'complete liberty to do whatever he wishes'" (22).

thereby wronging him. What's being assumed, of course, is that the other is in fact one's equal *qua* rational moral agent.

In what way am I not treating you as my equal *qua* rational moral agent when I treat you paternalistically? Presumably it's in my assuming that I know better than you what is good or right for you to do in this situation. In treating you paternalistically, I am assuming that your cognitive access to the relevant goods and rights is inferior to mine; therein is located my treating you as my inferior.

Everybody Regards As Permissible Some Paternalistic Treatment of Deliberative Adults

Let me make two responses. In what I have said just now, I have assumed that if to treat you paternalistically is to treat you as my inferior *qua* rational moral agent, then the treating-as-inferior must be located in my assuming that I know better than you what is good or right for you to do in this situation. The alternative would be to locate the treating-as-inferior not in my assuming that I have superior cognitive access but in the combination of that assumption with the pressure. But that makes no sense. If my assumption that I have superior cognitive access does not treat you as inferior, why would combining that assumption with putting pressure on you to conform constitute treating you as inferior?

But now notice that nobody thinks that to disagree with someone is, as such, to wrong him; nobody thinks that others all have a right against one that one not disagree with them. But when I disagree with someone, I perforce regard myself as having superior cognitive access in this case. So if paternalism as such is wrong, it can't be that what's wrong with it is that to treat the other paternalistically is to treat him or her as one's inferior *qua* rational moral agent. Either paternalism does not amount to treating the other as one's inferior *qua* rational moral agent; or it does, but that's not necessarily to wrong him.

My second response is that it is patently not true that paternalistic treatment of deliberative adults is wrong as such unless they voluntarily submit to it. There's no point in running through a list of other candidates for what it is about such treatment that makes it wrong as such, since it's patently not wrong as such. Here's why: we are all citizens of states that treat paternalistically not only those who are not fully deliberative adults but those who are. And not all such treatment by states of citizens is wrong.

Our states coerce us to do things that we would prefer not doing, and coerce us to refrain from doing things that we would prefer doing. No doubt for each of us there are some laws that do not function coercively;

we would do what the law requires even if there weren't the law. But for each of us there are many laws that do coerce us. For each of us there is some point at which our legislators treat us paternalistically. But surely we're not wronged in all such cases. So paternalistic treatment of non-consenting deliberative adults cannot be wrong as such.

THE RAWLS AND AUDI RESPONSE

I know of only one reply to this point, a reply proposed initially by John Rawls and then adapted by Robert Audi.[9] The reply concedes that states do in fact function paternalistically, but then goes on to argue that, in a liberal democracy, this is neither how it has to be nor how it should be.

Suppose that each of the deliberative adult citizens of a liberal democracy adopted the policy of supporting a proposed piece of legislation only if his or her reason for supporting the legislation was also viewed by all those of one's fellow citizens who are deliberative adults as a decisive reason for the legislation. No doubt some of the legislation adopted under this policy will treat children paternalistically; probably some will also treat paternalistically those adults who are not fully deliberative. But none of it will treat paternalistically any deliberative adult. It may coerce some of them on occasion; but if so, that will be because he or she, in addition to first-order desires that run counter to the legislation, has second-order desires to restrain or eliminate those first-order desires. It's those second-order desires that lead him or her to support the legislation.

Both Rawls and Audi explicitly note that such a policy is not for the world as it is. It cannot belong to the ethic of citizen of a liberal democracy. For even if, *mirabile dictu,* all my deliberative adult fellow citizens did in fact share my reasons for supporting some legislative proposal, how could I possibly know that? There are too many of them. But second, and more important, I can always be confident that some do not in fact share my reasons. I can be confident that, in every case in which I have reasons for supporting some proposed piece of legislation, there are fellow citizens of mine who either do not share my reasons or do not regard them as decisive. Experience teaches me this.

Thus instead of the policy mentioned, both Rawls and Audi propose that the citizens of a liberal democracy adopt a conditionalized variant thereon. Neither of them is entirely clear as to which conditionalized

9. I discuss the reply in considerable detail in my essay "The Paradoxical Role of Coercion in the Theory of Political Liberalism," *Journal of Law, Philosophy, and Culture* 1.1 (2007): 135-58.

variant they prefer. But for our purposes here, it doesn't matter. Suppose it's this: a citizen of a liberal democracy is to support a proposed piece of legislation only if she has good reason to believe that all her fellow citizens who are deliberative adults *would* share her reason for supporting it *if they were* fully reflective on the matter and adequately informed.

I hold that the depth and extent of diversity of opinion in contemporary liberal democracies are such that one always has good reason to believe that some of one's deliberative adult fellow citizens *would not* share one's reasons *even if they were fully reflective and adequately informed*. Thus for citizens to adopt the policy mentioned would be to immobilize themselves. But the more important point is the following. Suppose that one did have good reason to believe that all one's deliberative adult fellow citizens, were they fully reflective and adequately informed on the matter, would share one's reasons for supporting some proposed piece of legislation and would regard those reasons as decisive. One nonetheless knows that many of them *do not in fact* share one's reasons or *do not in fact* regard them as decisive. So if one proceeds to support the proposed legislation for one's own reasons, one will perforce support treating them paternalistically. If they were different in some idealized way, one might not be treating them paternalistically — who knows? But given what they do in fact believe, one is in fact treating them paternalistically. Yet surely it's not always unjust to support a proposed piece of legislation that one knows will treat paternalistically some of one's deliberative adult fellow citizens.

The paternalistic treatment of deliberative adults is not as such unjust. There is no natural right of such adults not to be treated paternalistically, no natural right to be treated as autonomous. When paternalism is unjust, as very often it is, the source of the injustice lies not in the paternalism as such but in the form it takes. Sometimes what's wrong is that pressure has taken a form that is wrong, the form of torture, for example. Sometimes what's wrong is that one is pressured to do something that one ought not to be pressured to do, worship God in a way contrary to one's conscience, for example.

MILL'S ACCOUNT OF WHAT MAKES SOME PATERNALISM UNJUST

Since we cannot dismiss all forms of paternalistic treatment of deliberative adults as wrong, it would be desirable if we could identify those forms of paternalistic treatment of non-consenting deliberative adults that are wrong and could provide an explanation of why they are wrong. In his famous essay, *On Liberty,* John Stuart Mill undertakes a project that falls short of this but is nonetheless bold. He identifies a prominent form of paternalism that is, so he argues, always and everywhere wrong. It was not his view that this is the only form of paternalism that is wrong.

The principle Mill proposed for marking out a form of paternalism that is always and everywhere wrong has come to be called *the harm principle* — or sometimes *the no-harm principle*. The principle is this: it is never acceptable to treat a non-consenting deliberative adult in a coercively paternalistic manner with respect to actions or inactions that would harm only himself; it is acceptable to do so only with respect to actions or inactions that would affect others in such a way as to harm them — in such a way as to be "prejudicial to their interests." With respect to actions or inactions on their part that harm only themselves, non-consenting deliberative adults have a right to be treated as autonomous.

> The sole end for which mankind are warranted, individually or collectively, in interfering with the liberty of action of any of their number, is self-protection. . . . The only purpose for which power can be rightfully exercised over any member of a civilized community, against his will, is to prevent harm to others. His own good, either physical or moral, is not a sufficient warrant. He cannot rightfully be compelled to do or forbear because it will be better for him to do so, because it will make him happier, because, in the opinion of others, to do so would be wise or even right. . . . The only part of the conduct of any one, for which he is amenable to society, is that which concerns others. In the part which merely concerns himself, his independence is, of right, absolute. Over himself, over his own body and mind, the individual is sovereign. (95-96)

Mill himself raises the objection that the distinction he employs, between actions that harm only oneself and actions that harm others, is untenable.

> How (it may be asked) can any part of the conduct of a member of society be a matter of indifference to the other members? No person is an entirely isolated being; it is impossible for a person to do anything seriously or permanently hurtful to himself, without mischief reaching at least to his near connections, and often far beyond them. (183)

Mill concedes that the point has force. So he qualifies his distinction just a bit: some actions that are harmful to oneself have no *significant* negative impact on the wellbeing of others. "No person ought to be punished simply for being drunk; but a soldier or a policeman should be punished for being drunk on duty. Whenever, in short, there is a definite damage, or a definite risk of damage, either to an individual or to the public, the case is taken out of the province of liberty, and placed in that of morality or law" (186). The implication is that in some cases of drunkenness there is no "definite damage" to others and no "definite risk of damage."

Suppose we grant, for the sake of the argument, this claim that there are some actions susceptible to coercive regulation which do not significantly impair anyone's wellbeing but that of the agent. The agapist, in caring about the neighbor, will care not only about actions of the neighbor that impair the flourishing of others but also about those that impair the flourishing of the neighbor himself. She will care about both. If Mill is right, the former of these concerns may sometimes take the form of coercive paternalism; the latter, never. Is he right?

Mill is not assuming that harming oneself is ethically neutral. Harming me when the harm brings about no greater good is bad no matter whether it's done by me or by you; harming you when the harm brings about no greater good is bad no matter whether it's done by you or by me.[10] But if that's true, why is it often acceptable to pressure others into not harming you but never acceptable to pressure you into not harming yourself? Why the asymmetry? Why are we to stand idly by in the face of self-inflicted harm but permitted to act coercively to forestall other-inflicted harm?

Again, Mill himself poses the question:

> If gambling, or drunkenness, or incontinence, or idleness, or un-cleanliness, are as injurious to happiness, and as great a hindrance to improvement, as many or most of the acts prohibited by law, why (it may be asked) should not law, so far as is consistent with practicability and social convenience, endeavour to repress these also? And as a supplement to the unavoidable imperfections of law, ought not opinion at least to organize a powerful police against these vices, and visit rigidly with social penalties those who are known to practise them? (184)

Mill offers two answers to the question concerning the rationale for the asymmetry. At one point he says that we should refrain from regulating self-inflicted harm "for the sake of the greater good of human freedom" (186). This reply invites us to rephrase our question: why is it acceptable to restrain a person's freedom when he threatens to impair the

---

10. I will avoid taking up the vexed question of what Mill means by "harm," and the equally vexed question of whether or not his harm principle is compatible with his utilitarian maximizing principle.

flourishing of another but not acceptable when he threatens to impair his own flourishing? Why the asymmetry?

The other answer Mill offers is that the person whom one is tempted to treat paternalistically is the one who is both "most interested in his own well-being" (178) and most knowledgeable as to what serves his wellbeing. "The strongest of all the arguments against the interference of the public with purely personal conduct is that, when it does interfere, the odds are that it interferes wrongly, and in the wrong place" (188).[11]

That paternalism is often mistaken in what it judges to be the wellbeing of another is certainly a reason for caution. But Mill's answer makes no sense. His entire argument rests on the assumption that we can make judgments not only about our own wellbeing but about that of others. To judge whether someone other than yourself is harming you, I have to make a judgment about your flourishing. But if I can make judgments about your flourishing when the issue is whether someone else is harming you, why can't I make judgments about your flourishing when the issue is whether you are harming yourself? Add to this the point made earlier, that we all voluntarily submit ourselves to paternalistic treatment in many situations. I assume, and my students go along with the assumption, that I know better than they what would be good for them to read in the course on Modern Philosophy that they have signed up for.

There is yet another inexplicability in Mill's thought. Mill was not of the view that it is wrong to chastise the person who, in one's opinion, is acting badly. "Remonstrating with him" is acceptable, as is "reasoning with him, or persuading him, or entreating him" (96). And more yet:

> There is a degree of folly, and a degree of what may be called
> (though the phrase is not unobjectionable) lowness or depravation
> of taste, which, though it cannot justify doing harm to the person
> who manifests it, renders him necessarily and properly a subject of
> distaste, or, in extreme cases, even of contempt: a person could not
> have the opposite qualities in due strength without entertaining
> these feelings. Though doing no wrong to any one, a person may so
> act as to compel us to judge him, and feel to him, as a fool, or as a
> being of an inferior order: and since this judgment and feeling are a
> fact which he would prefer to avoid, it is doing him a service to warn

11. By contrast, Mill says that "On questions of social morality, of duty to others, the opinion of the public, that is, of an overruling majority, though often wrong, is likely to be still oftener right; because on such questions they are only required to judge of their own interests; of the manner in which some mode of conduct, if allowed to be practiced, would affect themselves" (188).

him of it beforehand, as of any other disagreeable consequence to which he exposes himself. (179-80)

We may even "give others a preference over him in optional good offices" (180) and shun him if we think that would be for his own good (201).

So it turns out that Mill is not opposed to pressuring the person who is supposedly harming only himself to refrain from doing so; on two occasions he even describes "general disapprobation" as *punishment* (97, 177). It's not pressure as such that he thinks is wrong, but pressure that takes the form of attaching sanctions.

What's the relevant difference between pressure that takes the form of expressing disapprobation and pressure that takes the form of attaching sanctions? The relevant difference, says Mill, is that when pressure takes the form of disapprobation, the wrongdoer "suffers these penalties only in so far as they are the natural, and, as it were, the spontaneous consequence of the faults themselves, not because they are purposely inflicted on him for the sake of punishment" (180).

This won't do. Making the person who is harming himself feel like a fool, making him feel as if he belongs to an inferior order, shunning him, preferring others over him in hiring — these are not "the spontaneous consequence of the faults themselves." They are intentionally inflicted on the recipient. And for most people, they function far more coercively than do a wide range of sanctions.

Mill's principle is twofold: it's always wrong to coerce a nonconsenting deliberative adult to refrain from doing something that harms only himself; and only if the effect on others of some action constitutes harming them is it permissible to coerce a person to refrain from that action.[12] I have considered only the former of these two theses. Let me forego consideration of the latter thesis and conclude my discussion of Mill by supplementing my highlighting of inexplicabilities in Mill's defense of the former thesis with the citation of some counterexamples to the thesis. I borrow a passage from Feinberg for the purpose.

If we reject paternalism entirely, and deny that a person's own good is ever a valid ground for coercing him, we seem to fly in the face both of common sense and long-established customs and laws. In the criminal law, for example, a prospective victim's freely granted consent is no defense to the charge of mayhem or homicide. The state simply refuses to permit anyone to agree to his own disable-

12. In *Social Philosophy*, 41ff., Joel Feinberg considers whether offending someone, as distinguished from harming them, sometimes justifies coercion.

ment or killing. The law of contracts similarly refuses to recognize as valid contracts to sell oneself into slavery, or to become a mistress, or a second wife. Any ordinary citizen is legally justified in using reasonable force to prevent another from mutilating himself or committing suicide. No one is allowed to purchase certain drugs even for therapeutic purposes without a physician's prescription. . . . The use of other drugs, such as heroin, for mere pleasure, is not permitted under any circumstances. It is hard to find any convincing rationale for all such restrictions apart from the argument that beatings, mutilations, death, concubinage, slavery, and bigamy are always bad for a person whether he or she knows it or not, and that antibiotics are too dangerous for any nonexpert, and narcotics for anyone at all, to take on his own initiative.[13]

No General Principle in Sight

Now that we have rejected Mill's harm principle, it would be a happy turn of events if I could offer a replacement, a principle that identifies a feature shared by many if not all cases of unjust paternalism — other, of course, than the feature of being unjust. I have no such principle to offer and see no prospect of ever having one. I agree with Feinberg's conclusion that there is no "convincing rationale" that fits all or even most cases. We have to make our decisions without the help of a general rule. But of course we would have to do that even if we did have a general rule that we regarded as correct, since it's against our intuitions concerning the cases that we would have to test the rule for correctness.

Is Agapism a Menace to Liberal Democracy?

In his essay "Law Like Love,"[14] Jeffrey Murphy makes the wry observation that agapic love is not "cuddly." One of the things that's not cuddly about it, he says, is that it "is concerned not simply with satisfying preferences, alleviating distress, providing for people's material well being, and thereby making their lives more pleasant . . . but is also centrally concerned with *promoting their moral and spiritual good* — helping each one to grow in *virtue*" (22).

Murphy is right about this. The goods in the life of the neighbor that the agapist seeks to advance are not just the goods of states and events

13. Feinberg, *Social Philosophy*, 46.
14. *Syracuse Law Review* 55.1 (2004): 15-32.

in the person's life but the goods of actions and activities on his part — not only how well the neighbor is faring but how well he is doing. When the neighbor is impairing his flourishing, whatever form that impairment takes, moral, spiritual, or physical, the agapist does not remark "That's his business" and walk away indifferent. He cares about the neighbor.

An implication, says Murphy, is that "a legal order dominated by *agape* would almost certainly be more paternalistic than would be acceptable to the more value neutral and libertarian versions of political liberalism — e.g., the views found in the writings of John Rawls and Ronald Dworkin" (22). To use a term current in the literature of political theory, agapists will likely be more "perfectionist" in their views concerning desirable legislation.

As an example of the point, Murphy observes that "those driven by *agape* will probably seek greatly to restrain the corrupt and corrosive availability of pornography — refusing to see its production, distribution, and consumption as an important human liberty. They might very reluctantly allow it for instrumental reasons (if they think that it is impossible to design a legal prohibition that would not constrain legitimate expression) but they would never seek to protect it in principle under the general heading of a fundamental right of personal autonomy."

To speak more generally, agapists will "see conversation about the good life as being central to law and politics, not as in principle a 'private' matter that should be left out of the political and legal domain. This suggests that there may be interesting tensions between some forms of political liberalism and agapic love" (22-23).

I think that "menacing" is probably more apt than "not cuddly" to describe how political theorists of the sort Murphy has in mind will view the presence of agapists in a liberal democratic society should the theses I have defended in this chapter become widely accepted. Liberal democracy is often thought of as inherently anti-paternalistic, a defense not only against the terrors of generosity to which Coles pointed but against the suffocating intrusions of those who want to make other people good. Among the menaces against which liberal democracy is a defense is the menace of those who insist on loving their neighbors. The theses I have defended in this chapter seem to undermine this defense: the thesis that paternalistic treatment of non-consenting deliberative adults, even *coercive* paternalistic treatment, is sometimes acceptable; the thesis that there cannot be such a thing as a non-paternalistic state; and the thesis that we have no choice but to live without any such general rule as Mill's for setting limits to acceptable paternalism.

Let me address this worry, that widespread acceptance of the theses I have defended would undermine liberal democracy and make the presence of agapists in such a society menacing. The topic deserves a book; here I can give it only a few pages. To address the worry, I must first sketch out, ever so briefly, my own understanding of liberal democracy.

All human beings assume, so it appears to me, that free non-coerced action is a fundamental good, in the sense that coercion always has to be justified by some good that it achieves or some obligation that it fulfills. Coercion always bears the burden of proof; freedom from coercion never does. It's true that one sometimes asks, "Why are you allowing him to do that, why aren't you stopping him?" In such a case it appears that freedom is being asked to bear the burden of proof. But I take it that what lies behind this question is the assumption that though the burden of proof for coercing him has in fact been borne, he is nonetheless not being coerced.

If this suggestion is correct, that everyone assumes that coercion bears the burden of proof, then all political regimes are alike in that they treat freedom from coercion as the default option. Liberal democracy differs from other political structures in its particular pattern and extent of coercion and non-coercion, and in the rationale that it gives for coercion.

A fundamental feature of liberal democracy is the prominence it gives to limits on what the state may coerce its citizens into doing; liberal democracies are limited governments. And prominent in how limits on governmental coercion have traditionally been determined and specified is appeals to natural rights. Citizens have rights against the state that were not conferred by the state. Liberal democracies are natural-rights-based polities. Respect for the worth of human beings lies at the very basis of liberal democracy. This is a major part of what makes such a polity distinctive.

The rights of citizens against the state that set limits to what the state may coerce its citizens into doing are all, in the nature of the case, freedom rights: one's right against the state to be allowed to speak, one's right against the state to be allowed to assemble, one's right against the state to be allowed to exercise one's religion, and so forth. I suggest that it is the fact that permissible and impermissible coercion in a liberal democracy is in good measure determined by natural freedom rights that makes it appear that freedom has a more fundamental status in liberal democracy than in any other political structure. And so it does, in this specific way.

Let me now turn to a few historical observations. One of the developments that gave rise to liberal democracy was the spreading conviction, in northwest Europe and its colonies in the late sixteenth, seventeenth, and eighteenth centuries, that the risk had to be taken of experimenting with a new relation between the state and the religions of its citizens. In many places and at many times, the human beings living within a single political jurisdiction have seen themselves as all together forming a religio-moral community united by a common vision of God and the good, and they have seen government as the highest institutional expression of that shared vision. Traditional Islam, with its system of millets for Jews and Christians, was a variant on this pattern; the millets were small pockets of exception whose members were allowed, to a considerable extent, to live out their minority vision of God and the good.

Liberal democracy arose in situations of substantial religious pluralization within a single political jurisdiction; those living within a single political jurisdiction no longer constituted a single religio-moral community united by a shared vision of God and the good. Within the citizenry there was instead a multiplicity of such communities. The emergence of liberal democracy represented the risky experiment of declaring that all citizens were to have the civil right to practice their religion as they saw fit or to practice none at all; the original theorists held that this civil right to free exercise was grounded in the natural right to free exercise. The liberal democracy that emerged in the United States took the risky experiment even farther; it declared that no religion was even to be established.

It follows that liberal democracy is not the highest institutional expression of a religio-moral community united by a shared vision of God and the good. The citizens belong to a multiplicity of such communities; the polity constitutes an association of such communities.

The fact that the polity of a liberal democracy is not the highest institutional expression of a religio-moral community united by a shared vision of God and the good, but is instead an association of such communities, has been the source of much lament in recent years by communitarians and traditionalists. It is said that liberal democracy has no moral basis, that it is nothing more than a *modus vivendi*. But liberal democracy is not a mere *modus vivendi*. It's true that, in the nature of the case, its moral basis is not the vision of God and the good shared by one particular community within the citizenry; if that is the sort of moral basis one is looking for, then liberal democracy will indeed appear as an amoral arrangement of convenience. The moral basis of liberal democracy is the moral basis of this particular *association* of such communities. Liberal democracy is no more without a moral basis than is any other political structure. What the critics ought to be saying is not that liberal democracy lacks a moral basis but that they disagree with its moral basis — disagree, for example, with the assumption that citizens have natural rights against the state.

When one studies the political writings of James Madison and his contemporaries, it becomes clear that there is another important component in the core idea of liberal democracy. Madison and his colleagues believed deeply that every government official was to be accountable to the people; and they believed that an essential device for the exercise of such accountability was a free and fair vote. The chain of accountability may be long; but always, if one starts from some official and follows the chain to its end, one finds someone holding office by virtue of having been voted into it. Madison's principal reason for dispersion of power in the U.S. Constitution was his conviction that concentrated power inevitably becomes power that the people cannot hold to account by their votes. The Madisonian principle concerning the conditions for the legitimacy of coercion — the legitimacy of state paternalism — is that the state may coerce citizens for the sake of justice and the common good only if those officials who authorize the coercive law or policy are ultimately accountable to the people by free and fair elections.

There is one additional principle belonging to the core idea of liberal democracy — call it the principle of the *political equality* of adult citizens. Important though this principle is, both its recognition and the realization of its implications have been slow and halting. The founding fathers of the United States did not regard slaves as the political equals of non-slaves, nor did they regard women as the political equals of men.

To these structural features of liberal democracy, a point must be added about the role of citizen of such a polity. I hold that the fundamental question citizens should ask, when deciding whether or not to support some legislation, is not whether the legislation serves their own interests but whether it serves justice for all and the common good. And very often justice requires that one's fellow citizens be free to do what one regards as morally wrong for them to do. In making up their minds on what is required by justice for all and the common good, citizens should take seriously the considered views of their fellow citizens. It is in taking seriously the considered views of others that we treat those others with due respect as rational moral agents.

AGAPISM NOT A MENACE TO LIBERAL DEMOCRACY

The agapist is a supporter of liberal democracy as I have just now described it, not a detractor; and she affirms what I have described as the role of citizen of such a polity. It's her agapism that leads her to be a defender. She does not defend it as the best of bad options.

Perhaps the most prominent theme in my discussion has been that the agapist's care about the neighbor includes seeing to it that the neighbor is treated justly, that she not be wronged. Accordingly, the agapist affirms the right of citizens against the state to the free exercise of their religion, to their right to speak freely, to their right to assemble, to their right to habeas corpus, to their right not to be tortured, and so forth. She sees the neglect of these and other such rights as the source of the terror perpetrated over the centuries in the name of a love that was misguided and a care that was malformed.

When considering which legislation to propose and support, she will indeed have the total good of her fellow citizens in mind — moral, spiritual, physical, psychological — and the full panoply of their rights. But she will not look to the state as a cure-all for social ills, nor will she seek to inscribe into law whatever she regards as morally right. She is vividly aware of the dangers of an aggrandizing state. But given that she cares about the totality of goods and rights in the lives of her fellow citizens, her initial convictions about legislation will quite often differ, as Murphy suggested, from those of libertarians and traditional liberals. Before making up her mind, she will listen attentively to what they and others have to say. But finally the time arrives to vote. She votes for what she believes will serve justice for all and the common good. She insists that everybody's vote carry the same weight. And she pledges to live with the result.

PART FOUR

The Justice of God's Love

Chapter Twenty

THE JUSTICE OF GOD'S
GENEROSITY IN ROMANS

IN THE DISCUSSION, in Part Three, of real and alleged tension between benevolence and justice, I employed various of the parables of Jesus as examples, supplemented by real and imagined examples of my own. But in the founding documents of the agapist tradition we find more than brief stories told by Jesus to illustrate the relation between *agapē* and justice. In Paul's letter to the Romans we find a theologically dense and multifaceted articulation and defense of the justice of God's generosity. So I propose concluding our discussion on justice in love by looking at what Paul had to say on the topic. Not to do so would be like declining or refusing to talk about the elephant in the room.

I am told by specialists in the field that the medieval commentators on Romans took it for granted that the topic of the book was *justitia dei;* the Latin of the Vulgate made it almost inevitable that they would do so. No post-medieval interpretation of Romans that I know of takes that to be the topic. My interpretation is thus a post-Reformation return to the medieval interpretation.

Most interpreters would not deny that Paul has some things to say about love and justice in Romans, but they would resist the suggestion that the justice of God's love is the main topic. Protestants have traditionally held its main topic to be personal salvation. Some recent interpreters have argued that its main topic is God's covenant faithfulness. Let me begin my defense of the claim that the main topic of Romans is the *justitia dei* by setting out, in a bare-bones way, what I see as Paul's line of thought. The remainder of this chapter and the next will then fill in the details and defend this interpretation.

AN INTRODUCTORY SUMMARY

In an episode reported in all three synoptic gospels, a term is used that captures the pattern of Jesus' engagement with those he came in contact with: he showed "no partiality." The episode is that in which some opponents of Jesus tried to trap him with the famous trick question about the morality of paying taxes to the Roman emperor. In all three narrations, the interrogator prefaced his question with a reference to Jesus' reputation. Let me quote Matthew's version: "Teacher, we know that you are sincere, and teach the way of God in accordance with truth, and show deference to no one; for you do not regard people with partiality" (Matthew 22:16).[1] The reference to Jesus' reputation for teaching the truth is flattery; the reference to his reputation for showing deference to no one and not regarding anyone with partiality is preparation for setting the trap. How far is Jesus willing to go in showing deference to no one? Is he willing to go all the way up to the emperor?

This theme of no partiality is picked up in the book of Acts. A visionary trance leads Peter to conclude that he must give up his Jewish particularism. "I truly understand," he says, "that God shows no partiality, but in every nation anyone who fears him and does justice (*dikaiosunē*) is acceptable to him" (10:34-35).[2]

The book of Romans can be seen as a meditation on the theological significance of Jesus' actions and Peter's vision. Its major theme is that the generosity of God, as manifested in God's justification of sinners, is just in that it is impartial as between Jews and gentiles. "There is no distinction between Jew and Greek; the same Lord is Lord of all and is generous to all who call on him" (10:12). "God shows no partiality" (2:11). Paul's argument, dense and profound, is a prime exhibit in support of my claim that New Testament agape is care.

Jew and gentile are alike in having sinned; God is just in pronouncing a verdict of "guilty" on both. But God, out of love for humankind, offers justification to both Jew and gentile. In our discussion of just and unjust generosity in Chapter Eighteen I argued that a distribution of some good may be just even though it does not distribute the good impartially to all who might benefit therefrom. That argument must not lead us to forget that one way to defend the justice of some distribution is to point out that the good has been distributed impartially.

But what if God has made a covenant with the Jews that they would play a special role in the story-line of God's endeavor to redeem all humanity? That would raise two new questions of justice. Was it just of God to choose the Jews for this special role? Does this not represent "injustice on God's part" (9:14)? And if it was not unjust of God to make such

---

1. Cf. Mark 12:14: "Teacher, we know that you are sincere, and show deference to no one; for you do not regard people with partiality, but teach the way of God in accordance with truth." And Luke 20:21: "Teacher, we know that you are right in what you say and teach, and you show deference to no one, but teach the way of God in accordance with truth."

2. For "does justice," the NRSV has "does what is right."

a covenant, then does not God's offer of justification to gentiles as well as Jews amount to breaking that covenant and thus wronging the Jews? Does it not mean that "God has rejected his people" Israel (11:1)?

Paul addresses both of these subsidiary justice issues in the course of his argument. It is not unjust of God to choose some persons and some peoples for a special role in the story-line of redemption. And the Jews misunderstand God's covenant with them if they think that offering justification to Jews and gentiles alike on the same basis constitutes breaking the covenant.

For you and me, readers and interpreters of Paul, the claim that God's generosity is just is not yet entirely in the clear, however. Be it granted that the distribution is just in that God offers justification to Jews and gentiles alike. Be it also granted that such impartiality breaks no prior covenant with the Jews, and that that covenant itself is not unjust to non-Jews. But God's actual justification of some human being has an important condition attached, namely, that the recipient have faith. Is that condition available equally to all? It is available to at least some Jews and to at least some gentiles. But is it available to all of each?

Paul has often and long been interpreted as teaching that the faith in question has to be faith in Jesus Christ. But many Jews, and masses of gentiles, have never known of Jesus; faith in Jesus Christ has not been available to them. Further, in the course of discussing the pattern of God's redemptive action, Paul remarks that God "hardens" the hearts of some persons. This, along with other remarks that Paul makes in the same context, has long led many to interpret him as saying that faith is a gift that God bestows on some and not on others. If that is right, then faith for those whom God "passes over" is not a possibility even if they have heard of Jesus. Two grounds for you and me to doubt whether, in Paul's theology, God's generosity in his offer of justification is just after all. Paul does not himself directly address these grounds for doubt. The reason he does not, so I will argue, is that these doubts on our part are the result of misunderstanding what he is saying.

To all this must be added the fact that there's a question of justice concerning justification itself. Justification, so I will argue, is a close relative of forgiveness, close enough to pose a question that we raised earlier concerning forgiveness, namely, doesn't the offer of justification encourage antinomianism and thus undermine the practice of justice? Paul directly addresses this worry. Nowhere does he take note of Anselm's worry, that justification violates justice by foregoing punishment of the wrongdoer; quite clearly it was his view that foregoing punishment of the wrongdoer is not perforce a violation of justice. It was the charge that his teaching on justification encouraged antinomianism that he felt had to be addressed.

If these are indeed the main and subsidiary lines of argument in Romans, then the conclusion is irresistible that Paul's main topic is the justice of God's generosity in offering justification to Jews and gentiles alike. It's not the only topic in Romans, not even the only important topic; Paul also talks about "sanctification," about the proper function of governmental authority, etc. Nor is God's justice the only context within which one might set a discussion of God's justification of sinners; Paul sets it within a different context in Galatians. N. T. Wright, in all of his writings on the matter, sets his discussion of justification within the context of God's covenant fidelity. That is not a mistake. My contention is simply that that is not the context within which Paul sets his discussion of justification in Romans.

Those who hold that New Testament agape is pure gratuitous benevolence with no attention to justice have long held up Romans as their prime exhibit. That interpretation has some bit of plausibility if one ignores the first two and a half chapters of the book in which Paul lays out the overall structure of his argument and jumps in at the point where Paul begins talking about justification. That's how Protestants have traditionally treated Romans. I propose starting at the beginning and attending to the structure of Paul's argument as a whole.

"THE NEW PAUL"

The classic Protestant interpretation of Romans, initiated by Luther, is that Paul is addressing the anxieties of those who believe that "good works" will save them, the assumption being that Paul's fellow Jews, and Paul himself before his conversion, believed this. Paul's message to such people is said to be that their attempt to achieve salvation by works is both hopeless and misguided: hopeless because nobody ever achieves perfection in works, misguided because salvation is in any case not earned but graciously bestowed on us by God. The message of Romans, so it is said, is that salvation is earned by Christ's obedience unto death and extended to all who believe in Christ.

The current state of New Testament scholarship, as I understand it, is that there are few scholars who still defend this traditional Protestant interpretation. Two publications were decisive in giving birth to what is now called "the new Paul." The first was Krister Stendahl's now-classic article, "The Apostle Paul and the Introspective Conscience of the West," published in 1963.[3] By careful reading of the text, Stendahl dismantled the traditional interpretation piece by piece. Paul had not been wracked

3. *Harvard Theological Review* 56 (1963): 199-215.

by guilt and worried about his salvation; he does not come across as having been guilt-ridden, nor does he give evidence of having doubted that God would be gracious to him. He never held that God gave Torah to the Jews so as to heighten their awareness of their sinfulness and, through them, to heighten humankind's awareness of its sinfulness — though it may often have had that effect; he thought God gave Torah to the Jews so as to order their lives while they awaited the Messiah.

The second publication that revolutionized Paul interpretation was E. P. Sanders's *Paul and Palestinian Judaism,* published in 1977.[4] Sanders, who approached the issues from the side of history of religion rather than exegesis, argued that the "works righteousness" that Luther and most subsequent Protestants interpreted Paul as ascribing to his fellow Jews was a caricature of the Judaism of the day. Following the law was seen by Jews of the day as living faithfully within the covenant, not as a way of getting into the covenant in the first place. Sanders coined the phrase "covenantal nomism" for Judaism's pattern of thought. "Covenantal nomism is the view that one's place in God's plan is established on the basis of the covenant and that the covenant requires as the proper response of man his obedience to its commandments, while providing means of atonement for transgression" (75). *"Obedience maintains one's position in the covenant, but it does not earn God's grace as such"* (420).

My interpretation of Paul will be along the lines of "the new Paul" initiated by Stendahl and Sanders.[5] Sanders's argument, that the picture of Judaism ascribed by Luther and his successors to Paul does not fit the Judaism of Paul's day, leaves us with the choice between concluding that Paul seriously misinterpreted the religion of his own people and concluding that we have seriously misinterpreted Paul. Stendahl's argument compels us to choose the latter alternative.

Let me add that some of the "new Paul" interpreters strike me as overdoing their reaction to the traditional interpretation. Granted that Paul's main theme is not that justification by faith eases the uneasy conscience of the legalist; it does not follow that Paul has nothing to say to the legalist. He does. Stendahl explicitly made the point.

---

4. (London: SCM, 1977).

5. The "new Paul" books that I have found most helpful are James D. G. Dunn, *The Theology of Paul the Apostle* (Grand Rapids: Eerdmans, 1988), and a number of books by N. T. Wright: *What Saint Paul Really Said* (Grand Rapids: Eerdmans, 1997); *Paul: In Fresh Perspective* (Minneapolis: Fortress, 2005); and *Justification: God's Plan and Paul's Vision* (Downers Grove: IVP Academic, 2009). See also Wright's article, "Paul and Caesar: A New Reading of Romans," in *A Royal Priesthood? The Use of the Bible Ethically and Politically: A Dialogue with Oliver O'Donovan,* ed. Craig Bartholomew, Jonathan Chaplin, Robert Song, and Al Wolters (Grand Rapids: Zondervan, 2002). I have also found helpful Stanley K. Stowers, *A Rereading of Romans: Justice, Jews, and Gentiles* (New Haven: Yale University Press, 1994).

THE MAIN TOPIC OF ROMANS

After a few introductory comments, Paul declares that he is eager "to proclaim the gospel to you" who are in Rome (1:15). What is that gospel? It's the good news of "the power of God for salvation to everyone who has faith, to the Jew first and also to the Greek. For in it the *dikaiosunē* of God is revealed through faith for faith; as it is written, 'the *dikaios* will live by faith'" (1:16-17). Right there at the beginning the impartiality theme is sounded: to the Jew first but also to the Greek. How could one miss it?

We are plunged at once into an issue of translation that I have discussed in some detail elsewhere.[6] The noun *dikaiosunē* in the Greek of New Testament times could be used to mean a number of different things: justice, righteousness (rectitude), fidelity, or judicial innocence, with the first two of these probably dominant. The Greek adjective *dikaios* could likewise be used to mean just, righteous (upright), faithful, or innocent. In the passage just quoted, the NRSV translates *dikaiosunē* as "righteousness" and *dikaios* as "righteous."[7] Is that correct? Is Paul's topic the righteousness of God?[8]

I doubt it. Paul's theme, he says, is that God's conferral of his salvific power on all who have faith, Jew and Greek alike, is a revelation of God's *dikaiosunē*. Why would anybody think that such conferral is a revelation of God's *righteousness*? Suppose I bestow some good impartially on all those who can benefit from it when there is no relevant difference among them. Would anybody describe that as a revelation of my righteousness, my rectitude, my uprightness? It's not my rectitude that's revealed but my fairness, my justice. Impartiality in the distribution of some good, when the recipients are all alike in the relevant respect, was for Aristotle the paradigmatic form of justice. Translations that have Paul saying that his main topic is the righteousness of God are mistranslations, based, one guesses, on misinterpretations of Paul's thought.[9]

6. See, in particular, the fifth chapter of my *Justice: Rights and Wrongs*.

7. Also, the NRSV has the circumlocution "the one who is righteous" where the Greek has simply the article and the adjective: "the just," or if one prefers, "the righteous."

8. There is a long-standing dispute as to whether Paul's topic is the *dikaiosunē* possessed by God or the human *dikaiosunē* that comes from God; the genitive can mean either of these. In the course of his argument, Paul speaks about both of these. But here, when he states the main topic of his letter, we have to interpret it in the former way. See Richard Hays's article, "Psalm 143 as Testimony to the Righteousness of God," in his collection, *The Conversion of the Imagination* (Grand Rapids: Eerdmans, 2005), 50-60.

9. In the Latin text of his commentary on *Romans,* Calvin speaks regularly of *justitia* — naturally, since the Latin text with which he was working translated *dikaiosunē* as *justitia.* The English translator John Owen, working in the mid-nineteenth century, decided to

N. T. Wright offers what I regard as a better suggestion: *dikaiosunē* in this topic-stating passage means "covenant fidelity." Over and over in his writings Wright presses the suggestion. The arguments he gives in support differ somewhat from one writing to another; but the insistence never weakens. Had scholars not "lost their moorings completely," he says,

> drifting away from the secure harbor of ancient Jewish thought, not least the biblical thought where both Paul and his contemporaries were anchored, and had [they not] allowed the little ship of exegesis to be tossed to and fro with every wind of passing philosophy, nobody would have supposed that "God's righteousness" was anything other than his faithfulness to the covenant, to Israel and, beyond that, to the whole of God's creation. It would have been taken for granted that "God's righteousness" refers to the great deep plans which the God of the Old Testament had always cherished, . . . and, more especially, to God's faithfulness to those great plans.[10]

No ambiguity or hesitation here!

Though I judge that "fidelity" is better than "righteousness" as a translation of *dikaiosunē* in Paul's statement of his theme, the question is whether it is the best translation. I think not. First, a few linguistic points. In the second sentence of the passage in which Paul states his theme, he speaks both of God's *dikaiosunē* and of the *dikaios* person. I think we should assume, absent good evidence to the contrary, that the meaning of these two *dik*-stem words, coming as they do in close proximity, is the same. Those who think they do not mean the same bear the burden of proof. But now suppose we translate *dikaiosunē* as "covenant fidelity." What then shall we do with *dikaios*? It makes little sense to say that the *dikaios* person is the faithful person, since then we find ourselves saying that the faithful person will live by faith. Of course; how else would he live! Why bother saying it? But if we hold that God's justice is the topic, we get a coherent uniform translation: God's justice and the just person.

Add to this the consideration that if it were God's fidelity that Paul had in mind, there was available to him a Greek word for saying exactly that, *pistis*. Paul uses that very term in this same passage. And later, when

---

avoid the English word directly derived from the Latin *justitia* and instead to translate Calvin's *justitia* as "righteousness." I will leave it to others to decide whether Calvin would be happy to find himself talking about righteousness rather than justice. (The Owens translation was reissued by Eerdmans in 1947.)

10. *Justification*, 178.

in 3:3 he clearly and explicitly raises the issue of God's fidelity to the covenant, he uses *pistis* and grammatical variants thereon.

Let us go beyond these observations about usage to consider what Paul is saying. Everyone who accepts "the new Paul" agrees that the main topic of Romans is not personal salvation but God's justification of gentiles as well as Jews. Paul is defending his ministry to the gentiles (see 15:15-21), a central feature of which was his controversial practice of not requiring gentile converts to take on the practices of Judaism. So what is it about God that Paul declares God's justification of gentiles as well as Jews to reveal?

I hold that it is the justice of God's generosity that Paul declares to be revealed. When Paul declares that there is no partiality as between Jew and gentile, he is highlighting the *justice* of God's distribution of justification. He is carrying forward the Old Testament theme of God as just.[11] Wright, on the contrary, holds that what Paul declares to be revealed is God's fidelity to his covenant with Abraham. Paul's no-partiality theme is barely mentioned in Wright's discussions. Wright strikes me as skittish about giving prominence to justice, as are most other Protestant commentators on Romans.

Our disagreement is thus over what it is about God that Paul is highlighting with the "both Jew and gentile" theme. For Wright, Paul's claim that God treats Jews and gentiles alike serves as *evidence* for the conclusion that God is keeping covenant; it has no other significance than that. On Wright's view, Paul is praising God for keeping his covenant with Abraham, not praising God for the content of that covenant.

I agree, of course, that in his brief discussion of God's covenant with Abraham in Romans 4, Paul notes that the promise made to Abraham and his descendants, that their faith would be reckoned to them as *dikaiosunē*, was meant not just for those who are blood descendants of Abraham but for all who, like Abraham, have faith. But I hold that what Paul emphasizes in Romans is not the *mere fact* of God's fidelity to his covenant with Abraham but the *justice* of the *content* of that covenant. In 3:29-30, Paul gives a rationale for that content: "Or is God the God of Jews only? Is he not the God of Gentiles also? Yes, of Gentiles also, since

11. My former colleague Harry Attridge has suggested to me that Paul's point is anticipated by Psalm 96:10:

> Say among the nations, "The LORD is king!
>   The world is firmly established;
>   it shall never be moved.
> He will judge the peoples with equity."

I'm not sure. I think it more likely that the writer had in mind that the Lord will judge equitably as among the nations *other than* Israel.

God is one; and he will justify the circumcised on the ground of faith and the uncircumcised through that same faith." Note that Paul does not say here that God will justify Jews and gentiles alike because he has covenanted with Abraham to do so! He says that it would violate God's nature not to do so.[12] Paul gives a rationale for the content of the promise.

Some readers will regard this disagreement as hopelessly arcane. Perhaps thus far it is. The proof lies in the pudding. Does interpreting Paul as continuing the Old Testament practice of praising God as just give us a plausible and coherent account of Paul's argument as a whole and in its details?

Suppose it had been God's fidelity that was upfront in Paul's mind when writing Romans, not God's justice. Might he have used the term *dikaiosunē* to refer to that fidelity? Perhaps. The term could be used to mean fidelity. In some passages in Romans it is so used.[13]

THE SOURCE OF ACCOUNTABILITY

The picture hovering over the beginning of Paul's argument is that of God holding court. "God judges the world" (3:6). And God's judgment is just (*dikaios*, NRSV "righteous"; 2:5). Some of the corrective justice that God executes occurs by way of historical events (1:18-32), some by

12. Richard Hays, in "Psalm 143 as Testimony," says that "Paul's underlying purpose in 3:9-20 is to establish beyond all possible doubt the affirmation that God is *just* in his judgment of the world. In other words, 3:9-20 forms an extended rebuttal to the rhetorical suggestion in verses 5-7 that God might be considered unfair (*adikos*)" (57). This seems to me definitely correct. Yet when Hays speaks, a few pages earlier, of the meaning of "the *dikaiosunē* of God" in 1:17, he suggests that it means the *integrity* of God, which he understands as more or less the same as the faithfulness, righteousness, and truthfulness of God (54-55). But Paul has not changed the topic between chapter 1 and chapter 3; and to my mind, the character traits Hays mentions are all very different from the justice of God.

13. Consider, for example, 3:3-6: "What if some [Jews] were unfaithful? Will their faithlessness nullify the faithfulness of God? By no means! Although everyone is a liar, let God be proved true, as it is written, 'So that you may be justified in your words, and prevail in your judging.' But if our injustice (*adikia*) serves to confirm the justice (*dikaiosunē*) of God, what should we say? That God is unjust (*adikos*) to inflict wrath on us? . . . By no means! For then how could God judge the world?"

"Unfaithful" and "faithlessness," coming before the embedded quotation from Psalm 51:4, are precise translations of the Greek for lacking in faith, in *pistis*. But then *adikia* after the quotation should also be translated as "infidelity," and *dikaiosunē* as "fidelity," since Paul's point is clearly the same before and after the quotation. To translate differently is to make the English completely obscure. Presumably the reason Paul himself shifted terminology is that, in the passage he quoted, he was confronted with the verb *dikaioō*. However, *adikos*, in the final sentence should clearly be translated as "unjust," as it is in NRSV, since the issue now is whether God would violate the principles of retributive justice if he punished Israel.

way of the exercise of political authority (12:19–13:7), some on the final "day of wrath when God's just judgment will be revealed" (2:5).

In our society, judges do not originate the law but receive it. It's there already, a given. The judge takes the extant law, holds the facts of the case up to the law, and issues his verdict. The origin of the law that he applies lies not in himself but in common law or legislative resolution. In the case of God as judge, things are different. What the judge considers is whether the person before him has done what the judge himself holds him accountable for doing.

The workings of accountability to God take two forms. In 2:12 Paul says that "all who have sinned apart from the law will also perish apart from the law, and all who have sinned under the law will be judged by the law." The distinction here employed, between those who sin apart from the law and those who sin under the law, leaves unspecified which group of human beings falls into which category. Paul addresses that question almost immediately. In 2:14 he says that the gentiles "do not possess the law," in 3:2 he says that "the Jews were entrusted with the oracles of God," and between these two passages he refers to the Jew who relies on the law to know God's will and determine what is best (2:17-18). The inference is clear: Jews possess the law and live under it, gentiles do not possess the law and hence live apart from it. By law *(nomos)* in this context, Paul has to mean Torah — that is, the Mosaic legislation.[14]

A bit later he remarks that while at a certain point "law came in" (5:20), "sin was in the world before the law" (5:13). The idea is clearly that God held human beings accountable before Torah was issued — and that human beings violated their accountability.[15] Paul did not find it easy to characterize the workings of accountability for those who live "apart from" Torah. There is no hesitation on his part as to the epistemology of the situation: even those not acquainted with Torah know, or are capable of knowing, what God holds them accountable for. But how do they get that knowledge?

Accountability in their case does not come from outside themselves in the form of divine commandments or positive legislation. Rather, the gentiles are "a *nomos* for themselves" (2:14). That which God holds them accountable for is "written on their hearts," and they come to

---

14. This is also Dunn's view; see *Theology of Paul the Apostle,* 131-33.

15. In Galatians 3:10, after speaking of "the law," Paul speaks immediately of "all the things written in the book of the law."

In Romans 4:15 Paul remarks that "where there is no law, neither is there violation." And in 5:13, after saying "sin was indeed in the world before the law," he adds, "but sin is not reckoned when there is no law." This is a puzzling comment. I think what Paul has to mean is that sin was in the world before Torah, since there was law before God had issued Torah; but where there is no law of any sort, no *nomos,* there is no sin.

know what is there inscribed by their "conscience bearing witness" to it (2:25). When they obey this *nomos* of themselves for themselves, they "do by nature *(physis)* what *nomos* requires" (2:14).[16] The Jew can do what God holds him accountable for doing by hearing and obeying Torah; the gentile must do so "by nature." Vague words, no doubt about it! Though Paul clearly holds that there is natural law and that all human beings are acquainted with it, he makes no attempt to spell out the workings of that acquaintance.

A good deal of Torah consists of God taking that which by nature God holds all humankind accountable for and making that the content of legislation issued to Israel. What God holds a person accountable for is more clear when published as Torah than when present to the gentiles in the alternative natural form. Nonetheless, no gentile can plead that he did not know and could not have known what God held him accountable for. He could have known what God held him accountable for with respect to his fellow human beings; he could also have known that God held him accountable for honoring and giving thanks to God (1:21), for acknowledging God (1:28). "They are without excuse," says Paul; "for though they knew God, they did not honor him as God or give thanks to him" (1:20-21).

Neither can the gentile plead that he did not know and could not have known that God decrees punishment for wrongdoing. Speaking of those who are "full of envy, murder, strife," and so forth, Paul says that "they know God's decree *(dikaiōma),* that those who practice such things deserve to die" (1:32). Presumably Paul's thought is that the principles of God's corrective judgment are present to gentiles in the same way that the principles of God's primary justice are present to them, namely, as something written on their hearts to which their conscience bears witness.

The fact that the law relevant to the case is what the judge himself holds the person accountable for gives a most unusual structure to the juridical situation. The case before the judge is a case in which the judge himself has been wronged; the judge is one of the injured parties. A human being may also have been wronged. But in every case of wrongdoing that comes before the divine judge, the judge himself is a wronged party. For whatever be the wrong that the accused has perpetrated on his fellow human beings, God held him accountable for not doing that. And God has a right to our doing what God holds us accountable for doing. Accordingly, the person who does not do that thereby wrongs God, deprives God of that to which God has a right. We are "accountable to God" (3:19).

16. NRSV translates, "they do instinctively what the law requires."

That God is one of the wronged parties makes intelligible Paul's repeated references to the anger of God. As I observed in our discussion of forgiveness in Part Three, anger and indignation are emotions naturally and properly evoked by the perception of having been wronged. God's punishment of the wrongdoer is an expression of God's anger; and God's anger is God's response to being wronged.

IT'S WHAT ONE DOES THAT COUNTS

Paul's discussion of the accessibility to everyone of God's requirements comes in chapters 1 and 2. But rather than finishing what he has to say on the matter and then moving on to another topic, Paul, at the beginning of chapter 2, introduces the courtroom model and from there on for the remainder of the chapter interweaves what he still has to say about accessibility with ringing a number of changes on the theme that what the divine judge takes note of, as he prepares to issue his verdict, is not whether the person in the dock knew the law or employed it in issuing judgments on the behavior of his fellows, but what the person in the dock has himself done, how he has lived. The Greek verb that gets translated as "doing" is *poieō*. To most present day readers, this point, developed in detail, seems completely unnecessary; it goes without saying that the attention of the judge is focused on what the person in the dock has done. But evidently it did not go without saying for Paul's readership.

Paul gives some indication in chapter 2 of just what it is, in what the person in the dock has done, that the divine judge takes note of as he prepares to issue his verdict. But since Paul's focus is not on that but on the many forms of "non-doing" that do not impress the judge, the matter remains vague until Paul takes up the topic in its own right in 3:9 and brings what he has to say to a ringing climax in 3:20-21. We have to interpret the rather vague indications in chapter 2 in the light of that and other clarifications. I will do so toward the end of the next chapter, when we have all the necessary clarifications in hand.

Here's what Paul says concerning the many forms of "non-doing" on which human beings pride themselves but which leave the divine judge unimpressed. Condemning others for violating the law and affirming the justice of God's negative judgment on them, all the while excusing yourself, will not get you a pass from the judge. "Do you imagine, whoever you are, [Jew or gentile], that when you judge those who do such things and yet do them yourself, you will escape the judgment of God?" (2:3). Paul then turns to his fellow Jews. The fact that you "rely on the law [Torah] and boast of your relation to God and know his will and determine what is best because you are instructed in the law [Torah]" (2:17-

18) — that's not going to get you a pass from the judge. The fact that "you are sure that you are a guide to the blind, a light to those who are in darkness, a corrector of the foolish, a teacher of children, having in the law [Torah] the embodiment of knowledge and truth" (2:19-20) — that's not going to get you a pass from the judge. You "that teach others, will you not teach yourself? While you preach against stealing, do you steal? You that forbid adultery, do you commit adultery? You that abhor idols, do you rob temples? You that boast in the law, do you dishonor God by breaking the law?" (2:21-23). And as to circumcision, "if you break the law, your circumcision has become uncircumcision" (2:25).

PAUL'S PROTESTING JEW

Paul imagines one of his fellow Jews lodging a protest at this point: if all this is true, "then what advantage has the Jew?" (3:1). This is the first appearance in Paul's discussion of what I shall call *the protesting Jew*. His role in Paul's discussion as a whole is not to stake out a single objection but to be a sparring partner, trying out a number of related objections. We are to imagine a dialogue taking place between Paul and the protesting Jew. Reproducing the dialogue requires both rehearsing some points already made and anticipating some points to be developed later.

The protesting Jew has heard Paul say that in the Great Assize, God renders to each according to what he has done, Jews and gentiles alike. He doesn't much like this. That may hold for gentiles. But for Jews, it's enough that Torah be present among them. That enables the Jew to be "a guide to the blind, a light to those who are in darkness, a corrector of the foolish, a teacher of children," since he possesses "in the law [Torah] the embodiment of knowledge and truth" (2:19-20).

No way, says Paul. Do you really think that if you "preach against stealing" it doesn't matter whether "you steal"? That if you "forbid adultery" it doesn't matter whether "you commit adultery"? That if you "abhor idols" it doesn't matter whether you "rob temples"? "You dishonor God by breaking the law" (2:21-23) that you yourself preach.

Well, okay, says the protesting Jew, now shifting ground somewhat. We Jews are better than my comments may have suggested that we are. Not only is Torah present among us. We have kept Torah; our keeping of Torah gives us title to eternal life. And it is unfair of God to ask anything less of the gentiles — to give them eternal life if they just have faith while requiring of us that we labor long and hard in the vineyards of Torah.

No way, says Paul, you have not kept Torah; you deceive yourself if you think you have. When we who are Jews take an unflinching look at our relation to the whole of Torah, what we discover is not that we have fulfilled Torah but that Torah teaches us, as nothing available to the pagans teaches them, how many are the ways in which we wrong God. We learn not how good we are in measuring up to Torah but how sinful we are by falling short of Torah. "If it had not been for the law [Torah], I [Paul] would not have known sin" to the degree that I do. For example, "I would not have known what it is to covet," nor that coveting is wrong, "if the law [Torah] had not said, 'You shall not covet'" (7:7). Does this condemnatory function of the law mean that the law is bad? Of course not. "The law [itself] is holy, and the commandment is holy and just and good" (7:12).

And in any case, mere "keeping" of Torah is not the point. "Circumcision is of value if you obey the law; but if you break the law, your circumcision has become uncircumcision. . . . A person is not a Jew who is one outwardly. . . . Rather, a person is a Jew who is one inwardly" (2:25-29). Torah was given to the Jews as a way of giving expression to their faith in God, not as an alternative to faith in God. Israel, when it strove "for the *dikaiosunē* that is based on the law, did not succeed in fulfilling that law. Why not? Because they did not strive for it on the basis of faith, but as if it were based on works" (9:31-32). "Not all Israelites truly belong to Israel, and not all of Abraham's children are his true descendants" (9:6-7).

Faith always was the issue. Abraham had no Torah; Torah was still hundreds of years in the future. It was Abraham's faith that the Lord reckoned to him as righteousness (Genesis 15:6). What God has always asked, of Jews and gentiles alike, is faith. Before the coming of the Messiah, God asked of Jews that their faith take the form of obedience to Torah. Full obedience was never forthcoming until it was achieved in the obedience unto death of the Messiah. Now obedience to the Jewishness of Torah is no longer required.

So "then what advantage has the Jew? What is the value of circumcision" and all the rest? (3:1)? It all seems a pointless oppressive burden.

No way, says Paul. The glory of the Jews is that to them "were entrusted the oracles of God" (3:2). "To them belong the adoption, the glory, the covenants, the giving of the law, the worship, and the promises; to them belong the patriarchs, and from them, according to the flesh, comes the Messiah, who is over all, God blessed forever" (9:4-5).

The main point of Romans remains intact, namely, the justice of God's offer of justification to Jews and gentiles alike. That offer does not constitute breaking covenant with the Jews.

Chapter Twenty-One

WHAT IS JUSTIFICATION AND IS IT JUST?

THE QUESTION NOW BEFORE US is what Paul means when he speaks of God justifying human beings. Let me approach the topic by way of a short detour, looking first at the traditional understanding of justification and then once again raising a point of translation. What we learn on the detour will prove of use when we return to the main road.[1]

THE INCOHERENCE OF TRADITIONAL ACCOUNTS OF JUSTIFICATION

The account of justification that we get from the main theological tradition is incoherent on a point of central importance for interpreting Paul. The incoherence I have in mind can be nicely illustrated from Thomas C. Oden's book, *The Justification Reader*.[2] Oden's aim is to show that there is a core of consensus throughout the Christian tradition on the nature of Pauline justification. One of the many passages in which he states what he takes that core to be is this:

> God's justifying verdict is compared to a judicial act by which God declares the sinner free from guilt — acquitted. The Judge forgives the one who repents and believes in the unique way the Judge has provided for the sinner's release. On the basis of this pardon the person is declared right in the presence of the divine Judge. (53)

I do not propose combing the literature to assess Oden's claim that there is a core of consensus around this understanding of justification. For our purposes it is sufficient to note that Oden cites a good many formulations that do in fact express the thought that he articulates, formulations from several different ecclesiastical traditions.

There are two incompatible understandings of justification packed into Oden's three brief sentences. On one understanding, God's justifi-

---

1. A useful history of the doctrine of justification is Alister E. McGrath, *Justitia Dei: A History of the Christian Doctrine of Justification,* second edition (Cambridge: Cambridge University Press, 1998).
2. (Grand Rapids: Eerdmans, 2002).

cation of the sinner is compared to a judicial act in which a judge declares the accused innocent of the charges against him — in Oden's
words, "free from guilt — acquitted." On the other understanding,
God's justification of the sinner is compared to a judge forgiving or pardoning the offender. Acquitting and pardoning, declaring innocent
and forgiving, are not only distinct but incompatible. If the judge declares the accused innocent of the charge, that is, acquits him, then
there is nothing for anyone to forgive or pardon him for; conversely, if
someone forgives or pardons him, someone must already have declared
him guilty. Forgiving and pardoning presuppose the judgment of guilt.[3]
So is justification to be identified with forgiving, or does justification, as
a declaration of the innocence of the accused, forestall the possibility of
forgiving?

The *Joint Declaration on the Doctrine of Justification 1997* by Lutherans
and Roman Catholics[4] comes down quite squarely in favor of understanding justification as forgiveness. "Justification is forgiveness of sins"
(art. 11, and *passim*). Yet even in this text there is a bit of wavering. Article 22 says that "when persons come by faith to share in Christ, God no
longer imputes to them their sin. . . ." No explanation is given of what is
meant here by "no longer imputes." The *Joint Declaration* might mean,
no longer holds against. But if the phrase has its ordinary meaning, that
God no longer *ascribes* or *attributes* sin to them, then this is the intrusion
of an idea different from forgiveness. When I forgive you for some
wrong you did me, I do not cease to ascribe or impute that wrongdoing
to you; rather, in full recognition of the fact that you have wronged me,
I forgive you for doing so. To forgive you for wronging me presupposes
that I ascribe to you, impute to you, that you wronged me.[5]

---

3. Oden systematically confuses acquittal with pardon. He says, for example, that "at
the very conclusion of a trial in which one already is found guilty, one may be accounted
upright by executive clemency, wherein the penalty may be remitted on the principle of
pardon" (55). One might wonder, then, whether he is reading his own confusion on the
matter into the tradition. I think the evidence is clear that he is not, that he is instead reflecting the tradition on this point. Consider the following passage from the Augsburg
Confession: "It is also taught among us that we cannot obtain forgiveness of sin and righteousness before God by our own merits, works, or satisfaction, but that we receive forgiveness of sin and become righteous before God by grace, for Christ's sake, through faith,
when we believe that Christ suffered for us and that for his sake our sin is forgiven, and
righteousness and eternal life are given to us. For God will regard and reckon this faith as
righteousness" (quoted by Oden, 4). But if we are righteous before God, forgiveness is an
impossibility; there is nothing to forgive us for. And conversely, forgiveness does not make
a person righteous, that is, into a person who has not done wrong; rather, it does not hold
his wrongdoing against him.

4. The text is available in various places, including the Institute for Ecumenical Re-
search, Strasbourg, sponsored by the Lutheran World Federation.

5. The acquittal/pardon ambiguity also runs throughout N. T. Wright's discussion of

It might in principle be the case that the incoherence of the theological tradition reflects incoherence in Paul's thought. But the only way to arrive at either that conclusion or its opposite, that the theological tradition has misunderstood Paul, is to look closely at Paul's argument.

A MATTER OF TRANSLATION

The standard English translations of Romans destroy the linguistic unity of what Paul has to say about justification. We have already been confronted with mistranslation of Paul's opening statement of his theme, the result being that most readers of English translations never realize that his topic is the justice of God's generosity. The result of destroying the linguistic unity of his text is that it is all too easy to miss the unity of his thought.

Speaking of Abraham's justification in 4:1-12, Paul six times over uses the verbal phrase, "X was reckoned to Y as *dikaiosunē*," specifically, "Abraham's faith was reckoned to him as *dikaiosunē*" — translated as "righteousness" by NRSV. It's clear from the text that Paul is using "reckons as *dikaiosunē*" as a synonym of the verb *dikaioō*, which gets translated by the NRSV as "justifies." The advantage of the full phrase, "reckons X to Y as *dikaiosunē*," is that in addition to incorporating a reference to the person to whom the reckoning is done it incorporates a reference to the ground of the reckoning — that is, to the ground of the justification. In 4:22-25, the verbal phrase, to reckon as *dikaiosunē*, and the verbal noun, *dikaiōsis*, are used in direct parallel with each other:

> Therefore [Abraham's] faith "was reckoned to him as *dikaiosunē* [NRSV: righteousness]." Now the words, "it was reckoned to him," were written not for his sake alone, but for ours also. It will be reckoned to us who believe in him who raised Jesus our Lord from the dead, who was handed over to death for our trespasses and was raised for our *dikaiōsis* [NRSV: justification].

The linguistic unity in the Greek text between the phrase "reckoned as *dikaiosunē*" and the verbal noun *dikaiōsis* is destroyed for the English

---

justification. In one place he jams both understandings together into one sentence: "But since, in Romans 3, Paul's point is that the whole human race is in the dock, guilty before God, 'justification' will always then mean 'acquittal,' the granting of the status of 'righteous' to those who *had been* on trial — and which will then also mean, since they were in fact guilty, 'forgiveness'" (*Justification*, 90). If the judge determines that the man in the dock is guilty, he will not acquit him; if the judge does acquit him, there's nothing to forgive him for.

reader by the fact that NRSV translates the former as "reckoned as righ-teousness" and the latter as "justification."

This destruction of the linguistic unity of the Greek text is especially jarring in 4:5, which gets translated thus:

> But to one who without works trusts him who justifies the ungodly, such faith is reckoned as righteousness.

The Greek has the verb *dikaioō* and the noun *dikaiosunē*.

Of course the translators of NRSV would insist that though they have destroyed the linguistic unity of what Paul is saying, they were doing the more important thing of rendering into present day English what Paul meant: to justify someone is to reckon that person as righteous. I hap-pily concede that we do not have, in English, any single term that corre-sponds to the full range of *dik-* stem words in Greek. The question is whether *righteous* comes even close to describing the status of the per-son who has been justified. Let's turn to Paul's argument.

PAUL'S CONCEPT OF JUSTIFICATION

"Both Jews and Greeks are under the power of sin," says Paul in 3:9. What then follows is a chain of quotations from the Psalms, beginning with "there is no one who is *dikaios,* not even one," and continuing with hyperbolic descriptions of the depth and extent of human turpitude: "there is no one who seeks God," "there is no one who shows kindness," "the venom of vipers is under their lips," "their mouths are full of curs-ing and bitterness," and so forth. Some of my readers may be inclined to challenge my claim that Paul is speaking hyperbolically. But did Paul think that these accusations fit Abraham? Did he think that they fit Jere-miah and Isaiah? Did he think that they fit himself? Surely not.

Nonetheless, Paul clearly did think that sin is pervasive in human ex-istence, with the result that no one does all the "deeds prescribed by the law" (3:20) — not even Abraham. The Greek that gets translated as "deeds" here is not the word that Paul used for "doing" in the preceding chapter when he was making the point that what the divine judge at-tends to is what people have done. That was the verb *poieō;* the word here is the noun *ergōn.*

The fact that no one does all the wdorks or deeds prescribe by the law is due, in part, to the fact that we are under the *power* of sin, in its *grip.* Paul would regard the thousands of pages in present day philoso-phy devoted to discussions of evil and free-will as curiously shallow — or perhaps as *dangerously* shallow. Yes, we human beings do have free will.

But there is more to be said about the massive wrongs that we inflict on our fellows than that this represents free will taking some wrong turns. There are strange menacing forces loose in the world, and we human beings are constantly succumbing to them.[6] It's because of this strange power of sin working within him, says Paul, that "I can will what is right but I cannot do it. For I do not do the good I want, but the evil I do not want is what I do" (7:18-19).[7]

With these sobering observations as his preface, Paul declares that the justice of God, as attested by the law and the prophets, has now been disclosed, the justice of God through the fidelity of Jesus Christ for all who believe. "For there is no distinction, since all have sinned and fall short of the glory of God, they are now justified by his grace as a gift, through the redemption that is in Jesus Christ."[8] Let's add what Paul says just a few lines later: "For we hold that a person is justified by faith apart from works *(ergōn)* prescribed by the law. Or is God the God of Jews only? Is he not the God of Gentiles also? Yes, of Gentiles also, since God is one; and he will justify the circumcised on the ground of faith and the uncircumcised through that same faith" (3:28-30). God's justification of anyone is pure gift; it is not required by justice. But God's love is a just love, for God offers justification on the same basis to Jews and gentiles alike, viz., on the basis of faith.

So what does Paul mean, here and elsewhere, by his use of the verb *dikaioō*, translated by virtually all English translators as "to justify"? Every position ever taken on the matter has proved controversial. No doubt mine will prove so as well.

Paul cannot mean that to declare someone justified is to declare him or her innocent of wrongdoing, since he has just said that "no human being will be justified in [God's] sight by deeds prescribed by the law." As we shall see shortly, *declaring innocent* is a species of *declaring justified;* but the two are not identical. The actual condition of every human being except Christ is that the person before the judge is guilty. To declare him innocent would be to declare him to be what he is not and what the judge knows he is not.

6. Cf. the following episode reported in John's Gospel: "Then Jesus said to the Jews who had believed in him, 'If you continue in my word, you are truly my disciples; and you will know the truth, and the truth will set you free.' They answered him, 'We are descendants of Abraham and have never been slaves to anyone. What do you mean by saying, "You will be made free"?' Jesus answered them, 'Very truly, I tell you, everyone who commits sin is a slave to sin'" (8:31-34).

7. There has long been controversy over who is the "I" here. Is it Paul before his conversion? Is it Paul after his conversion? Or is the "I" simply *one:* "one can will what is right but one cannot do it"?

8. On the matter of gift, Paul remarks a bit later that "to one who works, wages are not reckoned as a gift but as something due."

Running throughout most English translations of Romans is the con-fusion between the character trait of righteousness and the person's sta-tus before the law, a confusion abetted, so I guess, not only by skittish-ness over interpreting Paul as talking about justice but by failure to keep sharply in mind what happens in a courtroom situation, this being the image that Paul is using throughout the opening chapters of Romans.[9] The judge does not declare the person before him *righteous* or *unrigh-teous;* those are not legal categories. *Innocence* and *guilt* are legal catego-ries. And the judge's verdict is not based on the character of the person; that's not relevant. N. T. Wright puts the point nicely: "the 'righteous-ness' which someone has when the court has found in their favour is not a moral quality which they bring into court with them; it is the legal status which they carry out of court with them."[10] Of course, in present day idiomatic English we would not say that the legal status a person car-ries out of court with her, if she has been declared innocent, is that of *be-ing justified.* We would say that she carries out of court the status of *hav-ing been acquitted.*

Was I perhaps too hasty in saying that to justify is not to declare inno-cent? Has the judge, before it comes time to issue his verdict, "infused" Christ's innocence into him, so that whereas previously he was not inno-cent, now, after the infusion, he is innocent; and does the judge, when it comes time to issue his verdict, recognize that the person is now inno-cent and hence declare him innocent — innocent of wrongdoing? This is one of the traditional understandings of justification, common espe-cially in the Catholic tradition. But I find no such doctrine of infusion in Paul. And when one thinks clearly about the metaphysics presup-posed — God bringing it about that whereas at a certain time it's true that I wronged God last Tuesday, at a later time it's not true that I wronged God last Tuesday — I think one can see that this is metaphysi-cally impossible.

If one keeps clearly in mind the courtroom situation, one comes to the same conclusion, namely, that infusion of innocence makes no sense. N. T. Wright makes the point with wit:

> If we use the language of the law court, it makes no sense whatever
> to say that the judge imputes, imparts, bequeaths, conveys or other-
> wise transfers his righteousness to either the plaintiff or the defen-
> dant. Righteousness is not an object, a substance or a gas which can

9. I confess that I too was guilty of having failed to keep the courtroom situation clearly in mind in an earlier article of mine on these matters: "Justice and Justification," in *Re-formed Theology for the Third Christian Millennium,* ed. B. A. Gerrish (Louisville: Westminster John Knox Press, 2003).

10. *What St. Paul Really Said,* 119.

be passed across the courtroom. For the judge to be righteous does not mean that the court has found in his favour. For the plaintiff or defendant to be righteous does not mean that he or she has tried the case properly or impartially. To image the defendant somehow receiving the judge's righteousness is simply a category mistake.[11]

I suggest that the best clue to what Paul means by *dikaioō* is to be found in the locution he uses when he considers Abraham's situation. Abraham's faith was reckoned to him as *dikaiosunē* (4:3-11). As we saw earlier, Paul uses the locution, "his faith was reckoned to him as *dikaiosunē*," as synonymous with "he was justified by faith."

What might it mean to say that Abraham's faith was reckoned to him as *dikaiosunē*? Does it mean that God *imputes* innocence to Abraham, reckons him as innocent, knowing all the while that he is not? This is another traditional understanding of Pauline justification, common among Protestants.[12] But what does imputation amount to? When the judge imputes innocence to the guilty man standing in the dock, does the judge pretend? What does he pretend? Does he pretend to declare him innocent while realizing that he is not innocent? What would that amount to? Does he really declare him innocent while pretending not to know that he is not innocent? What would pretending such ignorance amount to? I find the imputation interpretation dissipating upon close scrutiny. And in any case, there is no indication whatsoever in Romans that Paul held such a view. Note that Paul does not say that *Abraham* was reckoned as *dikaios;* that would have the ring of imputation to it. He says that Abraham's *faith* was reckoned to him *as dikaiosunē*.

So once again, what might Paul mean when he says that Abraham's faith was reckoned to him as *dikaiosunē*? Well, recall the situation. A person is standing before the divine bar of justice. The question before the judge is whether this person has violated what he, the judge, holds him accountable for. The facts of the case show that he has. So the judge cannot acquit him on the basis of his "works," his "deeds." But now something remarkable happens. The judge performs a certain "reckoning." While fully cognizant of the fact that the person before him has done what he, the judge, holds him accountable for doing, the judge

11. Wright, *What St. Paul Really Said,* 98. Wright himself understands justification as *acquittal* (see 99, 131).

12. The Westminster Larger Catechism, in Question 70, blends a pardon understanding of justification with an imputation understanding: justification is "an act of God's free grace unto sinners, in which he pardons all their sin, accepts and accounts their persons righteous in his sight, not for anything wrought in them, or done by them, but only for the perfect obedience and full satisfaction of Christ imputed to them and received by faith alone" (quoted by Oden, 39).

takes note of the fact that he has faith. The judge then reckons that to him as *dikaiosunē*. The idea, quite clearly, is that after the judge has done the reckoning, the one whose faith is reckoned to him as *dikaiosunē* has the same status before the law as the one who is declared innocent *(dikaios)* of misdeeds.

What might that same legal status be — given that it is not the status of having been acquitted? The status of there being no valid charges against him — the status of being in the clear with respect to the law. And how might that status come about, the status of there being no valid charges against him, if not by being acquitted of the charges? There are two ways in which it can come about that there are no valid charges against a person after court proceedings have been initiated. One way is by being declared innocent of the charges, acquitted. The other way is by having the charges dismissed. I suggest that for God to justify the sinner on account of his faith is for God to dismiss the charges on account of his faith.

Abraham's faith was reckoned to him in the way that Christ's innocence was reckoned to him, namely, as ground for dismissing the charges. As Paul puts it in the famous ringing sentence that opens chapter 8: "There is therefore now no condemnation for those who are in Christ Jesus." That is to say: for those who are in Christ Jesus there is no verdict of guilty, not because God has judged them innocent of the charges, for they are not innocent, but because God has dismissed the charges on the ground that the accused is "in" Christ — that he has faith. And it makes no difference whether the person is Jew or gentile; "there is no distinction." "All have sinned and fall short of the glory of God" and all are "now justified by his grace as a gift."

Pauline justification thus comes in two forms. In both forms it consists of the divine judge dismissing the charge that the person before him has failed to do what God holds him accountable for doing. One form consists of the judge dismissing the charge by declaring the person innocent of the charge; only Christ is justified in this way. The other form consists of the judge dismissing the charge on account of the person's faith.[13] This way is open to all, Jew and gentile alike. Either way, one is in the clear. Justification in both forms results in being in the clear as one leaves the courtroom.

Here is a close analogy in human affairs. Judges in the American legal system have the authority to dismiss charges. Usually when they dismiss

---

13. I take Paul to be making the same point in 2 Cor. 5:19 when he says that "in Christ God was reconciling the world to himself, *not counting their trespasses against them*" (my italics). Justification, in the second of the two above senses, amounts to not counting the sinner's trespasses against him or her.

charges they do so because they judge the charges too flimsy; only when the relevant law specifically permits them to do so are they allowed to dismiss charges for the sake of the good. Grand juries — the grand jury being an arm of the judiciary — have a good deal more latitude in this regard than do judges. One of the questions that the prosecutor puts to the grand jury when he presents a case is, "All things considered, should this person be indicted?" The jury is thereby given a virtually open-ended invitation to consider whether, even if they believe the accused guilty of the charges, considerations of the good outweigh proceeding with indictment. Perhaps the accused is old and infirm, perhaps his life has been spent in faithful service to the community, perhaps his indictment would cause a dangerous uproar, whatever. It is open to the jury not to "vote through a bill." God's justification of the sinner on account of faith is like that: God dismisses the charges (or if one prefers, decides not to press charges) on account of the faith of the accused. Justification is the juridical equivalent of inter-personal forgiveness.

But why faith? Why is it the person of faith that God justifies? Might God just as well have chosen something other than faith? Is God's selection of faith arbitrary? I will address this question in a later section, once we have discussed who it is that is the object of the faith in question.

DOES JUSTIFICATION UNDERMINE JUSTICE?

As I mentioned in the preceding chapter, nowhere in Romans does Paul address what worried Anselm about forgiveness and justification, namely, that foregoing imposing on a wrongdoer the punishment he deserves is a violation of justice. Paul did not believe that the moral order is violated if some wrongdoer is forgiven and not punished for what he did. I am well aware that one theory of the atonement, on the assumption that no sin may go unpunished, extrapolates from the Pauline text to hold that Christ paid the penalty for our sin on our behalf. But this is incompatible with Paul's doctrine of justification. If Christ paid the penalty for our sin on our behalf, then we were in fact punished for our sin, albeit vicariously. And if we were punished for our sin, then we were not declared justified with regard to that sin. The charge was not dismissed. Vicarious punishment and Pauline justification are incompatible.

The worry that Paul does address in Romans is that acceptance of his teaching concerning justification will encourage antinomianism and libertinism. Won't those who accept his teaching say to each other, let's go ahead and sin, since "we are not under law but under grace" (6:15)? Paul is dismissive: "By no means!" (6:15). Won't they be tempted to go yet farther and say to each other, let's "continue in sin in order that grace may abound" (6:1)? Again Paul is dismissive: "By no means!" (6:2).

I infer from this curt dismissal that Paul finds the objection silly, not worth taking seriously. Remember, God does not dispense justification hither and yon, no conditions attached. God justifies those who have faith. But faith is not a sort of supplement that one adds on to whatever else one may be doing. How could anybody think that? To come to faith is to be liberated from being a slave of sin to becoming a slave of *dikaiosunē* (6:17-18), a slave of God (6:22). Living as a servant of *dikaiosunē* is the polar opposite of being a libertine antinomian.

ARE SOME PREVENTED BY GOD FROM HAVING FAITH?

There is a long tradition of Pauline interpretation which holds that Paul in Romans teaches that faith comes by being implanted in a person by God and that God elects to implant faith in some and not in others, thereby electing to justify the former and not the latter. If that's how things go, is God not unjust? God may be just in bestowing justification on all who have faith, be they Jew or gentile. But God is not just in how he implants faith in people.

Here I can do no more than dip my toe into the ocean of controversy surrounding this interpretation of Paul's thought. Whatever may be said for this as a theological position, it is not what Paul says in Romans. The Augustinian interpretation that has so powerfully shaped Western Christianity cannot stand as an interpretation of the text.

It's easy to understand how the traditional interpretation arose. Consider, says Paul, what happened to Rebecca when she had conceived children, first Esau and then Jacob. "Even before they had been born or had done anything good or bad (so that God's purpose of election might continue, not by works but by his call), she was told, 'The elder shall serve the younger.' As it is written, 'I have loved Jacob, but I have hated Esau'" (9:10-12). It looks as if Esau never had a chance. Paul poses the obvious question: isn't this "injustice on God's part" (9:14)?

Paul's response is the now-familiar "By no means!" But instead of explaining why the charge of injustice does not hold, he amplifies his dismissal by offering another quotation from the Old Testament: "For God says to Moses, 'I will have mercy on whom I have mercy, and I will have compassion on whom I have compassion'" (9:15).

Paul goes on to mention Pharaoh's stubborn and hard-hearted attempt to prevent his Jewish slaves from leaving Egypt, and concludes by declaring that God "has mercy on whom he chooses, and he hardens the heart of whomever he chooses" (9:18). Apparently Pharaoh also never had a chance. But if God hardened Pharaoh's heart, "why then does God still find fault? For who can resist his will?" (9:19). Isn't it patently unjust for God to harden Pharaoh's heart and yet hold him responsible for his actions?

Paul responds with an image that one finds at a number of points in the Old Testament, the image of a potter. Who are you, O human being, to complain about your maker? Isn't the potter entitled "to make out of the same lump one object for special use and another for ordinary use" (9:21)?[14]

As I said, it's easy to see how the traditional interpretation arose. But let's look at the larger argument within which Paul's comments about Jacob, Esau, and Pharaoh occur; doing so will give those comments a very different import. Paul's questions about God's justice prove not to be the ones that you and I, given the traditional interpretation, want to ask.

Paul has just expressed his "great sorrow and unceasing anguish" over his own people Israel (9:2). To Israelites belong "the adoption, the glory, the covenants, the giving of the law, the worship, and the promises; to them belong the patriarchs and from them comes the Messiah" (9:4-5). But something is missing in the life of the Jewish people, giving Paul great sorrow. He doesn't here say what that is. But from other passages we can infer what it is: not all Israelites live by faith. Immediately Paul remarks that this does not mean that "the word of God has failed" (9:6). For it was never the case that "all of Abraham's children are his true descendants." Rather, "It is through Isaac that descendants shall be named for Abraham." What this means, says Paul, is that it is not Abraham's biological descendants who are "the children of God" but rather "the children of the promise" which God made to Abraham, namely, that "Sarah shall have a son." That's also how we should understand what "happened to Rebecca when she had conceived children by one husband, our ancestor Isaac. Even before they had been born or had done anything good or bad (so that God's purpose of election might continue, not by works but by his call), she was told, 'The elder shall serve the younger.'"

Paul's thought is beginning to emerge. He's not talking about who shares in the final redemption; he's talking about the pattern of God's action in history to bring about redemption. He's not talking about who God ultimately justifies; he's talking about the fact that God chooses certain peoples and certain persons for a special role in the story line of redemption. He's not talking about the divine strategy; he's talking

14. This is the NRSV translation. The RSV has this: "make out of the same lump one vessel for beauty and another for menial use."

about divine tactics. He's not talking about who God declares justified on the great day of final judgment; he's talking about who belongs here and now to "the children of God," to "the children of the promise." As to justification, he has already said that the right or just action *(dikaiōmatos)* of Christ leads to justification *(dikaiōsin)* and life for all (5:18). Presumably what he means is that God *offers* justification to all.

God's ultimate goal in dealing with God's fallen and wayward creatures is to "be merciful to all" (11:32). To accomplish that goal, God chooses some persons and some peoples for special use and leaves others for ordinary use. Notice that Paul did not say about the potter that he chooses some vessels for use and some for *destruction;* he said that the potter chooses some vessels for *special* use and some for *ordinary* use. This "special" use is two-sided, however. God chooses some persons in particular, and Israel in general, for a positive role in the story-line of redemption; God chooses others, such as Pharaoh, for what appears on the surface to be an obstructive role — though when we see the full picture, that proves not to be the case.

God hardened Pharaoh's heart toward the Israelites. God did not do so in order to make Pharaoh's acceptance of God's offer of justification forever impossible and thus to consign him to eternal damnation with never a chance. Pharaoh with his hardened heart played the role in the story-line of redemption of showing God's power so that God's name might be proclaimed to all the earth (9:17).[15] So too, the choice of Isaac over Ishmael and of Jacob over Esau for a special role in the story-line of redemption did not mean that the latter and their descendants were consigned to destruction; it meant that their role in the story-line was ordinary.

When Paul appropriates from Malachi the line, "I have loved Jacob but I have hated Esau," he is not talking about the final judgment; he is talking about the role of Jacob and his descendants, and of Esau and his descendants, in the history of redemption. And by appropriating the line to say what he wants to say with it, the term "hatred" gets used hyperbolically, whether or not it was so used by Malachi.[16]

It's about God's choosing of one over the other for a special role in redemptive history that Paul poses his question, "Is this unjust on

15. And even if it is only tactics, not strategy, does God just arbitrarily decide to harden some people's hearts? Maybe not. In the opening chapter of Romans, where he is discussing the pagans, Paul says that "they exchanged the glory of the immortal God for images resembling a mortal human being or birds or four-footed animals or reptiles," and that for this reason God "gave them up to degrading passions."

16. In the third and eleventh chapters of my *Divine Discourse* (Cambridge: Cambridge University Press, 1995), I discuss the phenomenon of one person appropriating the discourse of another.

God's part?" Whether someone plays a special role in the story-line of redemption "depends not on human will or exertion" but on God's selection (9:16). Is that unjust? Is it unjust for God to pick out in this way some people to play a special role? When Paul responds to that question with his now-familiar "By no means!" and quotes Exodus 33:19, "I will have mercy on whom I will have mercy and I will have compassion on whom I have compassion," he is talking about God's singling out of some persons and of some peoples for a special role in the story-line of redemption.[17]

To this must be added that being chosen or selected by God for a special "positive" role in the story-line of redemption is worlds away from being chosen for "worldly success" — fame and fortune. Those chosen often experience hardship, distress, persecution, famine, nakedness, peril, or the sword (8:35). Paul speaks often and openly about his own suffering.

A few chapters later Paul returns to his sorrow over his own people. The blood descendants of Isaac and Jacob were chosen for a special role in God's redemptive activity. But not all descendants have remained faithful to this call; a mysterious "hardening has come upon part of Israel" (11:25). It's clear from the context that Paul has in mind not only resistance to following Torah as a way of having faith in God but resistance to acknowledging Jesus as the Messiah. "As regards the gospel, they are enemies for your sake" (11:28), Paul says to his gentile readers. Among the Jews, there is resistance to the Messiah. Among the gentiles, some no doubt blood descendants of Ishmael and Esau, there is recognition of the Messiah. Strange reversal.

And as for this hardening of some of the Jews, or as he also calls it, this "stumbling," Paul observes that "through their stumbling, salvation has come to the Gentiles, so as to make Israel jealous. Now if their stumbling means riches for the world, and if their defeat means riches for Gentiles, how much more will their full inclusion mean!" (11:11-12). "Just as you [gentiles] were once disobedient to God but have now received mercy because of [the Jews'] disobedience, so they have now been disobedient in order that, by the mercy shown to you, they too may now receive mercy" (11:30-31). Strange reversals, one after another. It's as if history were the scene of divine jiu-jitsu. Add this: in order "to show his wrath and to make known his power, God has endured with much patience the objects of wrath that are made for [headed for]

---

17. And just as, when Paul appropriates from Malachi the line "I have hated Esau," the term "hated" gets used hyperbolically, so too, when he appropriates the line "I will have mercy on whom I will have mercy," the term "mercy" gets used to mean something different from what it was used to mean in its original context.

destruction" (9:22). Wickedness eventually leads to its own destruction. God's allowing this to happen is revelatory of God's anger with wickedness. As Paul said in the opening chapter, "the wrath of God is revealed from heaven against all ungodliness and wickedness" (1:18).

The hardening or stumbling of the Jews is not irreversible, however. Think of true Israel as a vine, says Paul. Some branches have been broken off — Jews who stumbled. Some branches have been grafted in — gentiles who acknowledge the Messiah. But the Jewish branches that have been broken off will be grafted back in "if they do not persist in unbelief" (11:23); and those gentile branches that have been grafted in will be cut off if they do not "continue in God's kindness" (11:22).

One might ask how this last point, about some gentiles not continuing in God's kindness, fits with the point Paul makes in a famous passage in chapter 8, that God justifies those whom he calls (8:30)? The answer is that God does indeed justify those whom he calls to a special role in the history of redemption, provided that they remain faithful to the call. The fidelity of Christ to those who believe in him remains constant and effective: "Who will separate us from the love of Christ?" (8:35). The same cannot be said of their fidelity to Christ.

To summarize: though we know the *telos* of God's redemptive activity in history, we are baffled by its details. The strategy we know; the tactics are beyond us. Electing, choosing, calling, hardening hearts, making jealous, causing to stumble, putting up with wickedness and its consequences. It's baffling. "O the depth of the riches and wisdom and knowledge of God! How unsearchable are his judgments and how inscrutable his ways!" (11:33).

The traditional view of Paul as teaching that faith comes by God's electing to implant it in some and not in others has no support in the text of Romans. Paul does not speak of God electing some people to be recipients of faith and others not. What he implies is that faith is *required* of us, required of all human beings. He says that justification is a gift; he nowhere says that faith is a gift. He offers no explanation of faith. Nor does he say that God elects some to be justified and others not. His use of the language of electing, calling, selecting, and so forth, is reserved for talking about God's choice of persons and peoples for a special role in the history of redemption; God foreknew them for their role, predestined them for it. What Paul does say is that those who accept God's call to be members of the people of God in the history of redemption can be assured of being justified. For they have faith.

The traditional interpretation rests on not recognizing that whereas Paul's topic in the opening chapters of Romans is God's offer of justification to all human beings and God's actual justification of all who have faith, his topic in the middle chapters is the pattern of God's redemptive activity in history, central to this pattern being God's calling or electing some for "special use." The two topics intersect at those points in the middle chapters where Paul assures his Christian readers that their confession of Jesus as Lord is sufficient for justification; they don't have to do something else in addition.

What Is the Faith of Those to Whom God Offers Justification?

One point remains before we can regard the justice of God's justification as established. God justifies those who have faith, Jews and gentiles alike. But who is the object of that faith? Is it Jesus the Messiah or is it God? To have faith in God, one must be sufficiently acquainted with God to make faith in God possible; in his opening chapter, Paul argued that all human beings do have such acquaintance with God. So too, to have faith in Jesus one must be sufficiently acquainted with Jesus to make faith in him possible. But vast numbers of human beings have had no acquaintance whatsoever with Jesus, Abraham among them. So if faith in Jesus is what is required for being justified, God's distribution of justification is surely on that account unjust. It's not an issue of justice that Paul himself raises, for a reason that will soon become clear.

Rather often Paul speaks of the faith required for being justified without specifying its object. Here are three examples from one brief passage: "a person is justified by faith," "God will justify the circumcised on the ground of faith," God will justify "the uncircumcised through that same faith" (3:28-30). But often it's clear, either explicitly or implicitly, that the faith Paul has in mind is faith in God, not faith in Jesus. Chapter 4, in which Paul is discussing Abraham, is full of examples: "Abraham believed God," "the *dikaiosunē* that Abraham had by faith," "it depends on faith," "those who share the faith of Abraham," and so forth. Nonetheless, the classic Protestant interpretation of Romans is that God bestows justification only on those who have faith in Jesus Christ. English-speaking Protestants can point to a number of well-known passages in their English Bibles which say exactly that: Romans 3:21, Romans 3:26, Galatians 2:16 (twice over), and Galatians 3:22.

The English of these passages says that what's required for being justified is faith in Jesus. But what does the original Greek say? The Greek of these passages has "faith" (*pistis*) in the nominative and "Jesus" (or "Jesus Christ") in the genitive. The normal translation of this construction would be "the faith of Jesus" or "the faithfulness of Jesus." "Faith in Jesus" is not grammatically impossible, however — though one would need a pretty strong reason for departing from the normal interpreta-

tion of the genitive. So which does Paul mean? Is he speaking of the fidelity *of Jesus* or of *our* faith *in* Jesus? Is there good reason for departing
from the normal interpretation of the genitive?

The issue has become highly controversial in recent years, and I do
not propose entering the fray any farther than to say that I, along with a
good many others, have been persuaded by the arguments of Richard
Hays that the fidelity of Jesus is what Paul was referring to.[18] Let me confine myself to remarking that, whatever is to be said about the other passages, this seems to me the only possible interpretation of a passage already quoted several times, Romans 3:21-22. Here is what Paul says:

> But now, apart from *nomos,* the *dikaiosunē* of God has been dis-
> closed, and is attested by the *nomos* and the prophets, the *dikaiosunē*
> of God through the faithfulness of Jesus Christ [or, through our
> faith in Jesus Christ] for all who believe.

How are we to understand that last phrase, "the *dikaiosunē* of God
through the faithfulness of [or, through our faith in] Jesus Christ"? Is
Paul here characterizing the justice that has been disclosed apart from
law, or is he characterizing its mode of disclosure? Suppose it is the latter. Then surely Paul is not saying that the apart-from-law disclosure occurs in our faith; he has to be saying that it occurs in the faithfulness or
fidelity of Jesus. Suppose, on the other hand, that he is characterizing
not the mode of disclosure of God's justice but the justice itself. Then
"the *dikaiosunē* of God through the faithfulness of Jesus Christ" would
mean the justice of God grounded in the fidelity of Jesus Christ — good
Pauline teaching. But what could "the *dikaiosunē* of God through our
faith in Jesus Christ" mean? The justice of God grounded in our faith in
Jesus Christ? Paul most certainly did not think that our faith grounds
the justice of God.

Let's go beyond these issues of translation to the overall thought of
Romans. Abraham was justified on the ground of his faith. But the faith
of Abraham did not have Jesus as its object; it had God as its object. So
too for all those descendants of Abraham living before the coming of Jesus who were "children of the promise." It was not possible for them to
believe in Jesus. It was God they believed in, thereby sharing the faith of
Abraham (4:16), thereby following the example of his faith (4:12).

But what then are we to make of a passage such as the following: "If

18. Richard B. Hays, *The Faith of Jesus Christ: An Investigation of the Narrative Substructure
of Galatians 3:1–4:11* (Chico, CA: Scholars Press, 1983). And "*Pistis* and Pauline Christol-
ogy: What Is at Stake?" in *Society of Biblical Literature Seminar Papers,* ed. David J. Lull (Atlanta: Scholars Press, 1991). James D. G. Dunn, in *The Theology of Paul the Apostle,* disagrees
with Hays.

you confess with your lips that Jesus is Lord and believe in your heart that God raised him from the dead, you will be saved" (10:9)? After his rather abstract theological discourse about justification in the opening chapters of Romans, Paul switches at the end of chapter 4 to the language of "we," "you," and "I," and maintains this mode of discourse for the remainder of the letter. The "we" here is we who confess that Jesus is Lord; it makes no difference whether we be Jew or gentile. We do not believe in Jesus *instead of* believing in God; rather, our faith in God *takes the form of* confessing Jesus as Lord. "We believe in him who raised Jesus our Lord from the dead" (4:24). In that way we are not unlike the Jew who, as a "child of the promise," lived by Torah. He did not live by Torah *instead of* believing in God; his faith in God *took the form of* living by Torah. His living by Torah was "on the basis of faith" (9:32).

The presence in our history of Jesus the Christ meant, for Paul, that the people of God has been re-constituted. The people of God, those human beings chosen for special "positive" use in the history of redemption, are now constituted of those whose faith in God takes the form of confessing Jesus as Lord. That conviction cast Paul into deep perplexity as to the role of his fellow Jews in the present stage of the history of redemption. He is deeply pained by the refusal of so many Jews to believe in the one whom he recognizes as the Messiah; that refusal appears to imply that even if in faith they follow Torah, they are not members of those who are chosen as God's people in this present age. But Paul cannot bring himself to say this. What he hopes for, what he even expects, is that ultimately, "when the full number of Gentiles has come in, all Israel will be saved" (11:25-26).

Rather than saying what he has traditionally been interpreted as saying, namely, that only those are justified whose belief in God takes the form of believing in Jesus, what Paul says with great emphasis is the converse, that those who believe in Jesus will be justified. Not, you will not be saved if you do not believe in Jesus, but you will be saved if you do believe in Jesus. Evidently Paul felt that his readers needed reassurance on this point. They can be assured that faith in God which takes the form of confessing that Jesus is Lord is sufficient. They do not, in addition, have to live by Torah. They do not, in addition, have to do what one or another form of paganism was urging them to do. No, "if you confess with your lips that Jesus is Lord and believe in your heart that God raised him from the dead, you will be saved. For one believes with the heart and so is justified, and one confesses with the mouth and so is saved." It makes no difference whether you believe in your heart or confess with your mouth. "There is no distinction between Jew and Greek. . . . Everyone who calls on the name of the Lord shall be saved" (10:9-13).

WHO ARE THE ONES WHO PATIENTLY SEEK GOOD?

We are now, at last, in the position of being able to deal with an issue that we raised in the preceding chapter when we were discussing Paul's argument in Romans 2, but then set off to the side until we had in hand the clarifications necessary for dealing with it. There I put it like this: what is it that the person in the dock has done that the divine judge takes note of as he prepares to issue his verdict? The background to the question is Paul's insistence that the divine judge attends to what the person has done, rather than to one and another form of non-doing.

In the course of making his point about the importance of doing, Paul declares that on the day of wrath, "God's just judgment will be revealed. For he will repay according to each one's deeds *(erga):* to those who by patiently doing (working, *ergou*) good seek for glory and honor and immortality, he will give eternal life; while for those who are self-seeking and who obey not the truth but wickedness, there will be wrath and fury." Paul immediately repeats the point: "There will be anguish and distress for everyone who does (works, *katergazomenou*) evil, the Jew first and also the Greek, but glory and honor and peace for everyone who does (works, *ergazomenō*) good, the Jew first and also the Greek. For God shows no partiality" (2:5-11).

Who are these people who patiently do good and who are, on that account, given eternal life, glory, honor, and peace? They cannot be those who, in the words of 3:20, do all the "deeds *(ergōn)* prescribed by the law," since there are none such, Christ excepted.

Well, recall Paul's reference in 1:21 to those who, "though they knew God, . . . did not honor him as God or give thanks to him." Recall also his reference in 1:28 to those who "did not see fit to acknowledge God." And recall his insistence that Abraham, though he too did not perform all the deeds prescribed by the law, nonetheless was justified because he had faith in God. Bring into the picture Peter's declaration, recorded in Acts 10:34-35, that "God shows no partiality, but in every nation anyone who fears him and does justice is acceptable to him." I think the conclusion is irresistible that the people Paul has in mind when he speaks of those who patiently do good are those that he will shortly speak of as people who have faith in God; they are the ones who see fit to acknowledge God. And when he says that God will give to these people eternal life, that is no different from saying that God will justify them.

But what then about the declaration which comes almost immediately after, that "it is not the hearers of the law who are *dikaioi* in God's sight but the doers (verbal nominative of *poiēo*) of the law who will be justified" (2:13)? Paul cannot here mean by "the doers of the law" what he means by those who do "the deeds prescribed by the law" in 3:20, since he there declares that no one will be justified by having done the deeds prescribed by the law. He must be referring to the same people that just previously he described as "patiently doing good" and as "doing good."

But if so, why would he describe them as "doers of the law," since it's almost inevitable that his readers would think that the ones he has in mind are those who do the deeds prescribed by the law? That's not hard to figure out. Throughout Romans 2, Paul is ringing various changes on the contrast between doers and non-doers. Here the non-doers are those who are merely hearers of the law. Hearers of the law as opposed to what? It would be hard to avoid saying, as opposed to *doers of the law.*

Justification on the basis of faith — alternatively expressed, the awarding of eternal life on the basis of having patiently done good, on the basis of honoring and acknowledging God — has always been part of God's way of dealing with wayward humanity. Justification did not enter the world when Jesus the Messiah was obedient unto death and rose again. Though the fidelity of Jesus grounds God's justification of sinners, justification of sinners did not await the fidelity of Jesus.

But how then are we to understand the ringing declaration, to which we have called attention several times, that "now, apart from law, the justice *(dikaiosunē)* of God has been disclosed, and is attested by the law and the prophets, the justice *(dikaiosunē)* of God through the fidelity of Jesus Christ for all who believe. For there is no distinction, since all have sinned and fall short of the glory of God; they are now justified by his grace as a gift, through the redemption that is in Jesus Christ" (3:21-24). We must understand it as meaning exactly what it says: the justice of God in offering justification to Jews and gentiles alike has now been *disclosed.* In 1:17 Paul spoke of it as *revealed.* Paul does not say that justification on the basis of faith is new; he says that the *disclosure,* the *revelation,* of God's impartial justification is new. Shortly he will quote one of the psalms of David:

Blessed are those whose iniquities are forgiven,
and whose sins are covered;
blessed is the one against whom
the LORD will not reckon sin. (Psalm 32:1-2)

God was always a forgiving God; the law and the prophets attested to that. But the attestation that God forgave Jews and gentiles alike, though not absent, was scarcely a ringing attestation; it was contested. One could scarcely describe the justice of God's impartial offer of justification as *revealed, disclosed,* in the law and the prophets. In Jesus Christ it is revealed. And it is on account of the fidelity of Jesus Christ that God forgives or justifies anyone at all.

Earlier I raised the question whether it is arbitrary that God would justify those who have faith. Might God just as well have decided to justify a different set of human beings than those who have faith? The answer should now be clear. If faith could be added on as a supplement to whatever else one might be doing, if it consisted, for example, of believing certain doctrines about God, then it would indeed be a mystery as to why God would choose faith. Why not choose some other add-on? But that's not how Paul understands faith. To have faith in God is to trust in God and seek to obey him, it is fully to acknowledge God as who God is. In the words of Peter, it is to fear God and do justice. So far is faith from being an add-on that it is one's life orientation; to have faith in God is to be oriented to God and to doing justice. To have faith in God requires repenting of all the ways in which one has wronged God and neighbor. The reason God justifies those who have faith and not some other set of human beings is that it is with these that God can become friends. How can God become friends with those who reject him?

JUSTIFICATION, SANCTIFICATION, AND RECONCILIATION

The defense of the justice of God's justification is now complete. But I think it would be a mistake not to conclude our discussion with a brief indication of the broader context within which Paul set his teaching concerning justification.

There has been a rupture in the relationship between God and humankind. God's desire for friendship with human beings has been frustrated. Both in failing to pay God due reverence, and in disobeying God by wronging our fellows, we have wronged God. God's justification of those who have faith in God is an indispensable component in God's way of healing the rupture. But healing the rupture is a process; and justification is only the first step in the process.

Think of Paul as having told an elaborate parable. The entry hall to the kingdom of God is like unto a courtroom. The judge opens the doors of the kingdom to the person of faith.[19] He does so neither by ex-

19. N. T. Wright would not like this image for what Paul was saying. Faith for Paul, he says, is "not a substitute 'work' in a moralistic sense. It is not something one does in order to gain admittance into the covenant people. It is the badge that proclaims that one already is a member" (*What Saint Paul Really Said,* 132). Faith is the badge, rather than the "works of the law" being the badge — sabbath observance, ritual cleanliness, circumcision, and so forth. Fair enough. But on the courtroom model, persons of faith do not just stroll into the kingdom of God on their own. They stand before the judge, awaiting his declaration. What the judge declares is that the persons wearing the badge of faith in God are to enter.

cusing this person nor by pardoning him after convicting and sentenc-
ing him; he does so by dismissing the charges on account of the person's faith, even though he knows that the charges are accurate. The
person who is justified now has "peace with God" (5:1).

But the peace with God that justification provides is only partial
peace. To see what more is needed, return to the example I offered, in
our discussion of forgiveness, of an abusive husband who, each time after flying into a rage at his wife, offers effusive apologies and expansive
professions of repentance, but who then later does the same thing all
over again. The apologies and professions of repentance need not be
insincere, nor need his wife regard them as insincere; because of his
penitence, she may decide to forgive him for his temper tantrums. And
she may feel no animosity toward him; she may in fact love him deeply.
But if he cannot control his temper, there cannot be full reconciliation.
Full reconciliation requires reformation of character.

Paul thinks of human beings as like the abusive spouse. Neither our
faith nor our being justified on the basis of our faith removes from us
the dynamics that propel or lure us into wrongdoing. We need a reformation of the moral dynamics of the self so that "the just requirement
(dikaiōma) of the law might be fulfilled in us" (8:4). Only then will we be
fully pleasing to God (8:8); only then can we be fully reconciled.

To understand how Paul thinks this re-formation occurs, we must
bring into the picture a point mentioned earlier. Paul is convinced that
wrongdoing is typically not just the consequence of weakness of will or
an error of judgment on the part of the wrongdoer. Our predicament as
human beings is that we are *impelled* and *lured* into wrongdoing by forces
within and beyond us — usually not irresistibly impelled and lured, but
nonetheless impelled and lured.

Did Paul have in mind some spooky invisible forces? I am not one to
dismiss all thought of invisible forces acting upon us. Do we have adequate empirical accounts of what drives the Hitlers, the Stalins, the Pol
Pots of our world to their frenzies of brutality? Not so far as I know. But
it would be a mistake to think of the forces Paul has in mind as forces
entirely beyond our ken. Bodily passions impel us into wronging others.
Negative emotions impel us — hatred, fear, jealousy, insecurity. And ideologies into which we have been inducted impel and lure us to trample
on the rights of others: nationalism, militarism, materialism, racism,
sexism, communism, capitalism, you name it.[20] Paul employs the lan-

20. The Latin Stoics had a strikingly similar outlook. In her discussion of Seneca in the
article mentioned earlier, Nussbaum speaks of him as regarding his fellow human beings
as in the "grip" of "cultural forces." "Before a child is capable of the critical exercise of reason, he or she has internalized a socially taught scheme of values that is in many ways diseased, giving rise to similarly diseased passions." Where Paul differs sharply from the

guage of enslavement to make the point. He says to his readers that they are "enslaved to sin" (6:6, 20). It was, of course, the familiar economic system of slavery that he had in mind when he used this metaphor; it would be appropriate for us to have in mind the enslavement of the drug addict to his drugs and of the alcoholic to his booze.

Paul's point is general. But the enslavement he spends most time analyzing, both because it is the one most relevant to the point at hand and the one that he himself and his Jewish readers were best acquainted with, was enslavement to legalism. "I am speaking to those who know the law" (7:1), he says. The context makes clear that it is the Torah he has in mind. Let us grant the argument of E. P. Sanders that Jews of Paul's days were not, in general, legalists. And let us keep in mind that Paul's argument in the first four chapters of Romans is not aimed at Jews who thought they could secure salvation by good works. Nonetheless, there can be no doubt that in chapters 7 and 8 of Romans it is legalists with respect to the Jewish law that Paul has in mind. Such legalism was among the ideologies that enslaved human beings. The Torah, meant as a guide for God's people until the Messiah comes, had been caught up into the enslaving power of legalism.

Let it be clearly and emphatically stated that it is not the law itself that Paul sees as enslaving but legalism concerning the law. He asks, should we say "that the law is sin"? His answer is the emphatic, "By no means!" (7:7). "The law is holy, and the commandment is holy and just and good" (7:12). But when the law gets caught up into legalism, then the power of sin "works death in [us] through what is good" (7:13). No doubt the same can be said about all 'isms': in all of them, something that is itself good gets caught up into an ideology that holds people in its grip.

I join countless other commentators down through the ages in finding Paul's analysis of the dynamics of legalism extraordinarily subtle and fascinating. But that analysis is not relevant to our purposes here. What's important for us is the general point that Paul is at pains to make, namely, that we human beings find ourselves impelled and lured into wrongdoing by forces within and beyond us. We find ourselves in the clutch of bodily lusts and psychological drives, emotions of hatred and jealousy, ideologies of nationalism and militarism.

One can anticipate what comes next. If we are to become well-pleasing to God,[21] we must be released from enslavement to those

---

Stoics is not in the diagnosis but the prescribed cure. It was the Stoic view that the forces that "take over the soul . . . can be eradicated, if at all, only by a lifetime of zealous and obsessive self-examination." (All quotations are from Nussbaum, "Equity and Mercy," 100.)

21. I mean the term "well-pleasing" both to pick up what Paul says in Romans 8:8 ("those who are in the flesh cannot please God") and to carry echoes of Kant's discussion,

forces that have us in their grip and that impel and lure us into wronging God and fellows. Given Paul's picture of the dynamics of the human self, what such release requires is that there be an alternative force at work within us that impels and lures us toward honoring rather than violating the requirements of *dikaiosunē*. We need an alternative "enslavement." That is what Paul sees God as bestowing on those whose faith in God takes the form of believing in Jesus. "God's love has been poured into our hearts through the Holy Spirit" (5:5) so that "we might no longer be enslaved to sin" (6:6). We have been set "free from the law of sin and of death" (8:2) so that "we might walk in newness of life" (6:4).

If you present yourselves to anyone as obedient slaves, you are slaves of the one whom you obey, either of sin, which leads to death, or of obedience, which leads to *dikaiosunē*. But thanks be to God that you, having once been slaves of sin, have become obedient from the heart to the form of teaching to which you were entrusted, and that you, having been set free from sin, have become slaves of *dikaiosunē*. . . . For just as you once presented your members as slaves to impurity and to greater and greater iniquity, so now present your members as slaves to *dikaiosunē* for sanctification. (6:16-19)

Paul was not of the view — how could he be? — that the forces that impel and lure toward wrongdoing have lost all grip on those who believe in Jesus. Instead the believer "groans" for full deliverance from those forces and awaits that deliverance with "eager longing" (8:18-27). In the meanwhile, injunctions are in order. Paul enjoins his readers not to "let sin exercise dominion in your mortal bodies, to make you obey their passions" (6:12).

A New Identity

We human beings are alike in having wronged God. The main burden of Paul's letter to the Romans is that we are alike in another way as well: God offers to justify all who have faith in God, Jews and gentiles alike. It is appropriate to see the pattern of Jesus' actions — the pattern that gained him the reputation of showing no partiality — as displaying what it is like to live out the acknowledgment of that fundamental unity. No

in *Religion within the Bounds of Reason,* of how we become well-pleasing to God. It would be fascinating to discuss the similarities and differences between Kant's account and Paul's. It is obvious from Kant's discussion that he was acquainted with St. Paul's account, though for him it was filtered through the lens of Lutheran and Pietist theological interpretations.

matter how far outside the bounds of respectability may be the human being who crosses my path, I am to treat her in a way that befits the fact that she is one to whom God offers justification. She is one with whom God desires to be a friend.

In various passages in his other letters, Paul highlights another identity created by God's offer of justification: the identity that holds among those whose faith in God takes the form of believing in Jesus Christ. Here is how he describes that identity in the best-known of these passages:

> In Christ Jesus you are all children of God through faith. As many of you as were baptized into Christ have clothed yourselves with Christ. There is no longer Jew or Greek, there is no longer slave or free, there is no longer male or female; for all of you are one in Christ Jesus. (Galatians 3:26-28)

The implications of this identity for how members of the church are to treat each other were vividly spelled out in the New Testament letter of James:

> My brothers and sisters, do you with your acts of favoritism really believe in our glorious Lord Jesus Christ? For if a person with gold rings and in fine clothes comes into your assembly, and if a poor person in dirty clothes also comes in, and if you take notice of the one wearing the fine clothes and say, 'Have a seat here, please,' while to the one who is poor you say, 'Stand there,' or 'Sit at my feet,' have you not made distinctions among yourselves, and become judges with evil thoughts? Listen, my beloved brothers and sisters. Has not God chosen the poor in the world to be rich in faith and to be heirs of the kingdom that he has promised to those who love him? Is it not the rich who oppress you? . . . If you show partiality, you commit sin and are convicted by the law as transgressors. (James 2:10)

God's no-partiality is to be reflected in the no-partiality of the church.

What I Have Not Tried to Do

Paul held that God justifies sinners on account of the fidelity of Jesus; Christ died *for us*. Though this is an extremely important part of Paul's thought, I have made no attempt to articulate how Paul thinks that works. My reason for not doing so is that my aim has not been to present

Paul's thought as a whole but to lay out the structure of his argument concerning the justice of God's love; I judged that doing this did not require explaining how the fidelity of Jesus grounds God's justification of the sinner. Let me just say that whatever conclusions one reaches on that latter topic have to fit within the framework that Paul himself establishes in Romans and that I have laid out; otherwise we are doing something other than interpreting Paul. It is my impression that this methodological principle has often been violated. Interpreters ignore Paul's overarching argument when interpreting elements of his thought that he himself placed within the framework. No note is taken of the fact that the justice of God's generosity in justifying sinners is Paul's overarching theme. I have tried to understand that overarching theme.

APPENDIX

I resolved not to read Karl Barth's now-famous exposition of election (*Church Dogmatics,* Volume 2, Part 2) until I had arrived at my own tentative interpretation of Romans. No one ever reads a text without being shaped in one's interpretation by pre-judgments of one sort or another. Nonetheless, insofar as possible I wanted to allow the text to talk back and tell me where my pre-judgments were mistaken. That proved difficult enough with respect to those pre-judgments that were the result of my indoctrination into, and membership within, the Reformed tradition of Christianity. I thought it best not to add additional pre-judgments.

I have now read Barth's exposition. A full engagement with what he says on the topic would require a very long essay. I have no substantial disagreements with what he says in the first two major parts of his exposition, "The Election of Jesus Christ" and "The Election of the Community." To the contrary, I find much of what he says here extraordinarily insightful, though excessively long-winded. His exposition of Romans 8–11 (213-33) is substantially the same as mine. Paul is here speaking about the calling out (choosing, electing) of Israel and the church for special service in the story-line of redemption, with the parable of the potter being "the focal point of the entire exposition" (223). It's when Barth gets to the third major part of his exposition, "The Election of the Individual," that I have my problems. Let me confine myself to indicating my main problem.

Barth says that "an elect man is in any case elect in and with the community of Jesus Christ; elect through its mediacy and elect to its membership. The people of Israel is elect in its Messiah, Jesus, and the Church in its Lord, Jesus" (410). This essentially repeats the point made in the preceding section; God elects Jesus, Israel, and the church. But then he says this: "There are in fact two classes of men, the called and the uncalled, the believing and the godless, and therefore the elect and the apparently rejected, the community of God and the world" (351). Now things are getting confused. Why are the uncalled equated with the godless? What has happened to those of whom Paul speaks in the first two chapters of Romans, people outside Israel and the church who nonetheless acknowledge God and patiently do good? And what is Barth implying when he equates the non-elect with the apparently rejected? Rejected for what?

Barth describes a "rejected" man as "one who isolates himself from God by resisting his election as it has taken place in Jesus Christ. God is for him; but he is against God. God is gracious to him; but he is ungrateful to God" (449). It would be possible to interpret Barth as here speaking of all those in every nation who do not acknowledge God. Unlike Paul, Barth uses the term "election" not only for the calling out of Jesus, Israel, and the church, but also for God's choosing to extend to each human being his redemptive love. Barth speaks of "the divine election of grace" (32) of which every human being is the recipient; in that sense, every human being is elect. Thus the rejected man, as described in the passage above, might include not only those who have met Jesus and refused to acknowledge him as Lord but those of all nations who do not acknowledge God. But Barth regards Judas Iscariot as the paradigmatic example of the rejected man (458ff.). And it was Jesus whom Judas rejected and betrayed; Judas rejected the call to be a member of the people of God chosen for a special role in the story-line of redemption.

So what does Barth say about Peter's claim that "God shows no partiality, but in every nation anyone who fears him and does justice is acceptable to him"? He never directly addresses the issue, not, at least, in his 500-page exposition of election. And what he says by the way that is relevant to the issue I find thoroughly confusing. From the very beginning of his discussion (see 19) he blurs the grace of justification with the grace of election; so far as I can see, that blurring continues throughout. One of my major points has been that if we do not distinguish the grace of justification from the grace of election, we cannot understand Paul.